Religion, Pluralism, and Reconciling Difference

We live in an increasingly pluralized world. This sociological reality has become the irreversible destiny of humankind. Even once religiously homogeneous societies are becoming increasingly diverse. Religious freedom is modernity's most profound if sometimes forgotten answer to the resulting social pressures, but the tide of pluralization threatens to overwhelm that freedom's stabilizing force.

Religion, Pluralism, and Reconciling Difference is aimed at exploring differing ways of grappling with the resulting tensions, and then asking, will the tensions ultimately yield poisonous polarization that erodes all hope of meaningful community? Or can the tradition and the institutions protecting freedom of religion or belief be developed and applied in ways that (still) foster productive interactions, stability, and peace?

This volume brings together vital and thoughtful contributions treating aspects of these mounting worldwide tensions concerning the relationship between religious diversity and social harmony. The first section explores controversies surrounding religious pluralism from different starting points, including religious, political, and legal standpoints. The second section examines different geographical perspectives on pluralism. Experts from North and South America, Europe, Africa, and the Middle East address these issues and suggest not only how social institutions can reduce tensions, but also how religious pluralism itself can bolster needed civil society.

W. Cole Durham, Jr., Susa Young Gates University Professor of Law, Founding Director of the International Center for Law and Religion Studies, J. Reuben Clark Law School, Brigham Young University, USA; recurring Visiting Professor of Law at the Central European University in Budapest, Hungary; Co-Editor-in-Chief, *Oxford Journal of Law and Religion*.

Donlu D.Thayer, Publications Director, International Center for Law and Religion Studies, J. Reuben Clark Law School, Brigham Young University, USA; Associate Editor, *Oxford Journal of Law and Religion*.

ICLARS Series on Law and Religion

Series editors:

Silvio Ferrari, University of Milan, Italy, Russell Sandberg, Cardiff University, UK, Pieter Coertzen, University of Stellenbosch, South Africa, W. Cole Durham, Jr., Brigham Young University, USA, and Tahir Mahmood, Amity International University, India

The *ICLARS Series on Law and Religion* is a new series designed to provide a forum for the rapidly expanding field of research in law and religion. The series is published in association with the International Consortium for Law and Religion Studies, an international network of scholars and experts of law and religion founded in 2007 with the aim of providing a place where information, data and opinions can easily be exchanged among members and made available to the broader scientific community. The series aims to become a primary source for students and scholars while presenting authors with a valuable means to reach a wide and growing readership.

Religious Freedom and the Australian Constitution
Origins and Future
Luke Beck

Islam, Law and the Modern State
(Re)imagining Liberal Theory in Muslim Contexts
Arif A. Jamal

Atheist Exceptionalism
Atheism, Religion, and the United States Supreme Court
Ethan G. Quillen

Lutheran Theology and Secular Law
The Work of the Modern State
Edited by Marie A. Failinger and Ronald W. Duty

Religious Freedom and the Law
Emerging Contexts for Freedom for and from Religion
Edited by Brett G. Scharffs, Asher Maoz and Ashley Isaacson Woolley

Religion, Pluralism, and Reconciling Difference
Edited by W. Cole Durham, Jr. and Donlu Thayer

For more information about this series, please visit: www.routledge.com/ICLARS-Series-on-Law-and-Religion/book-series/ICLARS

Religion, Pluralism, and Reconciling Difference

Edited by
W. Cole Durham, Jr. and Donlu D. Thayer

Routledge
Taylor & Francis Group
LONDON AND NEW YORK

First published 2019 by Routledge

2 Park Square, Milton Park, Abingdon, Oxfordshire OX14 4RN
52 Vanderbilt Avenue, New York, NY 10017

Routledge is an imprint of the Taylor & Francis Group, an informa business

First issued in paperback 2020

British Library Cataloguing-in-Publication Data
A catalogue record for this book is available from the British Library

Library of Congress Cataloging-in-Publication Data
Names: Durham, W. Cole, Jr., 1948-, editor. | Thayer, Donlu D., editor.
Title: Religion, pluralism, and reconciling difference / edited by W. Cole Durham, Jr., Donlu D. Thayer.
Description: New York, NY : Routledge, 2019. | Series: ICLARS series on law and religion | Includes bibliographical references and index.
Identifiers: LCCN 2018033987 | ISBN 9781472464071 (hardback)
Subjects: LCSH: Freedom of religion. | Religion and law. | Religious pluralism. | Sociological jurisprudence.
Classification: LCC K3258 .R445 2019 | DDC 342.08/52--dc23
LC record available at https://lccn.loc.gov/2018033987

ISBN: 978-1-4724-6407-1 (hbk)
ISBN: 978-0-367-52003-8 (pbk)

Typeset in Galliard
by Taylor & Francis Books

Contents

Contributors

Iain T. Benson holds a BA (Queen's University, Ontario, Hons), an MA Law (Cambridge UK), a JD Law (University of Windsor, Ontario), and a PhD Law (University of the Witwatersrand, Johannesburg, South Africa). He is Professor of Law, School of Law, University of Notre Dame Australia, Sydney; Professor Extraordinary, Faculty of Law, University of the Free State, Bloemfontein, South Africa, and Barrister and Solicitor of the Bars of British Columbia and Ontario, Canada. He serves on the Board of the Global Centre for Pluralism, a joint project of HH the Aga Khan and the Government of Canada, and was a member of the draft committee for the *South African Charter of Religious Rights and Freedoms.* He was retained by the Government of Canada to author material concerning Religion and Public Policy as an aspect of Federal Multi-Culturalism Policy. Author of more than 40 academic articles, he has been cited with approval by the Supreme Court of Canada and the Constitutional Court of South Africa. Author of *Living Together with Disagreement: Pluralism, The Secular and the Fair Treatment of Beliefs by Law Today* (2012). He is editor, with Barry W. Bussey, of *Religion, Liberty and the Jurisdictional Limits of the Law* (2017).

H. Victor Condé is a California lawyer whose legal ministry focuses on international law and freedom of religion and church–state relations issues, particularly in the United Nations and Council of Europe human rights systems. He received a BA in Classical Languages from the University of California Irvine, Juris Doctorate from UC Davis Law School, LLM in International and Comparative Human Rights Law from the University of Essex, England, MA in International Human Rights Theory and Practice from Simon Greenleaf Law School, Diplôme in International and Comparative Human Rights and Humanitarian Law from the International Institute of Human Rights in Strasbourg, France. He is a former professor of human rights law at Trinity Law School in California, and has taught human rights in the United States and in Europe, most recently at the University of Strasbourg, France. He has traveled to Canada, Nepal, Sudan, and Iraq to train lawyers in international religious freedom law and has served as an expert legal consultant on international human rights law to the Permanent Representative of the Holy See to the United Nations Human Rights Council.

W. Cole Durham, Jr. is Susa Young Gates University Professor of Law and Founding Director of the International Center for Law and Religion Studies (ICLRS) at the J. Reuben Clark Law School of Brigham Young University, United States. He is a graduate of Harvard College and Harvard Law School. He served as the Secretary of the American Society of Comparative Law from 1989 to 1994 and is a former member of the Organization of Security and Co-operation in Europe / Office for Democratic Institutions and

Human Rights Advisory Council for Freedom of Religion or Belief. He is an Associate Member of the International Academy of Comparative Law (IACL) in Paris and served as a General Rapporteur for the topic 'Religion and the Secular State' at the 18th Congress of IACL in 2010. He served as Chair both of the Comparative Law Section and the Law and Religion Section of the American Association of Law Schools. He was President of the International Consortium for Law and Religion Studies (ICLARS) from 2011–2016 and is a founding Editor-in-Chief of the *Oxford Journal of Law and Religion.*

Mohamed Saeed M. Eltayeb holds a Bachelor of Laws (University of Khartoum), post-graduate diplomas in international relations (University of Khartoum) and international law & organization for development (Institute of Social Studies, The Hague), masters degrees in international relations (University of Amsterdam) and international law (Lund University, Sweden), and a PhD in international human rights law (Utrecht University, Netherlands). He has worked at the Netherlands Institute for Human Rights (SIM), International Commission of Jurists (ICJ), Faculty of Law of the University of Khartoum and the Regional Institute for Gender, Diversity, Peace and Rights of the Ahfad University (Sudan) and has been a visiting researcher at institutes in Europe and United States, including the Swiss Institute of Comparative Law of the University of Lausanne, the Human Rights Centre at Essex University, the Law and Religion Program at Emory University School of Law, the Islamic Legal Studies Program at Harvard Law School, and Raoul Wallenberg Institute of Human Rights and Humanitarian Law at Lund University. He is currently working as a Human Rights Advisor at the Human Rights Department of the Qatari Ministry of Foreign Affairs.

Asher Maoz is Founder and Dean, Peres Academic Center Law School; taught at several universities in Israel, US, Europe, and Australia. Professor Maoz holds the degrees LL.B. and LL.M., *summa cum laude* (Hebrew U.), M.Comp.L. (U. of Chicago), J.S.D. (Tel-Aviv U.), and Honorary Doctorate (Ovidius U.). Founding Editor-in-Chief, *Law, Society and Culture*; former editor, *TAU Law Review*; member, Scientific Board, Review Dionysina; Academic Council, International Academy for Jewish Leadership; scientific committee, NEDES, 'Dimitre Cantemir' and the Romanian Chamber of Deputies; Academic Council, Shalem College; Senior Fellow, International Advisory and Research Council, Inter-University Center for Legal Studies, International Law Institute, George Washington University and International Center for Terrorism Studies; former member of the Board, ISPAC, United Nations. Chaired the Law Commission for Journalists' Privileges; served as academic advisor to the Knesset; served with many other law commissions and organizations. Author of numerous publications on the intersections of law and religion; member, G20 Interfaith Forum Advisory Council; Vice President of the Honorary Committee and member of the Board of Experts, International Association for the Defense of Religious Liberty, and Member, Steering Committee, International Consortium for Law and Religion Studies (ICLARS).

Javier Martínez-Torrón, Doctor of Law and of Canon Law, is Professor of Law and Director of the Department of Law and Religion, Complutense University of Madrid and Vice-President of the Section of Canon Law and Church–State Relations of the Spanish Royal Academy of Jurisprudence and Legislation. He is Honorary Foreign Member of the National Academy of Law and Social Sciences of Cordoba, Argentina; a former member of the Organization of Security and Co-operation in Europe / Office for Democratic Institutions and Human Rights Advisory Council for Freedom of Religion or

Belief; and a former member of the Spanish Advisory Commission for Religious Freedom within the Ministry of Justice. He helped found the first legal periodical in the Spanish language specifically focused on law and religion issues (*Anuario de Derecho Eclesiástico del Estado*) and is founding co-editor of *Revista General de Derecho Canónico y Derecho Eclesiástico del Estado*. His writings, published in twenty-three countries and in thirteen languages, include twenty books as author, co-author, or editor, and more than one hundred essays in legal periodicals or collective volumes.

Enyinna S. Nwauche is Professor of Law at Rhodes University Grahamstown South Africa. He has been Director of the Nigerian Copyright Commission; Dean at the Faculty of Law Rivers State University of Science and Technology; Member of the 8th & 9th Governing Councils of Rivers State University of Science and Technology; Director of the Centre for African Legal Studies Port Harcourt and member of the Rivers State Economic Advisory Committee. He is a member of the editorial board of the *Constitutional Court Review*; a tutor at the WIPO Worldwide Academy, and a member of the Executive Council of the International Association of Constitutional Law (IACL). He received his Bachelor and Master of Laws degrees from the Obafemi Awolowo University Ile-Ife. He also has a Doctor Legum (LLD) from the North-West University (Potchefstroom campus). He has held fellowship and visiting positions at the Max Planck Institute for Public International Law Heidelberg; the Max Planck Institute for Tax Competition and Intellectual Property Munich; the AHRC Research Centre for IP; IT Law University of Edinburgh Scotland, and the South African Institute for Advanced Constitutional Public Human Rights and International Law (SAIFAC).

Norberto Padilla is Full Professor of Constitutional Law, Faculty of Law, and for two terms Member of the High Council of Pontificia Universidad Católica Argentina 'Santa María de los Buenos Aires'. Was Assistant Professor at the University of Buenos Aires and is a Founding Member of the *Consejo Argentino para la Libertad Religiosa* (CALIR) and of the *Consejo Latinoamericano de Libertad Religiosa*, of which he is President since November 2017. Has served in the National Senate as an advisor to the Chairman of the Commission for Constitutional Affairs, was Advisor and Assistant-Secretary of the Secretariat of Religious Affairs, and Secretary of State of Religious Affairs, Ministry of Foreign Affairs and Worship with the rank of ambassador. Member of the Argentine Association of Constitutional Law and of the Editorial Board of *Criterio*. He is former President and Life Board Member of Fundación Navarro Viola, member of the Institute of Constitutional Politics of the National Academy of Moral and Political Sciences, and counselor of the Argentine Council for International Relations (CARI). Life member of the Argentine Institute for Genealogical Sciences, co-worker for the Argentine Bishops Conference Commission for Ecumenism and Interreligious Dialogue, and has been appointed on three occasions by the Pontifical Council for the Promotion of Christian Unity to ecumenical and Catholic-Jewish conferences.

Mary-Anne Plaatjies-van Huffel is a Senior Lecturer in Ecclesiology (Church Polity) at the Faculty of Theology, Stellenbosch University. She studied at University of the Western Cape, at the University of South Africa (UNISA), and at the University of Pretoria. She holds two Doctorates in Theology, one from UNISA and one from University of Pretoria. Among her publications are 'Patriarchy as Empire: A Theological Reflection'; 'Control, Secede, Vested Rights and Ecclesiastical Property'; and 'The Institutionalization of Christian Women's Organisations: From Docile Recipients to Agents of Change', all in

Studia Historicae Ecclesiasticae. Ordained as the first female minister of the Dutch Reformed family, she has served as minister in the Uniting Reformed Church in Southern Africa (URCSA) and on the decision-making structures of the URCSA as actuarius (church law expert) of the Regional Synod Cape and as vice-moderator of the General Synod. She was the first woman to be elected as moderator of the URCSA's General Synod. In 2013, she was appointed President of the World Council of Churches for Africa and was elected as one of eight presidents of the WCC General Assembly, the organization's supreme legislative body.

Russell Sandberg is Head of Law and Professor at the School of Law and Politics at Cardiff University where he specializes in Law and Religion, Legal History, Family Law, and interdisciplinary approaches to Law. He is the author of *Law and Religion* (Cambridge University Press, 2011) and *Religion, Law and Society* (Cambridge University Press 2014). He is co-author of *Religion and Law in the United Kingdom* (Kluwer Law International 2011; 2nd edn 2014) which forms part of the International Encyclopaedia of Laws Series. Russell is editor or co-editor of *Law and Religion: New Horizons* (Peeters 2010), *Religion and Legal Pluralism* (Ashgate 2015), *The Confluence of Law and Religion* (Cambridge University Press 2016), *Law and History: Critical Concepts in Law* (Routledge 2017) and *Law and Religion: Critical Concepts in Law* (Routledge 2017). He is also the author or co-author of more than 60 articles and book chapters addressed to legal, sociological, and general readerships. He is the editor or co-editor of three book series published by Routledge: Leading Works in Law, a new book series on Law and History, and the ICLARS Series on Law and Religion.

Reverend Piotr Stanisz is University Professor at John Paul II Catholic University of Lublin, Poland, where he has been President of the Department of Law on Religion, and former Dean (2012–2016) and Vice-dean (2008–2012) of the Faculty of Law, Canon Law and Administration. He has been Vice-president of the Polish Society of Law on Religion (*Polskie Towarzystwo Prawa Wyznaniowego*) and member of a number of scientific organizations, including International Consortium for Law and Religion Studies, European Consortium for Church and State Research and Consorciatio Internationalis Studio Iuris Canonici Promovendo. He has served on numerous editorial boards, including time as Editor-in-Chief of *Studia Prawnicze KUL* (Law Journal of John Paul II Catholic University of Lublin), *Studia z Prawa Wyznaniowego* (Studies in Law on Religion), and *Przegl⊠d Prawa Wyznaniowego* (Review of Law on Religion), and as Chair of the Editorial Board of the series *Publications of the Faculty of Law, Canon Law and Administration of the John Paul II Catholic University of Lublin.*

Jeroen Temperman is Associate Professor of Public International Law at Erasmus University Rotterdam and Editor-in-Chief of *Religion & Human Rights.* His research is focused on freedom of religion or belief, the right to education, freedom of expression and extreme speech, religion–state relationships, and equality. His book *Religious Hatred and International Law* is part of the Cambridge Studies in International and Comparative Law (prefaced by Heiner Bielefeldt, UN Special Rapporteur on freedom of religion or belief). Among other publications are *State–Religion Relationships and Human Rights Law* (2010), *The Lautsi Papers: Multidisciplinary Reflections on Religious Symbols in the Public School Classroom* (ed, 2012), and articles in *Human Rights Quarterly, Oxford Journal of Law and Religion, Netherlands Quarterly on Human Rights*, and *Annuaire Droit et Religion.* As Fulbright Scholar he was visiting professor at American University

Washington College of Law. He completed his doctoral degree at the Irish Centre for Human Rights.

Hans-Martien ten Napel is an Associate Professor of Constitutional and Administrative Law at Leiden University in the Netherlands and a Research Fellow of the Leiden Law School. He teaches the Bachelor of Laws Elective Course on Dutch parliamentary democracy and a Master Elective Course on Comparative Constitutional Law. He has also been a senior researcher at the School of Human Rights Research at Utrecht and taught in the Department of Political Science. He was a Post-Doctoral Fellow at the Minda de Gunzburg Center for European Studies at Harvard University and was a Research Fellow in Legal Studies at the Center of Theological Inquiry (CTI) at Princeton University. He is a member of the editorial board of the *Tijdschrift voor Religie, Recht en Beleid* (Journal for Religion, Law and Policy). His work has recently appeared in *European Constitutional Law Review, European Public Law, Journal of Markets and Morality, Muslim World Journal of Human Rights*, and the *Oxford Journal of Law and Religion.* His latest book, entitled *Constitutionalism, Democracy and Religious Freedom. To Be Fully Human* (Routledge), was published in 2017.

Donlu D. Thayer is Publications Director at the International Center for Law and Religion Studies at Brigham Young University Law School and an Associate Editor of the *Oxford Journal of Law and Religion.* She holds BA (French / English), MA (Literature), and JD degrees. She has been a family, juvenile court, and victim/offender mediator, and a university lecturer in writing. Publications include editorial roles for *Law, Religion, Constitution*, with Cole Durham, Silvio Ferrari, and Cristiana Cianitto (2013), *Religion and Equality: Law in Conflict*, with Cole Durham (2016), *Law, Religion, and Freedom: Conceptualizing a Common Right*, with Cole Durham and Javier Martínez-Torrón (forthcoming 2019), *Religion and the Secular State: National Reports*, with Martínez-Torrón and Durham, General Reporters (2015), the Brill *Encyclopedia of Law and Religion*, assoc. ed. with Gerhard Robbers and Cole Durham (6 vols. 2016), and the Durham / Brett Scharffs casebook, *Law and Religion: National, International, and Comparative Perspectives* (2nd edn 2018). She is a member of the Utah State Bar.

Sharon Thompson is a Senior Lecturer at Cardiff University. She researches the areas of divorce, family property, prenuptial agreements, and mid-twentieth-century legal history, with a particular focus on feminist perspectives. Publications include *Prenuptial Agreements and the Presumption of Free Choice: Issues of Power in Theory and Practice* (Hart 2015), which was shortlisted for the Peter Birks Prize for Outstanding Legal Scholarship in 2017 and both the SLSA Hart Socio-Legal Book Prize and the SLSA Socio-Legal prize for Early Career Academics in 2016. The book has been cited and applied by the High Court of Australia in *Thorne v. Kennedy* [2017] HCA 49. In 2018, she was awarded a SLSA grant for the project 'Married Women's Association: The Twentieth Century Campaigns that Family Law Forgot'. She is on the editorial board of *Feminist Legal Studies*, is co-editor of case notes for *Journal of Social Welfare and Family Law* and is a member of the Network on Family Regulation and Society.

Part I

Introduction

1 The paradox of pluralism

Towards a relational approach to religious freedom

Russell Sandberg and Sharon Thompson

The stories we tell

'Telling stories of all kinds is the major way that human beings have endeavoured to make sense of themselves and their social world'.[1] Law is all about stories: stories of individual cases; stories of the development of doctrines of law over time; stories about 'the law'; and stories about legal ideas and practices. Legislators, adjudicators, advocates, and scholars are constantly telling, accepting, and perpetuating stories; what Carole Pateman has termed 'conjectural histories'. Orthodox accounts and their implicit assumptions are perpetuated without question. The fact that they are authored and constructed is too easily forgotten. The ways in which these stories are framed; the assumptions, their biases and the fact that they are the product of human systems are overlooked. These stories of law can easily become constraining, rendering invisible alternative narratives and experiences. As Pateman's work illustrates, the stories that do not fit the narrative are silenced and forgotten.[2]

Legal disputes naturally narrow the focus to the often technical issues at hand. The technicolor lives of those involved are reduced to the monochrome constructs that the legal system can understand. The legal eye focuses on constructing a problem and solving a problem. Although cases may be cited by reference to the surnames of the parties, those people are depersonalized in the judgments. Legal argumentation silences or at least suppresses their voices.[3]

It is therefore welcome and important that bodies of scholarly work exist to question the accounts made from orthodox viewpoints. There is a need for scholarship that looks at the terrain from a different lens. The increasing literature on religious pluralism and the increased focus on the legal experiences of minority cultures provide an example of this. This literature starts from a different angle and asks different questions. It starts with an acceptance that diversity is the norm and that different religions and cultures will interact with the state and with the legal system in different ways. The pluralist literature recognizes religious pluralism as a social and legal fact. It problematizes the concept of religion by warning that the term cannot be defined by a conservative appeal to precedent and that the binary between religion and non-religion is by no means absolute.[4] The literature also recognizes

1 Carole Pateman, *The Sexual Contract* (Polity Press 1988), 1.

2 For an appraisal of *The Sexual Contract*, see Sharon Thompson et al., 'The *Sexual Contract* 30 Years On: A Conversation with Carole Pateman' (2018) 26 (1) *Feminist Legal Studies* 93.

3 For a discussion of how legal ideas can be misrepresented see Russell Sandberg, 'The Employment Status of Ministers: A Judicial Retcon?' (2018) 13 *Religion and Human Rights* 27.

4 For further discussion in the context of England and Wales see Russell Sandberg, 'Clarifying the Definition of Religion under English Law: The Need for a Universal Definition? (2018) *Ecclesiastical Law Journal* (forthcoming).

legal pluralism as a social and legal fact, problematizing too the concept of law. This again involves rejecting conservative understandings based on analogy with state law as the norm and debunking the notion that law is autonomous and detached from society and that a neat distinction can be made between law and non-law.[5]

The literature on pluralism has made a number of significant achievements. Indeed, it is striking how many of its presuppositions have become the norm.[6] Yet, this literature too has begun to perpetuate a particular story that is itself selective and constraining. Paradoxically, the pluralist focus is not pluralist enough. Ironically, although this literature has identified and critiqued a number of binary distinctions (most notably the public–private divide and understandings of religion/non-religion, law/non-law), the story it tells has perpetuated another binary focus: a dual spotlight upon the state and upon the religious group. This has overlooked the agency of individuals and failed to take into account the numerous interlocking power relationships that are in play. This means that, although the pluralist lens has meant that the picture painted is in no longer in broad brush strokes, it is still monochrome.

This introductory chapter will begin by exploring this paradox through looking at Ayelet Shachar's *Multicultural Jurisdictions: Cultural Differences and Women's Rights*, [7] a lauded work on religious pluralism and legal pluralism. This identifies the missing story but then ironically makes the same mistake in sidelining agency in the solutions that it proposes. Drawing upon our previous work,[8] we will then explain how a relational approach could overcome this, correcting the pluralist paradox. We conclude by asking the reader to keep this in mind as they read the chapters that follow which all tell stories about pluralism and religion.

The story of *Multicultural Jurisdictions*

Shachar's work is concerned with the 'minorities within minorities debate'. This explores whether the state should play a role in ensuring that members of religious or cultural groups should not be denied the rights that they would ordinarily enjoy by virtue of their citizenship of the state where the polity of the group differs from that of the state as regards gender roles. Shachar's argument is that the state should neither endorse a strong version of multiculturalism giving complete deference to groups nor have a blanket prohibition on the development and enforcement of group-based norms. Either approach would turn a blind eye to gender and other inequalities within the group. A stance of '"non-intervention" may effectively translate into immunizing wrongful behavior by more powerful parties' while

5 See, further, Russell Sandberg, 'The Failure of Legal Pluralism' (2016) 18 *Ecclesiastical Law Journal* 137 and the essays in Russell Sandberg, ed., *Religion and Legal Pluralism* (Ashgate 2015).

6 Socio-legal scholars have come to regard legal pluralism as 'an accepted fact of life': Anne Griffiths, 'Reviewing Legal Pluralism' in Reza Banaker and Max Travers, eds, *Law and Social Theory* (2nd edn, Hart 2013), 269.

7 Ayelet Shachar, *Multicultural Jurisdictions: Cultural Differences and Women's Rights* (Cambridge University Press 2001). This won the 2002 First Book Award, American Political Science Association, Foundations of Political Theory Section and was also cited by the Supreme Court of Canada in *Bruker v.Macovitz* 2007 SCTT 54.

8 Sharon Thompson, *Prenuptial Agreements and the Presumption of Free Choice: Issues of Power in Theory and Practice* (Hart/Bloomsbury 2015); Russell Sandberg and Sharon Thompson, 'Relational Autonomy and Religious Tribunals' (2017) 6 (1) *Oxford Journal of Law and Religion* 137.

prohibition would relegate 'religious traditions to the margins, labelled as unofficial, exotic, or even dangerous (unrecognized) law'.[9]

Shachar's work, therefore, focuses on when and in what circumstances the state should intervene. Like many feminist scholars,[10] Shachar rejects the binary option provided by what is often called the 'right to exit' argument, which states that the role of the state should be limited to ensuring that at-risk group members are able to leave if they do not agree with their group's practices. She argues that this 'right to exit offers no comprehensive approach at all' because it imposes 'the burden of solving conflict upon the individual' whilst 'relieving the state of any responsibility for the situation'.[11] Shachar is critical of how this approach is predicated upon a 'binary' notion of identity whereby individuals are either an adherent of the group or a citizen of the state. She is critical of such an 'oversimplified "either-or"- type understanding of legal authority that is not tailored to respect individuals' manifold identities'.[12] She argues that there is a need to recognize those people within religious groups – who she referred to as 'citizen-insiders' – as being both 'culture-bearers *and* rights-bearers'.[13] She highlights the agency of the citizen-insiders.[14] This criticizes the caricaturing of 'women who remain loyal to minority groups' cultures as victims without agency. She calls for attention to be paid to what she called the 'complex and multi-layered nature of multicultural identity', saying that we cannot 'remain blind to the web of complex and overlapping affiliations which exist between these competing entities'.[15]

However, while Shachar correctly diagnoses the problem, the cure she identifies is problematic. Shachar introduces her concept of 'joint governance'. This describes the idea that people can belong to, show allegiance to, and follow norms from more than one source of authority at any given time.[16] Joint governance seeks to overcome the problem of 'artificially compartmentalizing the relationship between the group and the state into a fixed inside–outside division [which] conceals the extent to which both are in fact interdependent'.[17] It 'promises to foster ongoing interaction between different sources of authority, as a means of improving the situation of traditionally vulnerable insiders without forcing them to adhere to an either/or choice between their culture and their rights'.[18]

Ironically, despite the fact that joint governance seems to focus upon the agency of the citizen-insiders, Shachar's articulation of joint governance sidelines this.[19] In emphasizing how individual identity is negotiated through membership of overlapping (and sometimes

9 Ayelet Shachar, 'Privatizing Diversity: A Cautionary Tale from Religious Arbitration in Family Law' (2008) 9 (2) *Theoretical Inquiries in Law* 573, 593. See also Shachar, *Multicultural Jurisdictions*, supra note 7 at 37, 40.

10 Anne Phillips, for example, denounces the 'right to exit' rationale as not attaching '*enough* significance to cultural belonging': Anne Phillips, *Multiculturalism without Culture* (Princeton University Press 2007), 133. She writes that it is based on a 'constructivist account of culture and universalist account of human nature' (135).

11 Shachar, *Multicultural Jurisdictions*, supra note 7 at 41.

12 Shachar, *Multicultural Jurisdictions* at 12.

13 Ayelet Shachar, 'Privatizing Diversity: A Cautionary Tale from Religious Arbitration in Family Law' (2008) 9 (2) *Theoretical Inquiries in Law* 573, 593.

14 As Phillips forcefully points out, reference to minority cultures is now 'widely employed in a discourse that denies human agency': Phillips, supra note 10 at 9.

15 Shachar, *Multicultural Jurisdictions*, supra note 7 at 15.

16 Shachar, *Multicultural Jurisdictions* at 81.

17 Shachar, *Multicultural Jurisdictions* at 40.

18 Shachar, *Multicultural Jurisdictions* at 88.

19 Russell Sandberg et al., 'Britain's Religious Tribunals: "Joint Governance" in Practice' (2013) 33 (2) *Oxford Journal of Legal Studies* 263.

competing) groups, her account fails to give adequate attention to the citizen-insider. The minority within the minority is treated as the object that the group and state fight over.[20] In her schema, 'it is in the self-professed interest of the group and the state to vie for the support of their constituents.'[21] She observes that 'each entity must "bid" for these individual's continued adherence to its sphere of authority.'[22] This takes a very passive and rational-minded approach to the question of agency. Her focus upon competition has been criticized for taking a 'rational actor view of the world' which is 'written in the language of the marketplace'.[23] When this perspective of the 'individual rights-bearer' is employed it arguably rests upon and perpetuates a liberal legal idea of the autonomous rational person.[24]

Shachar's diagnosis – that gender and agency must be central to understandings of the minorities within minorities issue – is sound. However, by viewing the state and the group as two competing entities, her solution ignores individual agency and the gendered nature of decision making. It fails to solve what Gillian Hadfield has referred to as a 'feminist puzzle' or 'dilemma of choice':[25] whether it is possible 'to protect women from the oppressive consequences of harmful, constrained choices … without divesting women of agency?'[26] Shachar's call for agency to be recognized is laudable but in the end is unrealized. The schemas suggested in *Multicultural Jurisdictions* focus on the state and the group as two competing and monolithic entities. While the story is about the citizen-insider, they themselves are not the main characters and their agency is ignored.

A relational approach

A relational approach is needed to recognize the ways in which people's identities are shaped by the relationships that they form.[27] It is needed in order to correct 'top-down' approaches that focus on the state and the group which deny the agency of minorities within minorities. And, crucially, it is also needed to ensure that the focus on minorities within minorities does not result in an individualistic approach based upon liberal legal assumptions of the autonomous rational person. Placing the citizen-insider as the main character in the story can often lead to an individualist approach. Focusing on whether the citizen-insider consents or can be said to have made an autonomous choice raises the problems caused by the 'right to exit' approach discussed above. Binary legal tests silence the voices of minorities within minorities distorting their situations to fit the story that the legal and political systems can deal with.

In the context of family law in England and Wales, Jonathan Herring has been critical of the rise of an 'individualist conception of autonomy' which claims that 'individuals should be allowed to make decisions for themselves and that those decisions should be respected by

20 Sandberg et al., 'Britain's Religious Tribunals' at 291.
21 Shachar, *Multicultural Jurisdictions*, supra note 7 at 118.
22 Shachar, *Multicultural Jurisdictions* at 117.
23 Phillips, supra note 10 at 153.
24 Joanne Conaghan, 'Reassessing the Feminist Theoretical Project in Law' (2000) 27 (3) *Journal of Law and Society* 351, 360–361.
25 Gillian K. Hadfield, 'The Dilemma of Choice: A Feminist Perspective on The Limits of Freedom of Contract' (1996) 33 (2) *Osgoode Hall Law Journal* 337.
26 Gillian K. Hadfield, 'Expressive Theory of Contract: From Feminist Dilemmas to a Reconceptualization of Rational Choice in Contract Law' (1998) 146 *University of Pennsylvania Law* Review 1235, 1237.
27 See, generally, Nick Crossley, *Towards Relational Sociology* (Routledge 2011).

others, unless the decision involves harming someone else'.[28] The pervasiveness of this approach has been shown by the encouragement of resolution of family disputes outside the courtroom, prompted at least in part by the removal of most legal aid for such family law disputes.[29] The importance now afforded to individual autonomy is epitomized by recent case law concerning prenuptial agreements,[30] which has stressed 'the need to recognize the weight that should now be given to autonomy' and stated that the 'new respect to be given to individual autonomy means that the fact of an agreement can alter what is a fair result and so found a different award to the one that would otherwise have been made'.[31] Family disputes are increasingly treated as private matters where the role of the law is to enable and encourage the couple to reach an agreement.[32] This assumes an equal playing field where the parties are able to make rational individualistic decisions. In other words, it assumes a 'legal fiction'[33] that people exist within a vacuum.

While Herring notes that 'independence and freedom have become the icons of our age', he claims that 'in the context of family law they are false gods'.[34] He therefore proposes an alternative conceptualization of autonomy which he claims is more suitable for family law matters. He suggests 'relational autonomy', which is defined in opposition to individualized autonomy: it stresses how our identities are constantly shaped and re-shaped through the relationships we form with others.[35] Relational autonomy can be particularly useful in relation to cases concerning religion and culture. It provides a means of focusing upon what Shachar refers to as the 'web of complex and overlapping affiliations' that characterize multicultural identities.[36] Indeed, the study of state law on religion ('religion law') can be defined as that area of law 'concerned with the recognition and regulation of certain religious *relationships*'.[37]

Approaches based upon relational autonomy have been employed (particularly by feminists) for some time.[38] However, while his critique of existing family law is both important and illuminating, the way in which Herring applies the term 'relational autonomy' could be seen as blunt. He suggests that any suspicion of the possibility of an adverse power relationship would mean that agreements would not be enforced. For Herring, 'a strong

28 Jonathan Herring, *Relational Autonomy and Family Law* (Springer 2014) 1. See also the essays in Marie-Claire Foblets, Michele Graziadei, and Alison Dundes Renteln, eds, *Personal Autonomy in Plural Societies* (Routledge 2018).

29 On which see, e.g., Jess Mant, 'Neoliberalism, Family Law and the Cost of Access to Justice' (2017) 39 *Journal of Social Welfare and Family Law* 246. See also Alison Diduck, 'Autonomy and Family Justice' (2016) 28 (2) *Child and Family Law Quarterly* 133.

30 Following the UK Supreme Court decision in *Radmacher v. Granatino* [2010] UKSC 42 where it was held that 'the court should give effect to a nuptial agreement that is freely entered into by each party with a full appreciation of its implications unless in the circumstances prevailing it would not be fair to hold the parties to their agreement' [78]. For a full discussion and critique see Thompson, *Prenuptial Agreements*, supra note 8.

31 *V v. V* [2011] EWHC (Fam) 3230, [36.]

32 Herring, supra note 28 at 7.

33 Marie-Claire Foblets, Michele Graziadei, and Alison Dundes Renteln. 'Individual Autonomy in Contemporary Plural Societies: How to Reconcile Competing Normative Standards?' in Foblets, Graziadei, and Renteln, supra note 28 at 2.

34 Herring, supra note 28 at 2

35 Herring, supra note 28 at 11.

36 Shachar, *Multicultural Jurisdictions*, supra note 7 at 15.

37 Russell Sandberg, *Law and Religion* (Cambridge University Press 2011), 11 (emphasis added).

38 See the essays in Catriona Mackenzie and Natalie Stoljar, eds, *Relational Autonomy: Feminist Perspectives on Autonomy, Agency and the Social Self* (Oxford University Press 2000).

argument against the enforcement of prenuptial agreements can be made from the perspective of relational autonomy' because 'only very rarely can there be an equality of bargaining power between parties contemplating marriage'.[39] However, setting an agreement aside because an individual's circumstances have rendered them 'non-autonomous' is not compatible with feminist aim to promote agency and to appreciate that individuals can be autonomous even in oppressive circumstances.[40] While relational autonomy can pay attention to this important reality, figuring out what autonomy means from a relational perspective can also be difficult in practice.[41] Relational meanings of autonomy are interpreted in different ways by different people[42] and are inevitably affected by societal assumptions. In theory, relational autonomy both challenges and undermines assumptions made by individualist conceptions of autonomy, but in practice the term is almost impossible to apply without the court falling back on norms based on individualistic approaches. It is therefore possible that the concept of relational autonomy (especially in the way applied by Herring) would not therefore have the desired practical impact of both recognizing relational inequalities and facilitating agency in a coherent way.[43]

Ultimately the term relational autonomy is a paradox: it recognizes by definition that complete autonomy cannot be achieved since we are all shaped and limited by our social interactions with one another.[44]The important word is 'relational' rather than 'autonomy'. The concept of relational autonomy is useful to identify and correct the dominant paradigm of individualist autonomy. However, as we have argued elsewhere,[45] there is a need to discard the reference to autonomy entirely because it is such an elusive concept. In its place there needs to be a reference to contract.

A contractual approach

As Pateman's work details, social contract theory has become one of the dominant stories told about the social world and the place of human beings within it. She notes: 'An explanation for the binding authority for the state and civil law, and for the legitimacy of modern civil government is to be found by treating our society as if it had originated in contract.'[46] Contract has become 'a principle of social association and one of the most important means of creating social relationships'.[47] Indeed, religious freedom can be understood as being contractual. In England and Wales, for instance, religious organizations are usually treated as

39 Herring, supra note 28 at 6.

40 See Diana T. Meyers, 'Intersectionality Identity and the Authentic Self?: Opposites Attract!' in Catriona Mackenzie and Natalie Stoljar, eds, *Relational Autonomy: Feminist Perspectives on Autonomy, Agency and the Social Self* (Oxford University Press 2000), 151.

41 Lucy-Ann Buckley, 'Relational Theory and Choice Rhetoric in the Supreme Court of Canada' (2014–2015) 29 *Canadian Journal of Family Law* 251, 256.

42 See Lucy-Ann Buckley, 'Autonomy and Prenuptial Agreements in Ireland: A Relational Analysis' (2010) 38 *Legal Studies* 164.

43 Sandberg and Thompson, 'Relational Autonomy and Religious Tribunals', supra note 8. There is also evidence to suggest that a relational autonomy approach does not lead to significantly different outcomes in practice: Buckley, 'Relational Theory and Choice Rhetoric', supra note 41 at 256.

44 Sandberg and Thompson, 'Relational Autonomy and Religious Tribunals', supra note 8 at 148.

45 Sandberg and Thompson, 'Relational Autonomy and Religious Tribunals' at 148 and Thompson, *Prenuptial Agreements*, supra note 8.

46 Pateman, supra note 1 at 1.

47 Pateman at 5.

voluntary associations where members have agreed to be bound together for common purposes and to undertake mutual duties and obligations.[48] The powers of the religious body derive from the agreement of its members. In the Australian case of *Scandrett v. Dowling*[49] it was held that 'the binding effect of the "voluntary consensual compact" …' arises from 'a willingness to be bound to it because of shared faith'. Religious freedom is seen as a quasi-contractual choice. There are examples of civil courts not only applying religious rules as terms of a contract but also applying religious agreements as contracts.[50]

This has perpetuated an individualist approach because it is based on a conception of contract that treats the parties as atomistic constructs, operating in a decision-making process which centers on the discrete moment of consent. Furthermore, as Pateman notes, the notion of social contract and 'the broader argument that, ideally, all social relations should take a contractual form' has entrenched the notion that 'individuals are normally free and equal to each other'.[51] This 'freedom' suffers from the defects of the 'right to exit' argument. It is 'assumed that individual attributes and social attributes always made it reasonable for an individual to give an affirmative answer to the fundamental question of whether a relationship of subordination should be created through contract'.[52] It is based on the assumption that human beings are all 'naturally free and equal (masculine) individuals'.[53]

It therefore may seem odd to rely on contract in order to develop a relational approach. However, a relational approach corrects and broadens the understanding of contract to understand it not in a narrow legal sense or even in the loose sense usually evoked by reference to 'the' social contract.[54] A contractual approach also benefits relational theory by shifting the focus away from autonomy to focus on the situations where social agreements are formed; where in the words of Martha Fineman, 'individuals are given the means to voluntarily and willingly assume obligations and gain entitlements'.[55] The fusion of contract and relational theory has been pioneered by Ian Macneil in his Relational Contract Theory (RCT).[56] Like Herring's explanation of relational autonomy, RCT brings the relationships of the parties to the fore. While orthodox and legalistic understandings of contract are

48 The legal status of the established Church of England and the formerly established Church in Wales differ: see Sandberg, *Law and Religion*, supra note 37 at ch. 3.

49 [1992] 27 NSWLR 483.

50 E.g., 'as a matter of contract arising out of the agreement which the parties had made … the judge was entitled in law to say that this was an enforceable agreement': *Uddin v Choudhury* [2009] EWCA Civ 1205 [15]. Cf. *Shahnaz v Rizwan* [1965] 1 QB 390. For discussion see Sandberg and Thompson, 'Relational Autonomy and Religious Tribunals', supra note 8 at 153–156. For a historical and comparative approach see respectively Amira Sonbul, 'Marriage Contracts in Islamic History' in Nadjma Yassari, ed., *Changing God's Law: The Dynamics of Middle Eastern Family Law* (Routledge 2016), 225 and M. Siraj Sait, 'Our Marriage, Your Property? Renegotiating Islamic Matrimonial Property Regimes' in Yassari, ed., at 245.

51 Pateman, supra note 1 at 39.

52 Pateman at 40.

53 Pateman at 41.

54 Martha Fineman explains the idea of social contract as 'a way of approaching the relationship between the individual and the systems of coercion and authority within which he or she lives': Martha Fineman, *The Autonomy Myth: A Theory of Dependency* (The New Press 2004) 212.

55 Martha Fineman, 'Contract and Care' (2001) 76 (3) *Chicago-Kent Law Review* 1403, 1408.

56 See, e.g, Ian R. Macneil, 'Relational Contract: What We Do and Do Not Know' (1985) *Wisconsin Law Review* 484; Ian R. Macneil, 'The New Social Contract: An Inquiry into Modern Contractual Relations' (1996) 15 (1) *Journal of Public Policy & Marketing* 157 and the essays in David Campbell, ed., *The Relational Theory of Contract: Selected Works of Ian Macneil* (Sweet & Maxwell 2001).

imbued with flawed notions of autonomy, RCT instead repurposes contract in a way that recognizes the relational context in which individuals make decisions.

Macneil's work criticizes orthodox contract for its focus on agreements as discrete one-off transactions, and for failing to recognize the relationships between the parties, as he argued that these relationships significantly influence the ways in which decisions are made. For Macneil, highlighting the parties' relationship necessitates a focus on important contextual factors in commercial transactions, such as duration and trade customs. By replacing neo-liberal assumptions that depict contracting parties as being purely self-interested and disconnected individuals with a relationship-orientated approach, RCT appreciates what Mulcahy refers to as the 'lived world of contracts'.[57] Once liberated from the narrow orthodox legalistic understandings that pay almost exclusive attention to what Pateman has referred to as the 'fictions of original agreements',[58] contract becomes a useful means of understanding relationships and arrangements. Indeed, this means that contract can be seen 'as a principle of social association and one of the most important means of creating social relationships'.[59]

Approaches based on RCT contextualize the discrete transactions within the overall relationships between the parties, highlighting the number of relationships that exist. This involves exploring in detail not just the agreement and the conditions surrounding it but a number of interlocking relationships over a much longer period. In the context of religious pluralism this would include looking at the entire relationship between minorities within minorities and the individual member and the group as well as family and community pressures and the role of authority structures within the group as well as their interaction with the state.[60]

However, this does not go far enough. It does not question the structures that exist and the power disparities and inequalities that exist as a result. As Pateman argues, the roots of contract are based in inequality and informed by a status quo that treats everyone in a neutral way.[61] It is noticeable that RCT was developed mostly within a commercial context and, although some work has extended it beyond this setting,[62] the original context continues to constrain it. There is a clear difference between commercial and domestic agreements: there are different expectations of their nature and enforcement and numerous different interlocking power relationships in play. This means that RCT needs to be developed. A relational approach broadens the story to look at the characters in relation to each other and to see them as products of their relationships. However, it still does not place them at the center ground. It continues to be shaped by the priorities, assumptions, and values of the pervasive neo-liberal culture. This can be overcome by changing the perspective through adopting the feminist approach which shaped Shachar's diagnosis, but which was less present in her cure.

57 Linda Mulcahy, 'Telling Tales about Relational Contracts: How Do Judges Learn about the Lived World of Contracts?' in David Campbell, Linda Mulcahy and Sally Wheeler, eds, *Changing Concepts of Contract: Essays in Honour of Ian Macneil* (Palgrave Macmillan 2013) 193.

58 Pateman, supra note 1.

59 Pateman at 5.

60 Sandberg and Thompson, 'Relational Autonomy and Religious Tribunals', supra note 8 at 157.

61 Pateman, supra note 1.

62 E.g., on marriage law: Lloyd Cohen, 'Marriage, Divorce and Quasi Rents; or, "I Gave Him the Best Years of My Life"' (1987) 16 (2) *Journal of Legal Studies* 267; Robert Leckey, 'Relational Contract and other Models of Marriage', (2002) 40 (1) *Osgoode Hall Law Journal* 1, 5.

A feminist approach

Pateman's *The Sexual Contract* highlights a disconnect between the myth – that all citizens are equal under the social contract – and the reality, that across institutions, women are subordinate to men. Her work asserts that the focus on the social contract has meant that it is rarely noticed that 'half the story' is missing: 'We hear an enormous amount about the *social* contract; a deep silence is maintained about the *sexual* contract.'[63] The conjectural history told presents the rise of the social contract as 'a story of freedom' where all adults enjoy the same standing and ability to contract and which is 'anti-patriarchal or post-patriarchal'.[64] This ignores the 'story of subjection' found in the sexual contract, which shows 'how men's patriarchal right over women is established through contract' because, rather than being universal, 'civil freedom is a masculine attribute and depends upon patriarchal right'. For Pateman, 'contract is far from being opposed to patriarchy; contract is the means by which modern patriarchy is constituted'.

Pateman's insistence that the invisible story of the sexual contract be told and the orthodox account be questioned and debunked provides an example of the subversive approach to storytelling that a feminist approach can take by telling the untold story; by making visible what was previously invisible. A feminist approach can be understood as a critical approach to law; that is, an approach that 'produces disturbances in the field – that inverts or scrambles familiar narratives of stasis, recovery or progress; anything that advances rival perspectives (such of those as the losers rather than the winners) for surveying developments, or that posits alternative trajectories that might have produced a very different present'.[65] Such approaches can be said to be subversive in that they disturb and challenge the narratives and sources used by and in conventional and orthodox historical accounts.[66]

Feminist approaches to law can be understood in this light: they provide a particular type of subversion. Although feminist approaches to law are varied,[67] as Conaghan notes it is possible and 'useful to identify some common, recurring features of feminist academic engagement with law and to do so without either essentializing feminism or denying the complexity and contestability of the features thus described'.[68] A feminist approach 'presupposes that gender has a much greater structural and/or discursive significance than is commonly assumed, a significance which is ideologically but not practically diminished by its

63 Pateman at 1.

64 Pateman at 2. For discussion of what Pateman means by the term patriarchy see chapter 2 of *The Sexual Contract*. As Vanessa Munro notes, an argument based on patriarchy does not necessarily imply that women and their interests have been ignored: 'Rather, the claim is often, more accurately, that the processes by which women's interests have been (re)presented, historically and currently, have been mediated (or "refracted") by male interpretations and understandings': Vanessa Munro, *Law and Politics at the Perimeter: Re-evaluating Key Debates in Feminist Theory* (Hart 2007), 12.

65 Robert Gordon, 'The Arrival of Critical Historicism' (1997) 49 *Stanford Law Review* 1023, 1024.

66 Russell Sandberg, 'The Time for Legal History: Maitland and Milsom Fifty Years On' (2018) *Law & Justice* (forthcoming).

67 This includes the identification of particular schools of feminist thought such as the liberal, radical, cultural and postmodern. The usefulness of such designated has been questioned by Pateman on the basis that 'the classification of feminists ... suggests that feminism is always secondary, a supplement to other doctrines': Pateman, supra note 1 at x.

68 Joanne Conaghan, 'Reassessing the Feminist Theoretical Project in Law' (2000) 27 (3) *Journal of Law and Society* 351, 358–359. See also Wishtik's framework for inquiry for feminist jurisprudence: Heather R. Wishnik, 'To Question Everything: The Inquiries of Feminist Jurisprudence (1986) 1 *Berkeley Women's Law Journal* 64, 72–75.

relative invisibility'.[69] By choosing to explicitly recognize this, in other words, to not be silent on the gendered dimensions, issues of power are placed at the core of the discussions rather than on the margins. A feminist approach alters the lens in which we see law and the social world by shedding light on structural and entrenched gendered disadvantages that are perpetuated.

Feminist scholarship focuses on structures and discourses that are often invisible in the conventional stories that are told. By choosing not be silent on the gendered dimensions, feminist scholarship questions and debunks conventional and traditional understandings about law and talk of law. Gender is never absent from a discussion about where fundamental values in law come from, particularly when examining the wider context of social relations in which values are constituted and accepted. A feminist approach acknowledges that ideas about gender are both affected and effect legal ideas. It looks at the situation from a different angle. Feminist scholarship is grounded. It dispenses the usual 'top-down' analysis to instead focus on actual lived experiences, operating from the ground up.

This means that attention is afforded to agency. A feminist approach does not assume that men necessarily have an oppressive role but it recognizes that there is a power dimension between men and women in social life as a whole and especially when they are legal actors given the gendered nature of legal institutions, discourse, and practices.[70] A theory that protects women *qua* women (and therefore as oppressed) fails to recognize the different contexts in which power imbalance occurs. Just because there are situations where women as minorities in minorities have less power and less autonomy, this does not mean these women are vulnerable or have less power because they are always weak in the face of inevitable male dominance. Indeed, it would be a mistake to presume a lack of agency. As Diana Meyers has argued, individuals experiencing multiple forms of oppression and structural inequality can still be partially autonomous, and it should not be assumed they are unable to be autonomous because of structural constraints.[71] A more worthwhile use of feminism is instead to focus any concerns on the interests of people who are affected by power imbalance.

A feminist approach can therefore provide a crucial corrective to conventional stories of religious pluralism and the role of the state which present a binary choice between paternalistic or laissez-faire stances, both of which fail to give attention to the agency of minorities within minorities. A feminist approach is required in particular because religious life is gendered, as shown by the significant position that women play in religious life and the fact that this is often not in correlation with male dominated decision-making processes, norms, and culture.[72] Moreover, the construction and articulation of religious freedom is also gendered. Its contractual nature and man-made architecture which assumes that individuals are free to act in economic rational ways means that it is based upon and perpetuates masculine notions of individualized autonomy. A feminist approach can identify and critique this. It can provide a means of deconstruction. However, a feminist approach need not be placed in

69 Conaghan at 359–360. It is possible to identify a shift in feminist legal literature moving from a focus on 'women and law' to 'law and gender': Emily Jackson and Nicola Lacey, 'Introducing Feminist Legal Theory' in J. Penner et al., eds, *Introduction to Jurisprudence and Legal Theory* (Butterworths 2002), 779, 781.

70 Thompson, *Prenuptial Agreements*, supra note 8 at 9.

71 Meyers, supra note 40 at 151.

72 Marie Failinger et al. view religious women as being 'not only part of religious communities [but] arguably, essentially DNA from which many rich religious cultures are built': Marie A Failinger, Elizabeth R. Schlitz, and Susan J. Stabile, 'Foreword' in Marie A. Failinger, Elizabeth R. Schlitz, and Susan J. Stabile, eds, *Feminism, Law, and Religion* (Ashgate 2013), xiii.

opposition to conventional accounts. Instead, it can improve those accounts by criticizing the law whilst operating within its confines.[73] It can provide a means of reconstruction.

Combining the approaches: feminist relational contact theory

As we have argued elsewhere,[74] an approach previously created and applied in relation to prenuptial agreements provides a way forward: Feminist Relational Contract Theory (FRCT).[75] On the surface, developing RCT by using feminist approaches seems to be mixing two contradictory approaches. David Campbell, a leading advocate of RCT, calls feminist contract theory 'something of an oxymoron' because in his view it sacrifices the liberal values implicit in RCT (most notably the respect for individual autonomy) for the prioritization of feminist equality.[76] However, FRCT is designed to overcome the incompatibility identified by Campbell by recognizing as problematic and discarding the liberal values implicit in RCT and by applying an explicitly feminist approach which develops RCT to pay attention not only to the tacit understandings affecting intimate relationships, but to also critique and subvert them. As the name of the theory suggests, it seeks to build upon RCT using the subversive nature of feminist legal studies to question the values implicit in RCT by altering the lens in order to place gender inequalities at the fore.[77]

FRCT builds upon the strengths of both relational autonomy and RCT. It incorporates feminist perspectives that explicitly address power imbalances (especially those that are gendered) where RCT otherwise would not, directing critical fire at how social and legal structures reinforce power imbalances. FRCT places emphasis upon the various overlapping relationships which people have and the effect that this has. It involves examining social agreements within the wider context of multiple power relationships paying particular attention to inequalities caused by gender by taking a 'bottom up' approach which focuses on the gendered aspects of various interlocking relationships and the decision-making process and court personnel.[78]

Crucially, agency is not abandoned when feminist understandings of power are combined with relational contract's understanding of context.[79] FRCT does not view choice as being a binary ultimatum between agreeing or disagreeing. It recognizes instead that it is possible to follow a third route: staying within the group and negotiating a compromise.[80] FRCT can see that it might not be rational or practical for minorities within minorities to walk away and that this does not mean that we should presume that they lack agency. FRCT also pays much more attention to how the relationship has changed over time. FRCT places agency to the fore. It fully recognizes the web of relationships by regarding them as social contracts, and it accepts that power imbalances exist and that the role of the law is to decide when

73 Munro, supra note 64, ch. 2.
74 Sandberg and Thompson, 'Relational Autonomy and Religious Tribunals', supra note 8.
75 This was first developed in Thompson, *Prenuptial Agreements*, supra note 8.
76 David Campbell, 'Afterword: Feminism, Liberalism and Utopianism in the Analysis of Contracting' in Linda Mulcahy and Sally Wheeler, eds, *Feminist Perspectives on Contract Law* (Routledge 2005), 161, 165.
77 It is part of a trend within feminist legal studies which moves on from the critique of the liberalism tradition to engage with it: Munro, supra note 64, ch. 2.
78 Sandberg and Thompson, 'Relational Autonomy and Religious Tribunals', supra note 8 at 158.
79 For an application of a contextual approach see the Australia decision in *Thorne v Kennedy* [2017] HCA 49 as discussed by Sharon Thompson, '*Thorne v Kennedy*: Why Australia's Decision on Prenups is Important for English Law' (2018) 39 (4) *Family Law* 415.
80 Thompson, *Prenuptial Agreements*, supra note 8 at 115.

those power imbalances are significant enough to override freedom of (social) contract. FRCT therefore goes further than Shachar's work on joint governance or Herring's work on relational autonomy in that it provides a means by which courts and other decision-making bodies can recognize and take into account the various relationships involved and the resulting power imbalances. An approach based on FRCT recognizes the effects of various relationships focusing upon contract as a concrete form of social association without being infected by the liberal and neo-liberal obsession with individualized autonomy.

Unlike Shachar's work on joint governance, FRCT advances matters in a way which unlocks the promise of recognizing agency whilst simultaneously appreciating the effect of gendered power issues. Shachar's work stresses that 'the action and agency of individuals, groups and states is situational, that is, it varies in different institutions settings and to some extent is shaped by them'.[81] FRCT takes this further to regard action and agency as situational *and* relational: being shaped by complex interlocking social relationships and social statuses. Adding an explicitly feminist approach to RCT alters the lens and provides us with a multicolor picture using a feminist perspective to place issues of power at the center. FRCT therefore provides us with a way whereby stories about law can be challenged. The paradox of much of the literature on pluralism is not only overcome but is transcended. A relational approach overcomes the binary focus on the group and the state by recognizing a number of interlocking power relationships that develop over time. A feminist approach complements and furthers this by changing the lens to focus upon the power inequalities that exist, placing them and the lived experiences of those affected at the fore without denying them agency. Shachar's ambition is to find a way that does not provide religious groups with a blank cheque but also does not prohibit their activities. FRCT provides this. It recognizes that minorities within minorities more often than not do not have an entirely free choice but that this does not mean that the compromise they reach should automatically be disregarded. Rather than adopting a paternal approach based on assumptions, a grounded approach is taken based on evidence.

The stories to come

This introduction has discussed how a relational and feminist perspective drastically changes our view on legal responses to religious pluralism. Such a perspective takes us away from an orthodox legal binary view of choice and a twofold relationship between the state and the group. It moves us towards an understanding of the many and varied ways in which people really make decisions and the social, economic, and legal pressures they are under when making these decisions. It allows us to see what is otherwise often invisible. The chapters that follow provide a plethora of perspectives on pluralism, exploring religious pluralism from several different angles and in a variety of settings. They all tell stories about pluralism and the law, which provide new questions. Moreover, since those chapters and their authors do not exist in a vacuum, they all reflect pervasive stories about religion and about law that exist. This should be kept in mind when reading each chapter and the stories about law that they present. Each chapter provides a snapshot giving a particular story; taken as a whole, they provide a plurality of perspectives on pluralism.

81 Shachar, *Multicultural Jurisdictions*, supra note 7 at 89.

The book features selected revised papers from the third ICLARS conference on 'Religion, Democracy, and Equality'.[82] It falls into two sections. The first, entitled 'Starting Points', introduces a range of different vantage points from which the topic of religious pluralism can be approached. These include both legal and religious starting points. Chapters 2 and 3 set the scene by focusing on what has been identified as the two halves of law and religion scholarship: the rules and norms enacted by secular authorities at the international, national, and sub-national levels affecting religion ('religion law') and the rules and norms enacted by religious groups themselves ('religious law').[83] Chapter 2 by H. Victor Condé, 'Human Rights and the Protection of Religious Expression', sets the scene in religion law terms by exploring the international legal frameworks concerning religious freedom. It is by no means a primer, however. It is rather not only a foundation for the chapters that follow but also a radical call to reexamine the legal texts, concepts, and rules of interpretation; the building blocks of the stories that this book and others like it seek to tell. The chapter is a welcome reminder that these legal ideas and articulations are constructs and therefore can be revisited and reconstructed.[84] Chapter 3 by Iain T. Benson, 'The Search for Pluralism in Islam, Roman Catholicism, and Judaism', sets the scene in terms of religious law looking at how pluralism is understood in these three religions. It focuses on the understandings of pluralism put forward in the works by particular writers in each faith, exploring the stories they tell about the nature and purpose of pluralism in their faith tradition. Chapter 4 develops this. In 'Religious Freedom and Tolerance: A Judaic Perspective', Asher Maoz explores the Jewish attitude towards other religions. This provides yet another vantage point seeing how a particular religion views other religions and as the author notes this focus needs to be selective, concentrating on articulating what he refers to as the attitude of mainstream contemporary Judaism. This highlights the effect that the starting point taken can have upon the story that is being told.

Hans-Martien ten Napel's Chapter 5, 'Western "Civic Totalism", Sovereignty of the People, and the Need for Limited Government', provides a different starting focus: the role of the State, with a much-needed insight from political philosophy that is often omitted in the legal stories told about religious pluralism. Chapter 6 begins from a different place, focusing on international initiatives to deal with religious freedom. 'From Rabat to Istanbul' by Mohamed Saeed M. Eltayeb examines the Rabat Plan of Action and the Istanbul Process as being complimentary and as operating within a quest for wider implementation strategies for combating religious hatred. Jeroen Temperman's Chapter 7, 'The Prohibition of Advocacy of Religious Hatred that Constitutes Incitement to Discrimination, Hostility, or Violence', develops the focus on the law on religious hatred found in Chapter 5 but zooms in to explore what the author considers to be 'the oddity' of Article 20(2) of the UN International Covenant on Civil and Political Rights. This chapter provides an example of a

82 This was held in Virginia, the United States in Richmond, Williamsburg, and the University of Virginia in Charlottesville from 21–23 August 2013. A selection of other papers delivered at that conference has been previously published in W. Cole Durham, Jr. and Donlu Thayer, eds, *Religion and Equality: Law in Conflict* (Routledge 2016).

83 Sandberg, *Law and Religion,* supra note 37 at ch.1 and ch. 9.

84 This is one of the key reasons why a historical approach to law is important: see Russell Sandberg, 'The Time for Legal History', supra note 66 and Russell Sandberg and Norman Doe, 'Textual and Contextual Legal History' in Norman Doe and Russell Sandberg, *Law and History – Critical Concepts in Law* (Routledge 2017) 1. For an example of an approach tracing the changing meanings of words and the way in which this affects legal discourse see Sharon Thompson, 'In Defence of the "Gold-Digger"' (2016) 6 (6) *Oñati Socio Legal Series* 1225.

different story-telling device: the micro-examination of a particular law which seeks to explore its nature and future. The juxtaposing of Chapter 5 with Chapters 6 and 7, as with the contrasting Chapter 2 with Chapters 3 and 4, is telling. By revealing very different starting points, these chapters underline how the stories told about pluralism are shaped by the foundations upon which they are based and that these foundations are themselves constructed and reconstructed as part of the story-telling process.

The second section, 'Perspectives', grounds the analysis by focusing on a particular geographical context to examine how states and supra-state institutions have responded to religious pluralism. Norberto Padilla's Chapter 8, 'Religious Pluralism: The Argentine Experience', starts by looking at a country whose history is littered with political intolerance and divisions. Padilla argues that religion has and does play a significant role in reconciling differences in Argentina. The historical predominance of Catholicism now complemented by other religions has, for Padilla, created a society capable of solidarity in matters of religious and social harmony. Chapter 9, 'The Quest for Religious Pluralism in Post-Apartheid South Africa', by Mary-Anne Plaatjies-van Huffel also looks at another country that is often characterized as being very religious. The chapter explores how the management of moral and religious diversity is one of the challenges facing post-apartheid South Africa. It calls for an 'ethic of concern' to develop whereby individuals need to learn to co-exist and develop bonds of solidarity with one another and whereby religious groups and the state need to engage with one another. Chapters 8 and 9 therefore look at the stories of legal regulation at a state level taking a broad often historical sweep to contextualize today's issues. These are not narratives of progress, however, but are rather stories of 'works in progress' through which the legacy of history is being modified by changes in social mores, political policy, and legal reform. One significant change in the last century has been the move towards globalization. Now the nation state no longer has complete authority over the story that they want to tell. This is underlined by Chapter 10, which provides a continental-level analysis to show the effect and potential of supra-State legal norms. In 'National Human Rights Institutions and the Accommodation of Religious Diversity in Africa', Enyinna Nwauche notes that the fact that Africa is made up of 53 countries means that discussions about accommodation of religious diversity across the continent are complex. The chapter proposes that discussion of National Human Rights Institutions (NHRI), constitutional and statutory bodies established by African States for the protection and promotion of human rights, can provide a step forward.

The book concludes by reference to European experiences, again starting with an examination of a particular state and how they have dealt and how they deal with the regulation of religious freedom before mirroring Enyinna Nwauche's chapter by providing a continental-wide analysis, here focusing on the jurisprudence of the European Court of Human Rights. In Chapter 11, 'The Status of Religious Organizations in Poland', Piotr Stanisz explores how the Polish constitution embraces the 'cooperation model' by promoting cooperation and agreements between the state and religious organizations.[85] Stanisz identifies a number of tensions that emerge from this constitutional stance and emphasizes the importance of recognizing the unique character of individual religious groups. The narrative expressed in constitutional norms can often drown out the idiosyncratic nature of different

85 For discussion and critique of the models of church–state relations that are said to exist in Europe see Norman Doe, *Law and Religion in Europe. A Comparative Introduction* (Oxford University Press 2011) and Russell Sandberg, 'Church–State Relations in Europe: From Legal Models to an Interdisciplinary Approach' (2008) 1(3) *Journal of Religion in Europe* 329.

religions making them conform to a discourse that the legal system understands. This risk is even more pronounced where regulation of religion occurs at a level above the nation state. This is reflected in Chapter 12. In Javier Martínez-Torrón's appraisal of 'State Neutrality and Religious Plurality in Europe' the focus moves the regional level and in particular looks at the role of a particular court. This chapter provides a *tour de force* of recent case law by the European Court of Human Rights and interrogates the language used by the Court to reveal the underlying principles that underpin the Court's developing jurisprudence. Cases before the Court provide a range of heterogeneous stories about the nature and accommodation of religion shaped by national and sub-national histories and experiences. The unenviable task of the Court is to determine such claims within the confines of a pan-European legal order which needs to balance the need to respect diversity in approach though the 'margin of appreciation' doctrine whilst ensuring that there are pan-European norms since otherwise the institution has no reason to exist. Martínez-Torrón's chapter explores the stories about religious freedom that are accepted, created, and perpetuated by the Court.

Taken as a whole, the chapters showcase a plurality of perspectives on pluralism. This is examined in the concluding chapter by the editors W. Cole Durham Jr and Donlu D. Thayer who ask the provocative question, 'Religious Pluralism: Peace or Poison'. Given mounting worldwide tensions concerning the relationship between religious diversity and social harmony, the questions raised, explored, and critiqued in this volume are timely, stimulating, and difficult. Tensions exist about the place of religion in public life generally, manifested in disputes about employment, education, and the family and shaped by and shaping media coverage of religion.[86]There are no easy answers to the dilemmas posed. However, reference to differing perspectives and a move away from binary solutions provides a step forward. The paradox of pluralism – that debates about pluralism and religious difference focus on the state and the group and therefore give inadequate attention to the lived experiences and agency of minorities within minorities – needs to be overcome. It needs to be remembered that the stories we tell about religious pluralism are precisely that: stories. They are constructed ways of making sense of the world and our role within it, which provide but one perspective and render other stories invisible.[87]

86 For a legal and sociological discussion see Russell Sandberg, *Religion, Law and Society* (Cambridge University Press 2014).

87 Cf. Pateman, supra note 1 at 1.

Part II

Starting points

2 Human rights and the protection of religious expression

Manifestation of religion as *Lex Specialis* of freedom of expression

H. Victor Condé

Abuse of religious freedom: a crucial global issue

This chapter addresses the danger of misapplying or misinterpreting international human rights legal standards in dealing with religious freedom issues, particularly about religious expression. The abuse of religious freedom is one of the crucial global issues of our day. Though freedom of religion is said to have been historically the first human right, and is a most important part of human rights law, many now perceive that right is in danger. More and more often today, what that religious speaker can say is being prevented, limited, or punished.[1]

The focus here is not on the effect, impact, or damage caused by a religious message, nor is it on the harm or injured feelings of someone who finds such expression offensive or blasphemous. The focus is rather on the speaker, on the rights of the religious person to manifest religion via religious expression, to express *religious* truths, whether about one's own religion's doctrines or about another religion, or about a moral or even a political issue. The focus of this chapter, in other words, is on the extent of religious speakers' human rights to express themselves religiously,[2] and it is about the religious organization's freedom of expression, religious expression to be exact, in a world increasingly antagonistic to religion and its truth claims.

In looking at international human rights law and what it says about how much government can restrict religious expression, the chapter takes us to the wording of human rights legal texts and specifically to the norm of 'manifestation of religion', a phrase which covers any religious expression. This is examined in relation to general freedom of expression, which leads us to the legal principle of *Lex Specialis*,[3] by which freedoms of religion and expression are related.

Increasingly louder voices today express beliefs that some religious speech constitutes hate speech, or an incitement to violence or discrimination, particularly regarding morality issues

1 Heiner Bielefeldt, 'Freedom of Religion or Belief—A Human Right Under Pressure', (2012) 1 *Oxford Journal of Law and Religion* 1, 15–25.

2 See Heiner Bielefeldt, 'Equality and Diversity in Conceptualizing Freedom of Religion or Belief', Foreword to W. Cole Durham, Jr. and Donlu Thayer, eds, *Religion and Equality: Law in Conflict* (Routledge 2016), xv: 'Due to its nature as a human right, freedom of religion or belief protects human beings rather than religions or belief systems in themselves.'

3 From *lex specialis derogat legi generali* ('specialized laws prevail over general laws'). 'The Principle is based on the presumption that, in enacting a law or drafting a contract provision, a lawmaker or contract drafter does not want to create a law or contractual provision that would be devoid of any scope of application. This would be the case if the general rule always prevailed.' See Trans-lex Law. Commentary to Trans-Lex Principle, http://www.trans-lex.org/910000.

and minority religions. This has given rise to the use of the law as a tool to stifle religious expression about other religions, about morals, and about various minorities. In such a view, the religious voice has no more place in the marketplace of ideas. Political correctness is the spirit of the day, reflecting a professed attempt to bring about the magnanimous idea of tolerance and broadmindedness. To some, however, this spirit reflects, rather, evidence of uniformity, intolerance, and narrowmindedness towards religion.

Of course, not all expressions concerning religion, or statements made by religious persons, are absolutely protected. But legitimate religious expression is now under attack, as individuals, organizations, and governments seek to silence the pulpit, the street preacher, the evangelist, the Mormon missionary, the Jehovah's Witness, the parent teaching her children, even the religious politician, whose views they do not like or that are deemed contrary to 'modern' social values.

This chapter is a call to the legal, political, and academic communities to reexamine our legal concepts, texts, and rules of interpretation regarding religious expression and its legal limits. Most importantly, this chapter seeks to show a failure in the international legal and political arenas to apply the correct legal standard to religious expression because of an incorrect use of the legal texts involving freedom of religion and freedom of expression. In short, the restriction clauses of freedom of expression are too often applied to issues for which the freedom of religion restriction clauses should be applied. An understanding of the legal principle of *Lex Specialis* can explain how religious freedom should correctly be legally protected and how protection of religious expression can be maximized.

Why is religious freedom, including religious expression, important?

Anyone watching the media has to be aware of issues of religious persecution and discrimination in the world today. Many such events involve punishing religious expression. This often involves claims that the religious expression constitutes a hate crime or an offense to the religious sensitivities of another religion or its members, is a manifestation of extremism,[4] or concerns an incitement to religious hatred or discrimination against a certain group in society.

One classic example is the 2006 academic lecture of Pope Benedict XVI in Regensburg, Germany. This lecture, wherein the Pope quoted a medieval scholar on the latter's views on Islam, set off riots and caused fatalities, as it was perceived to have been defamatory of Islam. It was argued that the Pope should not have said what he did even to a Catholic academic audience at a Catholic University. It was argued that he did not have the right to say such things, that it was defamatory and incited hatred of Muslims. This chapter would argue that under existing human rights law the Pope had every legal right to so speak, and that the Pope's expression was legally merely 'manifestation of religion' through teaching, within the permissible scope of international human right law.

To illustrate only a few other examples of religious expression being attacked:

- Egypt 2013: A Coptic school teacher was convicted of insulting Islam, accused by three students of insulting the prophet Muhammad by saying the late Coptic Pope Shenouda performed more miracles than the Prophet.

4 We may consider, for example, Russia's application of July 2016 amendments to its anti-extremism law, which led in April 2017 to a ban on activities of Jehovah's Witnesses in the country and a seizure of the church's assets, followed by ongoing legal battles.

- London 2016: A lay Christian Evangelist was arrested during open air evangelizing for 'using homophobic speech that could cause people anxiety, distress, alarm or insult'.[5]
- Spain 2016: Efforts were being made to criminally prosecute five Spanish bishops for writing and speaking out against a new law on protection of LGBT rights.

Many other such attacks against those disseminating religious expressions could be cited, most of them involving legal claims against the speaker, denounced as either hate speech, so-called defamation of religion, blasphemy, or incitement to religious hatred. All, in essence, involve claims that speakers did not have the right to say what they said, and this denial of a right to speak has been most often, and wrongly, based on the restriction of freedom of expression, not freedom of religion.

Once in a while one sees a legal forum giving religious expression its proper place, despite public disapproval, by finding it legally protected. In one such example from 2013, Costa Rica's Electoral Supreme Court said that the church hierarchy has the right to speak about social and moral issues, proclaiming its teaching freely in order to inform the nation's voters. It can 'take stances on the country's social problems, as well as to preach the faith with authentic freedom, teach its social doctrine, exercise an earthly mission without interference and issue moral judgments, even on issues related to public order and others of interest to it.'[6] Such legal victories, however, are the exception, not the rule. And this is partly because expressions are judged by expression norms, not religion norms.

In almost all such cases a religious person is making a religious expression. In human rights law, we call this a 'manifestation of religion'. It is not just about freedom of expression. It is about freedom of religion by manifestation of religion through teaching, practice, worship, and observance. Religious expression is being judged the same as non-religious expression. Under the principle of *Lex Specialis*, this is legal error.

Without freedom of religion one cannot conceptualize any human rights, much less understand the concept and value of inherent human dignity, which is the juridical basis of all human rights. Full freedom of religion is important because where the state limits freedom of religion more strictly than human rights allows, the state is violating human rights, and the full exercise of all other human rights is imperiled. This is because all human rights are interdependent in principle. The related human right to freedom of expression is itself dependent upon freedom of religion for its effectiveness. All religions strongly favor the communication of religious doctrines, experiences, and views. For some it is a spiritual mandate, a divine obligation. This requires a legal protection of freedom of religion, especially its teaching and communicative aspects.

Freedom of religion is also important because it is the main source of a believer's identity and understanding of reality and the meaning of life. It is for many the prime mover of human emotions, the highest truth, the source of personal growth and development, the main source of law, moral values, cohesion of most societies. Such freedom can be helpful in avoiding or resolving social, national, or international conflicts. As the first recognized

5 'U.S. Street Preacher Arrested in London for Saying Homosexuality Sinful', *LifeSiteNews*, 9 July 2013, https://www.lifesitenews.com/news/u.s.-street-preacher-arrested-in-london-for-using-homophobic-language.

6 'Costa Rica Court: Church Has Right to Speak on Social Issues', *Catholic News Agency*, 30 October 2013, http://www.catholicnewsagency.com/news/costa-rica-court-church-has-right-to-speak-on-social-issues/.

human right, freedom of religion is considered by most scholars to be the 'lynchpin of all human rights'.[7]

One reason we know that freedom of religion is important in international human rights law, at both global and regional levels, is that it is given special legal protection in that body of law. Protection of freedom of religion, often coupled with belief ('religion or belief') has found a place within the legal norms of what is called international human rights law, a part of public international law. As a genre of human rights, protection of freedom of religion is called a right to moral integrity. It is that which allows an individual and collection of individuals to decide what creeds and values a society holds and wishes to protect by law, and what actions and expressions and beliefs are acceptable in society.

The importance of religious freedom in contemporary international affairs was well articulated in the first international-level human rights case involving a substantive human rights legal norm taken from the European Convention on Human Rights (ECHR) Article 9.[8] In its 1993 judgment in *Kokkinakis v. Greece* [9] the European Court of Human Rights (ECtHR) said the following:

> As enshrined in Article 9 (art. 9), freedom of thought, conscience and religion is one of the foundations of a 'democratic society' within the meaning of the Convention. *It is, in its religious dimension, one of the most vital elements that go to make up the identity of believers and their conception of life*, but it is also a precious asset for atheists, agnostics, sceptics and the unconcerned. The pluralism indissociable from a democratic society, which has been dearly won over the centuries, depends on it.
>
> While religious freedom is primarily a matter of individual conscience, *it also implies, inter alia, freedom to '**manifest [one's] religion**'. Bearing witness in words and deeds* is bound up with the existence of religious convictions.
>
> According to Article 9, freedom to manifest one's religion is not only exercisable in community with others, 'in public' and within the circle of those whose faith one shares, but can also be asserted 'alone' and 'in private'; furthermore, it includes in principle the right to try to convince one's neighbour, for example through 'teaching', failing which, moreover, 'freedom to change [one's] religion or belief', enshrined in Article 9, would be likely to remain a dead letter.[10] (emphasis added)

This case was about protection of religious expression, namely proselytism,[11] specifically, door-to-door evangelizing by a Jehovah's Witness in Greece. The ECtHR was recognizing the legal status of Mr. Kokkinakis's religious expressions, and protecting his human rights to manifest his religion in teaching.

7 See Thomas Farr, 'Is Religious Freedom Necessary for Other Freedoms to Flourish?', Berkeley Center for Religion, Peace & World Affairs, Georgetown University, 7 August 2013, http://berkleycenter.georgetown.edu/rfp/essays/is-religious-freedom-necessary-for-other-freedoms-to-flourish.

8 European Convention for the Protection of Human Rights and Fundamental Freedoms, 213 UNTS 222 (1950) entered into force 3 September 1953.

9 *Kokkinakis v. Greece*, App. No. 14307/88 (ECtHR, 25 May 1993).

10 *Kokkinakis* para. 31.

11 Though 'proselytism' is often used pejoratively, it is not, by definition, a wrongful or harmful act. It is simply the attempt to persuade another person to convert to another religion or world view.

A more recent example of an international organization expressing the value of protecting freedom of religion, including religious expression, comes from the European Union in mid 2013, in its *Guidelines on the Promotion and Protection of Freedom of Religion or Belief.*[12]

> 1. The right to freedom of thought, conscience, religion or belief, more commonly referred to as the right to freedom of religion or belief (FoRB) is a fundamental right of every human being. As a universal human right, freedom of religion or belief safeguards respect for diversity. Its free exercise directly contributes to democracy, development, rule of law, peace and stability. Violations of freedom of religion or belief may exacerbate intolerance and often constitute early indicators of potential violence and conflicts.

The protection of religious expression in human rights law occurs in relation to two specific human rights: freedom of religion and freedom of expression, such as found in ECHR Articles 9 and 10, and in Articles 18 and 19 of the UN International Covenant on Civil and Political Rights (ICCPR)[13] and Articles 12 and 13 of the American Convention on Human Rights (ACHR).[14] ECHR Article 9 and ICCPR Article 18 deal specifically with freedom of religion, but all too often the international community resorts to Article 10 of the ECHR and Article 19 of the ICCPR to apply to *religious* expression, manifestations of religion, where the scope of permissible restriction of religious expression is greater than the scope of restriction in Articles 9 and 18. This means that religious expression enjoys less legal protection under the freedom of expression norms than it does under the freedom of religion norms.

The fullest and most effective legal means of protection of legal expression will be accomplished by using the legal norms most suited and meant for protection of expressions that are religious. All expression is not alike in international human rights law. Some expression is special. Religion is different from all ideas, philosophies, and ideologies. Religious expression is special; it is an act of religion, the exteriorizing of the religious truth of what one believes. This specialness is reflected in the present legal theory and texts of human rights laws. Religious expression must be judged and restricted, if at all, only under the freedom of religion norm, under the principle *Lex Specialis.*

Legal theory of religious freedom

In the field of human rights law the subject of protection of a person's religion is comprised of two aspects: the internal forum (*forum internum*), what one believes in the inner being of self, and the externalization of religious belief in the external forum (*forum externum*). In the legal theory of human rights law, the internal forum is inviolable, absolutely protected from interference by man or state. The external forum, the manifestation of religion, is not inviolable and absolute. The exercise of a human right to manifest religion can be limited by the state. Too often in the world today states apply abusive limitation on the exercise of religious expression.

12 'EU Guidelines on the Promotion and Protection of Freedom of Religion or Belief, Council of the European Union', Foreign Affairs Council Meeting, Luxembourg, 24 June 2013.

13 GA res. 2200A (XXI), 21 UN GAOR Supp. (No. 16) at 52, UN Doc. A/6316 (1966), 999 UNTS 71, entered into force 23 March 1976.

14 OAS Treaty Series No. 36, at 1, OAS off. Rec. OEA/Ser.L/V/II. 23 doc.rev.2, 1144 UNTS 23, entered into force 18 July 1978.

A consideration of legal protection of religious freedom and of freedom of expression in general brings us to three international human rights legal texts: the International Covenant on Civil and Political Rights (ICCPR, United Nations), the European Convention on Human Rights (ECHR, under the Council of Europe); and the American Convention on Human Rights (ACHR, under the Organization of American States). Each of these three instruments treats general expression and religious expression separately and distinctly.

The key international legal texts and their interpretation: freedom of religion and freedom of expression

International Covenant on Civil and Political Rights (United Nations)

Article 18.

1 Everyone shall have the right to freedom of thought, conscience and religion. This right shall include freedom to have or to adopt a religion or belief of his choice, and freedom, either individually or in community with others and in public or private, to manifest his religion or belief in worship, observance, practice and teaching.
2 …
3 Freedom to manifest one's religion or beliefs may be subject only to such limitations as are prescribed by law and are necessary to protect public safety, order, health, or morals or the fundamental rights and freedoms of others.

Article 19.

1 Everyone shall have the right to freedom of expression; this right shall include freedom to seek, receive and impart information and ideas of all kinds, regardless of frontiers, either orally, in writing or in print, in the form of art, or through any other media of his choice.
2 The exercise of the rights provided for in paragraph 2 of this article carries with it special duties and responsibilities. It may therefore be subject to certain restrictions, but these shall only be such as are provided by law and are necessary:

   a For respect of the rights or reputations of others;
   b For the protection of national security or of public order (*ordre public*), or of public health or morals.

European Convention on Human Rights (Council of Europe)

Article 9 (Freedom of Religion)

1 Everyone has the right to freedom of thought, conscience and religion; this right includes freedom to change his religion or belief, and freedom, either alone or in community with others and in public or private, to manifest his religion or belief, in worship, teaching, practice and observance.
2 Freedom to manifest one's religion or beliefs shall be subject only to such limitations as are prescribed by law and are necessary in a democratic society in the interests of public safety, for the protection of public order, health or morals, or the protection of the rights and freedoms of others.

Article 10 (Freedom of Expression)

1 Everyone has the right to freedom of expression. This right shall include freedom to hold opinions and to receive and impart information and ideas without interference by public authority and regardless of frontiers.
2 The exercise of these freedoms, since it carries with it duties and responsibilities, may be subject to such formalities, conditions, restrictions or penalties as are prescribed by law and are necessary in a democratic society, in the interests of national security, territorial integrity or public safety, for the prevention of disorder or crime, for the protection of health or morals, for the protection of the reputation or the rights of others, for preventing the disclosure of information received in confidence, or for maintaining the authority and impartiality of the judiciary.

American Convention on Human Rights (Organization of American States)

Article 12. Freedom of Conscience and Religion

1 Everyone has the right to freedom of conscience and of religion. This right includes freedom to maintain or to change one's religion or beliefs, and freedom to profess or disseminate one's religion or beliefs, either individually or together with others, in public or in private.
2 Freedom to manifest one's religion and beliefs may be subject only to the limitations prescribed by law that are necessary to protect public safety, order, health, or morals, or the rights or freedoms of others.

Article 13. Freedom of Thought and Expression

1 Everyone has the right to freedom of thought and expression. This right includes freedom to seek, receive, and impart information and ideas of all kinds, regardless of frontiers, either orally, in writing, in print, in the form of art, or through any other medium of one's choice.
2 The exercise of the right provided for in the foregoing paragraph shall not be subject to prior censorship but shall be subject to subsequent imposition of liability, which shall be expressly established by law to the extent necessary to ensure

   a respect for the rights or reputations of others; or
   b the protection of national security, public order, or public health or morals.

Note that the wording and the scope of the limitations clauses in the freedom of expression norms are different from those of the freedom of religion norms. The state may make fewer, more limited restrictions to manifestations of religions, compared with freedom of expression in general. It is therefore legally clear that among all types of expression international human rights law protects religious expression more broadly than non-religious expression.

Juridical justification for differential treatment of manifestation of religion: the *Lex Specialis* principle

Manifestation of religion is one small area of the whole field of expression. In legal terms one says that manifestation of religion is the *Lex Specialis* of general freedom of expression.

It is a special law covering one kind of expression, religious expression. As a broadly held legal principle, *lex specialis derogat generali*: a specific/special law prevails over (derogates) a general [law].[15] Thus, the legal provisions covering manifestation of religion and its permissible restrictions prevail over the provisions of freedom of expression and its permissible restrictions.

From a juridical perspective, the difference in treatment of religious expression from non-religious expression lies in *Lex Specialis*, a principle of interpretation and application found in International Law. The term describes a certain law by its character and scope, in relation to another law. It occurs that sometimes the legislator or treaty drafting body deals with a broad area of conduct or rights but wants to give a specific area of conduct or rights a different, special legal treatment. That specially treated law is known as the *Lex Specialis*. In any legal text containing a *Lex Specialis* there generally exists a *Lex Generalis* and the *Lex Specialis*. Otherwise stated, we take a broad area of law, such as expression, which covers all sorts and media of expression, and that area constitutes the *Lex Generalis*. Under the *Lex Generalis* it says that, generally speaking, most expressions in this area are governed a certain way. In the same legal text, however, or sometimes in a separate legal text, a certain portion of that field or expression, for example *religious* expression, is governed by law differently. It is set apart for special coverage. Because of their character, those things which by their nature are covered by the *Lex Specialis* are given a separate and different and special scope and protection.

Referring to our legal texts, ICCPR Article 19, ECHR Article 10, ACHR Article 13 are the *Lex Generalis* of expression in their respective treaty legal regimes. On the other hand, ICCPR Article 18, ECHR Article 9, and ACHR Article 12, are the *Lex Specialis* norms expressly protecting, inter alia, religion and manifestation of religion or belief by teaching, practice, worship and observance. Once again, all expressions are not the same in international human rights law. Religious expression is different.

The legal notion of Lex Specialis

The rule of *Lex Specialis* has a long legal history, but it is being challenged today. The reason for the challenge is the perceived 'fragmentation' of international law caused by many new areas of law, such as the so called 'self-contained regimes' of human rights and environmental law, which are deemed to require special treatment in international law. The popularity and pedigree of *Lex Specialis* was treated in the Koskenniemi Report for Study Group on Fragmentation under the International Law Commission.[16] That Report stated:

> The idea that special [law] overrides general [law] has a long pedigree in international jurisprudence. Its rationale is well expressed already by Grotius: 'What rules ought to be observed in such cases [i.e. where parts of a document are in conflict]. Among agreements which are equal ... that should be given preference which is most specific and approaches most nearly to the subject in hand, for special provisions are ordinarily more

15 See, for example, Silvia Zorzetto,'The *Lex Specialis* Principle and its Uses in Legal Argumentation. An Analytical Inquire', found at *Euronomie*, http://eunomia.tirant.com/?p=1164. See also Anja Lindroos, 'Addressing Norm Conflicts in Fragmented Legal Systems: The Doctrine of *Lex Specialis*', (2005) 74 *Nordic Journal of International Law* 27–66.

16 International Law Commission, Fragmentation of International Law: Difficulties Arising from the Diversification and Expansion of International Law—Report of the Study Group of the International Law Commission UN Doc. A/CN.4/L.682 (Apr. 13, 2006), as corrected UN Doc. A/CN.4/L.682/Corr.1 (Aug. 11, 2006) (finalized by Martti Koskenniemi) [Koskenniemi Report].

effective than those that are general.' (Hugo Grotius, *De Jure belli ac pacis. Libri Tres*, Book II Sect. XXIX).[17]

This passage refers to two reasons for why the *Lex Specialis* rule is so widely accepted. A special rule is more to the point ('approaches more nearly to the subject in hand') than a general one, and it regulates the matter more effectively ('are ordinarily more effective') than general rules do. This could also be expressed by saying that special rules are better able to take account of particular circumstances. The need to comply with them is felt more acutely than is the case with general rules. They have greater clarity and definiteness and are thus often felt 'harder' or more 'binding' than general rules, which may stay in the background and be applied only rarely.[18]

Without referring to the *Travaux Preparatoires*, the Preparatory Works of the three respective general human rights treaties above, it is reasonable to believe that historically the drafters of these treaties were very concerned about the safety of religious beliefs and expression in the post World War II East–West world where many governments found religion to be poison, the 'opiate of the people', and were intent upon ridding the world of religious belief. Special treatment of religious expression would be a logical object and purpose for these freedoms of religion in human rights texts.

Whatever the case, it is clear that religious expression is not considered in the world of international law the same as other types of expression. The period shortly after World War II, arguably more respective of traditional religion than today, chose to give religious expression legal pride of place in international human rights law, compared to freedom of expression, which was also a cornerstone of western liberal democracy. A free orientation to the ultimate truths of reality and the transcendent, and the freedom to express the deepest depths of *homo sapiens* were the goals of those who shaped the post war world and its global and regional intergovernmental organizations. It was the victory for two of the Four Freedoms announced by Roosevelt in 1941: Freedom of speech and freedom of worship. The latter subsumed all of religions outworking: worship, observance, practice and teaching. It is particularly teaching where the present issue of this chapter is most at issue, and teaching should be understood very broadly.

In summary, the norms applying to manifestation of religion trump the norms of freedom of expression and are to be applied whenever the expression manifesting religion are at issue. If done, this will provide greater protection of religious expression.

There is one qualification to this application of *Lex Specialis* to freedom of religious expression. In legal theory the protections of the freedom of expression at the same time apply to religious expression, but only as they provide backup or supplemental protection to religious expression. As has been stated, the expression norm cannot be applied as the primary applicable norm for religious expression, particularly the restriction clause terms. Religious expression is protected both in a special way per the *Lex Specialis* principle and in a general way as expression under the freedom of expression norm, but only to the extent that the latter norm maximizes protection, not the contrary. The freedom of expression norm can be used to increase protection of religious expression but not to diminish it.

It then becomes an issue where one applies only freedom of expression norms to religious expression and ignores the greater protection of the freedom of religion norm. We are, of course, talking mainly about application of the restriction clauses of freedom of religion

17 Koskenniemi Report at 59.
18 Koskenniemi Report at 60.

versus freedom of expression. Religion and expression norms offer religious expression different degrees of protection.

The question then becomes: So what does that mean in terms of the scope of protection of religious expression? What can the preacher preach? What can the evangelist-proselytizer proclaim/announce? How is manifestation of religion to be applied legally and how can it be restricted in human rights law?

Interpretation of the Lex Specialis *norm of 'manifestation of religion': what constitutes a manifestation of religion?*

While no one juridical source gives us a definitive description of what makes an expression a 'manifestation of religion' expression, as opposed to a general expression, there are several helpful distinctions that can be made, depending on how the norms are interpreted.

There are legal tools to help in the application and interpretation of these freedom of religion norms, particularly the restriction clauses, where the real battle for freedom of religious expression is waged. In interpreting and applying international law one must first have resort to the Vienna Convention on the Law of Treaties.[19] This is the treaty about treaties. Any restriction norms applying to manifestation of religion must be interpreted consistent with the principles of the VCLT. On the way to interpret treaty provisions the VCLT states:

> *Article 31: General rule of interpretation [of treaties]*
> 1. A treaty shall be interpreted in good faith in accordance with the ordinary meaning to be given to the terms of the treaty in their context and in the light of its object and purpose.

This rule applies to each and every part of a treaty text. Thus, freedom of religion norms must be interpreted in good faith, in accordance with the ordinary meaning of their terms in light of the object and purpose of the treaty, in order to fully protect religious freedom involving a manifestation of religion.

For our purposes here, we employ a broad definition of religion and its manifestation: orientation of the individual to the ultimate truths of reality, and the externalization of those truths in teaching, worship, practice, and observance alone or with others and in private or in the public domain. A more human rights law definition, or at least characteristics of religious belief can be found in the ECtHR judgment of *Campbell and Cossans v. UK*, [20] which requires that beliefs possess 'a certain level of cogency, seriousness, cohesion and importance' in the life of the believer.

These terms, manifestation and religion, are to be interpreted consistent with the object and purpose of each of those three respective human rights instruments. That object and purpose is usually spelled out in the preamble of the treaty. In any case, the object and purpose of a special norm on manifestation of religion will be to most fully protect freedom of religion or belief, including its expression, its manifestation. A good faith interpretation of the manifestation clauses would require a broad scope of what constitutes religion, belief,

19 Vienna Convention on the Law of Treaties (with annex). Concluded at Vienna on 23 May 1969, available at https://treaties.un.org/doc/publication/unts/volume%201155/volume-1155-i-18232-english.pdf.

20 *Campbell and Cosans v. The United Kingdom*, App. Nos 7511/76; 7743/76 (ECtHR, 25 February 1982).

manifestation, teaching, practice, worship, and observance. If one applies the freedom of expression norm to a religious expression then none of these terms comes into play, and the expression will be judged by the wrong standard of expression.

Permissible restrictions to manifestation of religion

> For all the due emphasis on freedom, it is a truism that the exercise of any right has its limitations. In cases of direct conflicts with other human rights or with important public order interests, restrictions may be justified. However, the decisive point in human rights is that the onus of proof always falls on those who argue on behalf of restrictions, not on those who defend a right to freedom.
>
> ...
>
> Freedom of religion or belief should therefore not be seen in isolation but rather as forming an *integral part of the entire system of human rights.* A particularly close relationship exists between freedom of religion or belief and freedom of expression, freedom of assembly, freedom of association or other 'communicative' rights of freedom that can mutually reinforce each other in the on-going project to shape societies based on respect for the dignity and freedom of all.[21]

A good faith interpretation of the manifestation of religion norms would require a narrow interpretation of the restriction/limitation clauses, which the state must prove.

Applying the above principles to the manifestation clause and their restriction clauses any measure restricting the exercise of manifesting religion must comply with the restriction clauses of Articles 18.3, 9.2, and 12.3, respectively, where applicable. As has been shown, religious expression is articulated in the human rights treaty norm of freedom of religion as 'manifestation of religion by teaching, practice, observance and worship'. This is part of the substantive right to freedom of religion. As also stated, this norm is not absolute. It is known as a Prima Facie or a conditional right. This means that the state can permissibly restrict the exercise of the substantive right in certain limited circumstances. Once again, it is in these limitations/restriction/clawback clauses that the battle for protection of religious expression takes place. In most instances where an interference with the exercise of the right is found the state will always raise the defense that the measure taken was a legitimate restriction. The issue here is: under which restriction clause does one analyze a particular expression and measures restricting its exercise (manifestation)?

How does this apply in a specific case of an alleged human rights violation under one of these three human rights treaties? In analyzing whether a conditional human right has been violated alleged in a petition against a state, a legal or quasi-legal forum, such as the UN Human Rights Committee, will first determine whether a case is 'admissible', meaning whether that forum has the legal authority ('competence') to even hear and decide the case. This involves issues such as legal standing to file a case (admissibility *ratione standi or locus standi*) and other criteria such as whether the alleged offender is a state party to the human rights treaty (*ratione personae*), whether the interference transpired within the geographical territory of a state party to the treaty (*ratione loci*), whether the case was timely filed after exhaustion of domestic remedies (*ratione temporis*) and whether the subject act falls within the material scope (*ratione materiae)* (like subject matter jurisdiction) of the protection of the article of the treaty allegedly violated. Once it have been determined that a matter is

21 Bielefeldt, supra note 1 at 22.

admissible the forum can proceed to handle the 'merits' of the case, whether the facts support the claim that a violation of the treaty norm has occurred as a matter of law.

The first thing to be decided is whether there was, in fact, an 'interference' by the state in the exercise of the substantive right. If so, then the forum will proceed to determine whether any measures taken by the state, for example, closing down a church building for safety reasons, are legitimate aims, according to the provisions of the restriction clause. This involves, roughly, the following analysis of the state measure taken.

If the forum finds an interference with the exercise of a human right in the treaty it will then ask whether the measure taken by the state meets the following criteria:

Was the measure prescribed by law?

This means that the measure is consistent with the Principle of Legality in that it meets all the following sub criteria:

a It was issued by a proper legal authority who had the legal power and right to establish or take the measure under domestic (national) law;
b The measure is accessible to persons, they can find out what it is and what is required; and
c It is sufficiently clear and precise enough that persons can know the foreseeable consequences of compliance or non-compliance, so as to be able to regulate their conduct accordingly.

Does the measure meet a legitimate aim specified in the treaty text?

Every state measure which interferes with the exercise of freedom to manifest religion must seek to achieve a specified 'legitimate aim'. By this is meant that the reason for which the state took the measure was to achieve a specific objective and a goal beneficial to society, which object or 'aim' is expressly listed in the limitation clause.

The legitimate aims set forth in the freedom of expression restriction clauses are not the same as those in the freedom of religion clauses. Freedom is the rule, limitation the exception. Thus, the listing of the only permissible legitimate aims of the three subject treaties, applied to manifestation of religion, to religious expression, are as follows:

> ICCPR: public safety, public order, health, morals, the fundamental rights and freedoms of others.
> ECHR: public safety, protection of public order, health, morals, protection of the rights and freedoms of others.
> ACHR: public safety, order, health, morals, the rights or freedoms of others.

Only those aims listed in the restriction clause and fully corroborated by the state will serve to justify a measure of restriction. Note that not even protection of national security constitutes a legitimate aim to restrict manifestation of religion or belief. This is not so in freedom of expression, thus showing the stronger protection of freedom of religion.

Is the measure necessary/necessity (ECHR: necessary in a democratic society)?

Assuming it is both prescribed by law and meets a legitimate aim or aims set forth in the restriction clause, in order for the measure to be permitted it still must then pass the test of whether it is 'necessary' (or necessary in a democratic society ECHR) to pass that measure to fulfill the state's obligations towards respect for and protection of human rights. This issue requires analysis of the measure in light of the following criteria:

a The measure meets a 'pressing social need'. Since freedom is the rule and limitation of freedom by the state is the exception, there must be a real and genuine need to take this measure to achieve the legitimate aim. In this respect the Europe Court will allow the state a 'margin of appreciation', some slack, leeway, the benefit of the doubt, in determining the basis for the measure. There is no 'margin of appreciation' as such, in the ICCPR and ACHR regime;
b The measure must be 'justified in principle'. This means that the measure taken is really being taken for the reasons asserted by the state, and the measure is consistent with achieving respect for human rights. They cannot be used in a discriminatory way, nor for discriminatory purposes, nor be used to undermine any other human rights. The result of the restriction will end up being beneficial for both the society and the person affected.
c Principle of Proportionality: The measure is 'proportionate' to the aim, the publicly beneficial goal sought to be achieved. In order to be accepted as a legitimate limit of the exercise of a right the state is authorized to interfere with individual freedom only to a degree that is necessary to meet the legitimate aim. There must be a relation of proportionality between the measure taken, such as a criminal punishment or dissolution of a group, and the legitimate aim, for example, control of violence or a threat to the rights and freedoms of others. Regarding all measures taken by states to restrict or control religion or belief one must *always* ask whether the measures are proportionate to the aim sought. Even if it is prescribed by law and there is a legitimate aim there will be no pressing social need found if the measure taken is disproportionate to the aim. That will render the measure legally invalid and impermissible and a violation of the treaty norm will be found. In the context of the European Court this is all part of the Court's determination that there has been a 'fair balance' of interests between the individual and the state, between the individual's freedom and the needs of state to properly and legally regulate society.
d The measures must be relevant and sufficient/adequate to accomplish the legitimate aims sought.

Again, as to any restriction of manifestation of religion, of religious expression, we must run that measure through *all* these criteria to determine if the measure is legally valid under international human rights law requirements. The implication of this is that protection of religious expression requires a sound knowledge of the textual content and mechanics of analysis of religious freedom treaty norms, especially the restriction clauses. Those challenging the state's assertion that its restriction measures against religious expression are legitimate and justify an interference must be able to go through this whole analysis and not assume the truth or correctness of the state's claim. Sometimes states can be wrong, or take measures for wrong reasons, often as a subterfuge. We must emphasize most strongly that the element of proportionality is an element often overlooked and almost never analyzed by those seeking to protect religious expression. So often a measure taken against religious expression violates the principle of proportionality either by the breadth of what a measure covers or the punishment or prohibition imposed by the state.[22] Remember: freedom is the rule; restriction is the exception. Legal vigilance is called for.

One example of the correct application of this distinction between religious and non-religious expression are the *Eweida and Chaplin v. UK* cases from the European Court of Human Rights.[23]

This case involved two women who wanted to wear their Christian crosses at work. One was a nurse and one an airline employee. The Court ruled in favor of the airline employee and against the nurse. The Court analyzed the case as one of freedom to manifest religion under Article 9, and applied the restriction clause analysis of Article 9.2. Wearing a cross was considered a religious expression, even if not an expression required by their faith. It may reasonably be asserted that *Chaplin*, as well as the two companion cases *McFarlane and Ladele*, were all decided wrongly. However, the Court did apply the correct substantive norm and its restriction clause in *Eweida* and *Chaplin*:

> Religious freedom is primarily a matter of individual thought and conscience. This aspect of the right set out in the first paragraph of Article 9, to hold any religious belief and to change religion or belief, is absolute and unqualified. However, as further set out in Article 9 § 1, freedom of religion also encompasses the freedom to manifest one's belief, alone and in private but also to practice in community with others and in public. The manifestation of religious belief may take the form of worship, teaching, practice and observance. Bearing witness in words and deeds is bound up with the existence of religious convictions (see Kokkinakis) ... Since the manifestation by one person of his or her religious belief may have an impact on others, the drafters of the Convention qualified this aspect of freedom of religion in the manner set out in Article 9 § 2. This second paragraph provides that any limitation placed on a person's freedom to manifest religion or belief must be prescribed by law and necessary in a democratic society in pursuit of one or more of the legitimate aims set out therein.
>
> *Eweida* at para. 80.

The *Eweida/Chaplin* judgments are more of an exception than the rule as far as use of the correct legal standard of treatment of religious speech. In other human rights fora, such as the UN General Assembly and Human Rights Council and in the European Union, most discourse about speech involving a religion focuses on the phenomenon of harmful or offensive speech, with a view to protecting the victim. So far so good. But we seldom see any treatment of the issues, such as hate speech or so-called defamation of religion, from the point of view of the speaker, of expressors and their rights when they are making religious expressions found to be offensive. The analysis becomes one solely of freedom of expression and its restriction. Again, that is the wrong legal standard.

22 The European Court of Human Rights has ruled that 'a lack of proportionality may be demonstrated where there is an alternative, less intrusive way of protecting the public interest' and 'where there were alternative ways in which social policies might be pursued the state was not entitled to choose a way which violated an individual's rights': David Harris, Michael O'Boyle, Edward Bates, and Carla Buckley, eds, *Harris, O'Boyle & Warbrick, European Convention on Human Rights* (Oxford University 2nd edn 2009), 359, commenting on *Campbell v United Kingdom* 13590/88 [1992] ECHR 41 (25 March 1992).

23 *Eweida and Others v. The United Kingdom*, App. nos. 48420/10, 59842/10, 51671/10 and 36516/10, ECtHR (15 January 2013). Eweida and Chaplin judgments only. para. 80.

Other tools applied to restrictions on religious expression

Other tools that are pertinent to a juridical understanding of the application of such restriction clauses include General Comment 22[24] of the UN Human Rights Committee, on ICCPR Article 18, and the Siracusa Principles on Limitations and Derogations to the International Covenant on Civil and Political Rights.[25] While these documents do not constitute binding legal instruments, its drafters were of highest academic caliber, General Comment 22 coming from the experts of the Human Rights Committee, and the Siracusa Principles by preeminent academic and NGO. These Principles have been cited numerous times and are in common legal use. They could at best be considered soft law, as a road map to how to comply with the hard law of the ICCPR. The Siracusa Principles offer, inter alia, scholarly guidance on the application of the restriction clauses of the ICCPR, but can be helpful in application of such clauses, *mutatis mutandis*, in any general human rights treaty, like the ECHR or ACHR.

The General Comment No. 22 to the ICCPR states in Paragraph 8:

> In interpreting the scope of permissible limitation clauses, States parties should proceed from the need to protect the rights guaranteed under the Covenant, including the right to equality and non-discrimination on all grounds specified in articles 2, 3 and 26. Limitations imposed must be established by law and must not be applied in a manner that would vitiate the rights guaranteed in article 18. The Committee observes that paragraph 3 of article 18 is to be strictly interpreted: restrictions are not allowed on grounds not specified there, even if they would be allowed as restrictions to other rights protected in the Covenant, such as national security. Limitations may be applied only for those purposes for which they were prescribed and must be directly related and proportionate to the specific need on which they are predicated. Restrictions may not be imposed for discriminatory purposes or applied in a discriminatory manner.

The *Siracusa* interpretive principles related to the restriction/limitation clause of the ICCPR are as follows:

A. General Interpretative Principles Relating to the Justification of Limitations

1 No limitations or grounds for applying them to rights guaranteed by the Covenant are permitted other than those contained in the terms of the Covenant itself.
2 The scope of a limitation referred to in the Covenant shall not be interpreted so as to jeopardize the essence of the right concerned.
3 All limitation clauses shall be interpreted strictly and in favor of the rights at issue.
4 All limitations shall be interpreted in the light and context of the particular right concerned.
5 All limitations on a right recognized by the Covenant shall be provided for by law and be compatible with the objects and purposes of the Covenant.
6 No limitation referred to in the Covenant shall be applied for any purpose other than that for which it has been prescribed.
7 No limitation shall be applied in an arbitrary manner.
8 Every limitation imposed shall be subject to the possibility of challenge to and remedy against its abusive application.

24 General Comment No. 22 (48) (art. 18), UN GAOR Hum. Rts. Comm., 48th Sess., Supp. No. 40, at 208, 209, UN Doc A/48/40 (1993).

25 American Association for the International Commission of Jurists, Siracusa Principles on Limitations and Derogations to the International Covenant on Civil and Political Rights, April 1985.

9 No limitation on a right recognized by the Covenant shall discriminate contrary to Article 2, paragraph 1.
10 Whenever a limitation is required in the terms of the Covenant to be 'necessary,' this term implies that the limitation:

a is based on one of the grounds justifying limitations recognized by the relevant article of the Covenant,
b responds to a pressing public or social need,
c pursues a legitimate aim, and
d is proportionate to that aim.

11 Any assessment as to the necessity of a limitation shall be made on objective considerations.
12 In applying a limitation, a state shall use no more restrictive means than are required for the achievement of the purpose of the limitation.
13 The burden of justifying a limitation upon a right guaranteed under the Covenant lies with the state.
14 13. The requirement expressed in Article 12 of the Covenant, that any restrictions be consistent with other rights recognized in the Covenant, is implicit in limitations to the other rights recognized in the Covenant.
15 14. The limitation clauses of the Covenant shall not be interpreted to restrict the exercise of any human rights protected to a greater extent by other international obligations binding upon the state.
16 …

These interpretive principles go on to explain the meaning of the specific legitimate aims, such as public safety and the rights and freedoms of others. Two examples are as follows:
vii.'public safety'

1 Public safety means protection against danger to the safety of persons, to their life or physical integrity, or serious damage to their property.
2 The need to protect public safety can justify limitations provided by law. It cannot be used for imposing vague or arbitrary limitations and may only be invoked when there exist adequate safeguards and effective remedies against abuse.

viii.'rights and freedoms of others' or the 'rights or reputations of others'

1 The scope of the rights and freedoms of others that may act as a limitation upon rights in the Covenant extends beyond the rights and freedoms recognized in the Covenant.
2 36. When a conflict exists between a right protected in the Covenant and one which is not, recognition and consideration should be given to the fact that the Covenant seeks to protect the most fundamental rights and freedoms. In this context especial weight should be afforded to rights not subject to limitations in the Covenant.

Legal importance of freedom to manifest religion: a non-derogable human right and an interdependent human right

In the legal theory of human rights there are two principles which militate for a high degree of protection for manifestation of religion. The first is the fact that the freedom of religion norm is a non-derogable human right, meaning it can never be suspended in time of public emergency. The second is that other all other human rights are interdependent on freedom of religion.

A non-derogable human right

Freedom of religion norms have a special characteristic in two of the above treaties: they are expressly deemed non-derogable in the derogation clauses of two of the instruments, the ICCPR and ACHR. This means that these norms can never be suspended in time of public emergency of any kind, and that they apply in all situations in the state. In ACHR 27.2, and ICCPR 4.2, the derogation clauses, freedom of religion, including manifestation of religion, are listed as non-derogable. In the ECHR article 9 is not listed as non-derogable right, but the Court has so much as said that protection of the *forum internum* is non-derogable, and the *forum externum*, is tantamount to such. Despite such status all three treaties have religious expression still subject to reasonable limitations under the restriction etc. clauses.

There are several features of the freedom of religion norms like this that testify to their being different and special and deserving of a unique and elevated scope and type of legal protection.

Interdependent human rights: freedom of religion and freedom of expression

Again, in legal theory all human rights are interdependent. As stated above, under this principle the fulfilment of one right depends, wholly or in part, upon the fulfilment of other human rights. Thus, freedom of expression is interdependent on freedom of religion, and thus freedom to manifest religion. Without the freedom to orient oneself to the ultimate truths of reality one could never express anything about anything. All expression depends on freedom of religious expression, in theory. But what happens when one limits freedom of religious expression by applying to it larger restrictions taken from the freedom of expression norm? This threatens not only freedom of religion but all other human rights, including freedom of expression.[26]

By treating religious expression under the strictures of freedom of expression generally there is a violation of the principle of inter-dependence of human rights. This principle says that every single human right is dependent upon the full exercise of each and every other human right in order for itself to be fully enjoyed. If full freedom of expression is dependent upon the full exercise of freedom to manifest religion, then to force someone to not exercise their freedom of religion, or to restrict it beyond what is provided in the religion restriction clause, would undermine both the human right to freedom of religion and freedom of expression. Freedom of religious expression depends on freedom of expression and freedom of expression depends on freedom of religious expression. One cannot say that two things are interdependent, that they each depend on the other, and then deny the use or limit the exercise of either. This is conceptually inconsistent.

Where there is a so called ‘conflict of rights’ between two different human rights the state must make every attempt to reconcile and allow the two rights to both be exercised to the greatest extent possible, at least by means of reasonable accommodation. Freedom to manifest religion by teaching is primarily protected under the freedom of religion or belief norm and only secondarily by the freedom of expression norm. By this is meant that freedom of

26 See EU Guidelines, supra note 11 at para. 31.

religious expression actually has a double protection: both the freedom of religion norm and the freedom of expression norm applied consistent with the object and purpose of the religion norm. However, and here is where the problem lies, the scope of the freedom of expression norm *ratione materiae* does not hold religious expression within its scope and, religious expression cannot be restricted within the scope of the freedom of expression restriction clauses. Freedom of religious expression, though interdependent on freedom of expression, was meant to have larger berth, greater scope, broader protection than that of general expressions. It is this that most of the international discourse on religious expression is missing, or even intentionally avoiding.

When international human rights discourse, adjudication, and standard-setting do not recognize, accept and implement this uniqueness of manifestation of religion all human rights are in placed in jeopardy. Where the incorrect legal standard is applied to restriction of the manifestation of religion, religious believers can be adversely affected and legal religious expression deemed illegal general expression. Freedom of religion suffers.

Manifestation of religion and 'defamation of religion' and related concepts and processes

The premise of this chapter is that too often issues of religious expression and human rights are not being analyzed under the correct legal standard, freedom of religion, but the incorrect standard: freedom of expression. And even where the correct standard is used, there is often an apparent subordination of religion to other norms, for example, non-discrimination based on sexual orientation.

One area where the failure to distinguish between religious expression and general expression concerns so-called 'defamation of religion'. This issue, which concerns an attempt to prohibit expressions that offend the sensibilities of a religious group, has been highly contentious on the international level, and particularly at the United Nations. While so-called defamation of religion focuses on the impact on the feelings or reputation of the demeaned group or religion, our topic is the right of the religious speaker to make religious expressions, even when they are found offensive by the targeted religion. Our focus regarding defamation is the legal standard applicable to a religious voice making a religious expression which offends the sensitivities of another religion's members. We are looking at the speaker of the message, not the victim religion, and then only as it relates to the speaker being a religious voice, for example, a bishop instructing his flock on avoiding false religions. What is the scope of the religious speaker's right to manifest religion by teaching etc. which happens to offend another religion, much like the Pope's Regensburg lecture?

Beginning in the late 1990s, the Organisation of the Islamic Council (since 2011 the Organisation of Islamic Cooperation), a group of 57 states that represents 'the collective voice of the Muslim world', pushed annually for UN resolutions to prohibit such claimed 'defamation of religion'. In its resolutions the OIC sought through use of various human rights norms, principally freedom of expression, to claim that expressions which offend religions are not really expression protected by human rights law, or that they can be restricted under the freedom of expression norm restriction clause. There was never a mention of the legal standard to be applied where the person making the expression was a religious voice. All claimed defamatory expressions were either deemed to be non-protected or to be prevented or punished under the freedom of expression norm, not as freedom to manifest religion. This resulted until 2011 in annual UN Human Rights Council resolutions, approved by the General Assembly,[27] condemning so-called defamation of religion but always in reference to freedom of expression or ICCPR Article 20.[28]

On the confusion over the relation between the rights of freedom of religion and freedom of expression Bielefeldt stated:

> Apart from obscuring the issue of the right holders, this restrictive and anti-liberal thrust constituted the most problematic feature of the resolutions against defamation of religions. Now, by somehow amalgamating freedom of religion or belief with the fight against 'defamation of religions', the false impression could even emerge that there exists an inherent antagonism between two human rights: freedom of religion versus freedom of expression. Some people actually seem to think that it is the purpose of freedom of religion to put a limit to an 'overly extensive' use of freedom of expression. From such an antagonistic assumption, however, what gets lost is the fundamental insight that freedom of religion and belief and freedom of expression closely belong together as *two interrelated legal safeguards of communicative freedom.* Although not completely identical in their content, they can and have to mutually reinforce each other....[29]

Bielefeldt has written and lectured much about this one issue. As Special Rapporteur on Freedom of Religion or Belief (2010–2016) he raised similar concerns with the defamation movement and the effect it has in the public square:

> The wording of the various defamation resolutions gave the impression that religions per se should receive a protection of their reputation. This idea would be clearly incompatible with a human rights approach, because from a human rights perspective the only rights holders are human beings, as individuals or in community with others. In addition, the defamation resolutions could be perceived as giving support to blasphemy laws which in many countries have a chilling effect on public debates. This would go not only against freedom of expression, but also against freedom of religion or belief which includes the rights of religious dissenters and critics to hold and manifest their convictions even if they are deemed 'blasphemous' by some religious authorities.[30]

The fear here is that any expression that a certain religion finds offensive to it would be deemed by it to be a defamation of that religion and thus could be suppressed or punished, regardless of who the speaker was or what the speaker's intentions were. A clear implication from the mind of the former Special Rapporteur is that those expressing a religious teaching can both hold and express views which some consider religiously blasphemous or offensive to feelings. This is the human rights law. No one can claim to have a legal right to have a religion that is free from criticism or debate. The subjective feelings of members of a religion that has been offended cannot trump the freedom of those who hold and express beliefs that are found to be offensive. It is up to education and public sensitization of religious audiences

27 See for example 'Combatting Defamation of Religion' draft resolution by Pakistan for the OIC. A/HRC/13/L.1, 11 March 2010; UN General Assembly.

28 ICCPR Article 20: Any advocacy of national, racial or religious hatred that constitutes incitement to discrimination, hostility or violence shall be prohibited by law.

29 Bielefeldt, supra note 1 at 30.

30 'Protecting and Implementing the Right to Freedom of Religion or Belief: Interview with Heiner Bielefeldt', (2011) 3 *Journal of Human Rights Practice* 3, 229–244.

to bring them to accept hearing and reading such offensive expressions. Education of those who make offensive expressions is also required. Teaching how to express religious truths respectfully, and, as much as possible without offending should be the goal of every religion. Education is the key, not manipulating legal texts to prohibit otherwise permissible religious expressions.

This does not mean, of course that all religious expression short of ICCPR Article 20 advocacy should be without limit. At the point when religious expressions by a religious voice create an objective atmosphere wherein members of a maligned religious group become too subjectively afraid to practice their religion, to go to their temple, their synagogue, their church, their assembly, and when the fear is objectively reasonable, then society can take measures to prevent or punish such expressions. This can work so long as there is an independent, impartial, and accessible judiciary providing effective remedies to assure compliance with the law, and no abuse of the restriction clause by the state to stifle a minority or disfavored religion. Otherwise, we place subjective fear over objective freedom to believe and to act and to express ideas that might help the world of ideas to develop. The antidote for offensive speech is more speech, not preventing speech. Again, religious expression that protects the right of every person to orient themselves in complete individual autonomy to the ultimate truths of reality, is too important in the canon of rights to be subordinated to mere feelings. The state is legally required to fulfill its positive obligation under the freedom of religion norms to create an environment wherein religious expression can be most free. This is true in our world characterized by increasing chaotic subjectivism in politics and law. Legal protection of human feelings can only go so far.

Only the high standard of ICCPR Article 20, and the strictly interpreted measures of the restriction clauses, should serve as legal bulwarks against extreme and actionable religious expression. It is not that all religious expression is legally permissible, or sacrosanct, but only that its limitations have not been properly applied, and its importance vis-à-vis other rights has not been respected in law and politics. Religious expression has seen a descent in its legal protection, and few are recognizing this and recognizing the detriment to freedom, democracy, diversity, and tolerance that this suppression of religious expression is and will continue creating.

The incorrect use, interpretation, and application of the legal norms of freedom of religion and freedom of expression and ICCPR Article 20 (threatening to ban any expression that incited hatred and offended religious feelings, leaving out the wording 'any advocacy of national, racial or religious hatred') were all added to undermine the integrity and the very legal basis and foundation of *all* human rights, not just as to freedom of religion. So-called defamation of religion sought to protect a religion, not a human being, the latter alone being the holder/bearer of human rights. The main point of all this is that in the discourse of so-called defamation of religion there was a general failure of all involved, non-governmental organizations,[31] international intergovernmental organizations, scholars, and even advocates for free religious expression, to factor in the scope and restriction clauses of freedom of religion as to one of the potential sources of the offensive religious expression.[32] As the discourse on religiously offensive expression was proceeding, all persons making such

31 See for example Article XIX, the Camden Principles on Freedom of Expression and Equality, June 2009, especially principles 11 and 12. It seems clear that these principles are primarily motivated by the defamation-blasphemy-hate speech-incitement type issue.

32 Roger Kiska and Paul Coleman, 'Freedom of Speech and Hate Speech: Unravelling the Jurisprudence of the European Court of Human Rights', (2012) 5 *International Journal of Religious Freedom* 1, 129–142.

expressions would be judged under the same legal norm, freedom of expression, and its restriction clause.

Offensive expression and intersectionality

In their 'defamation of religion' UN resolutions, the OIC sought to bring religiously offensive expression under the banner of the racism and racial discrimination norm using the concept of 'intersectionality' of human rights, also known as multiform discrimination. Intersectionality consists of examining adverse social phenomena found at the convergence of several different rights, for example religion, gender, and racial discrimination. The supporters of 'defamation of religion' sought to find a way to suppress anti-religion expressions against Islam. They attempted to link anti-Islamic expression with racism and religion, conflating race and religion as to Islam.[33] This was most pronounced in the Human Rights Council's Durban II Conference process. There the proponents of so-called defamation of religion attempted to bring that non-right to full center of the Council's last Conference and a place it in its outcome document. Much activity also took place in the Committee on Elimination of Racial Discrimination, and an attempt was made to park so-called defamation of religion in that legal garage. This largely failed.

An attempt continued in relation to the Durban II process and the Racism Convention to establish a binding legal norm against this offensive expression. Such a norm would allow states parties to legally prohibit and be obligated to prohibit what the OIC considers to be expressions of defamation of religion. Legally, this was an attempt to bootstrap Article 4 of the Racism Convention to allow forced suppression of anti-religious expression deemed racist. The Ad Hoc Committee on Elaboration of Complementary Standards, under the HRC Durban Conference process, was tasked to examine if the need for a new legal norm is warranted to cover this anti-religious expression lacuna. In Durban II they sought to focus on the perceived link between defamation of religions and racism. There was an attempt to get this committee to make defamation of religion prohibited under a new protocol to the International Convention on the Elimination of All Forms of Racial Discrimination (CERD). This ongoing process continues was much contested and divisive. Such norms would work against freedom of religious expression where such expression were deemed to offend religious sensibilities, particularly if it were religious expression that also crossed racial lines.

In the Human Rights Council the Special Rapporteur on Contemporary Forms of Racism, Racial Discrimination, Xenophobia and Related Intolerance was even asked to submit to the Human Rights Council a report on 'all manifestations of defamation of religions, and in particular on the serious implications of Islamophobia, on the enjoyment of all human rights by their followers'.[34] Even religious expression issued by religious voices could

33 'Freedom of expression and incitement to racial or religious hatred.' OHCHR side event during the Durban Review Conference, Geneva, 22 April 2009. Joint statement by Mr. Githu Muigai, Special Rapporteur on contemporary forms of racism, racial discrimination, xenophobia, and related intolerance; Ms. Asma Jahangir, Special Rapporteur on freedom of religion or belief; and Mr. Frank La Rue, Special Rapporteur on the promotion and protection of the right to freedom of opinion and expression.

34 UN Human Rights Council, A/HRC/12/38, 1 July 2009, Racism, Racial Discrimination, Xenophobia and Related Forms of Intolerance: Follow-Up to and Implementation of the Durban Declaration and Programme of Action: Report of the Special Rapporteur on contemporary forms of racism, racial discrimination, xenophobia and related intolerance, Githu Muigai, on the manifestations of defamation of religions, and in particular on the serious implications of Islamophobia, on the enjoyment of all rights by their followers.

have been banned or punished under the racism or religious intolerance, if found offensive to a religious group, and restrictions on expression by such religious persons would be judged not as a manifestation of religion and hence under the restriction of the freedom of religion norm, but under a stricter norm prohibiting racism and similar intolerance.

This legal confusion between so-called defamation of religion, hate speech, blasphemy, negative stereotyping, and incitement to religious hatred, and the growing opposition surrounding 'defamation of religion resolutions' gave rise to what some have called the 'Battle of Terminology' regarding religiously negative expression. 'Defamation of religion' was a social science concept dressed up as a legal prohibition. Fortunately, in 2011, after many years of UN resolutions concerning 'combatting defamation of religion', as the international community woke up to the confusion and potential damage to human rights posed by accepting such as bogus notion, the OIC presented a different resolution (HRC resolution 16/18) dropping the term 'defamation of religion'. The new reference would be to 'Combatting Intolerance, Negative Stereotyping and Stigmatization of, and Discrimination, Incitement to Violence and Violence against Persons Based on Religion or Belief'.[35] It condemned any advocacy of religious hatred that 'constitutes incitement to discrimination, hostility or violence, whether it involves the use of print, audio-visual or electronic media or any other means'. The OIC is now emphasizing the term 'incitement' to religious hatred, discrimination, and violence in its campaign to protect the reputation of Islam and feelings of Muslims.[36]

Many different efforts sprouted up in the international community to deal with negative expression against religions and their members, mainly in the UN between the UN Human Rights Council, its Special Rapporteurs on Religion, Expression, and Racial Intolerance, and the UN High Commissioner for Human Rights. Among these efforts were the following:

Rabat Plan of Action on the prohibition of advocacy of national, racial or religious hatred that constitutes incitement to discrimination, hostility or violence

The 'Rabat Plan' issued from meetings of NGO experts under the UN High Commissioner for Human Rights, focusing on 'the relationship between freedom of expression and hate speech'.[37] It was about 'restrictions to freedom of expression deemed to incite hatred'. It focuses a lot on ICCPR Article 20 as the upper level of protection against such incitement inducing expression.

As this Plan affects religious expression it ignores and nowhere considers the 'manifestation of religion' norm and religion's permissible restrictions, staying clearly within the realm of freedom of expression and its restrictions. Religious freedom and religious expression by

35 UN General Assembly, A/HRC/RES/16/18, 12 April 2011.

36 However, in the light of the reaction to the Charlie Hebdo event in Paris in 2015, the OIC again began calling for a resolution on defamation of religion. However, the sociological notion of 'defamation of religion' is now all but discarded. It is impossible to fit such a concept within existing international human rights law. Defamation is a legal term signifying the expression of a false fact about someone that causes real damage. There is no human forum which could adjudicate whether a given fact about a religion, particularly about its doctrine, is false or not. So-called defamation of religion looks only at the adverse effect of an expression on the feelings of members of a religious community, not on the truth or falsity of the expression.

37 UN Office of the High Commissioner for Human Rights [OHCHR] Rabat Plan of Action on the prohibition of advocacy of national, racial or religious hatred that constitutes incitement to discrimination, hostility or violence para. 18, http://www.ohchr.org/Documents/Issues/Opinion/SeminarRabat/rabat_draft_outcome.pdf.

religious voices are not protected in this process. This process ignores the norm of freedom of manifestation of religion. It sets up three criteria for judging whether a prohibition of an expression is valid, and then it sets up a six-factor threshold test to determine if an expression meets the Article 20 legal threshold. Those six factors are the (1) context, (2) speaker, (3) intent, (4) content or form, (5) extent of speech, and (6) likelihood of violence, including imminence. These criteria could make a distinction of when the speaker is a religious voice, such as a bishop, and the intent of the expression, such as would allow consideration of a religious voice expressing a message not intended to incite or offend, e.g. Pope Benedict at Regensbuerg. However, other than as relates to ICCPR Article 20 this process suffers the same legal infirmity as those others. All religious expression under the Article 20 threshold will be judged under the freedom of expression norm and its restriction clause. What would be expressed by the religious voice, such as the pulpit or an evangelist, would be seen as general expression, not a manifestation of religion.

The Istanbul Process

The Istanbul Process was set up between the OIC and the US as a follow up to Res.16/18, held outside of the Human Rights Council.[38] This process was to implement two prongs of that resolution: enforcing anti-discrimination laws, and training officials to engage with religious communities. Secretary of State Clinton saw this as primarily setting up a list of best practices for minimizing religious violence and discrimination. According to her this process was to work 'together to protect two fundamental freedoms – the right to practice one's religion freely and the right to express one's opinion without fear.' This process does nothing directly to protect the manifestation aspect of freedom of religion as distinct from other expression. It does emphasize the public education and sensitizing all involved and attempts to lower the temperature of inter religious or anti-religious discord. The US policy seems to be protection of general expression and not particularly religious expression.

EU Guidelines on the Promotion and Protection of Freedom of Religion or Belief

In addition to these global level processes a regional process affecting these legal issues in the European Union culminated in the 2013, *Guidelines on the Promotion and Protection of Freedom of Religion or Belief.* This document does seek to address various religious freedom issues, including religious expression. And this document comes as close as any other to recognize the distinct character of freedom of religion and the distinction between freedom of religion and freedom of expression. But when all is said and done this document too, misses the crucial *Lex Specialis* distinction necessary to best protect manifestation of religion.

1 25. Freedom of religion or belief is intrinsically linked to freedom of opinion and expression, ... Expression of a religious or non-religious belief, or of an opinion concerning a religion or belief, is also protected by the right to freedom of opinion and expression enshrined in Article 19 of the ICCPR.

38 US Department of State, Report of the United States on the First Meeting of Experts to Promote Implementation of United Nations Human Rights Council Resolution 16/18, December 2011, http://www.universal-rights.org/wp-content/uploads/2015/02/1st-Meeting-Conference-Report.pdf.

This paragraph expresses correctly the fact that an expression of a religious belief concerning a religion or belief is also protected under freedom of expression, indicating the dual protection of manifestation of religion, such as under both ICCPR arts. 18 and 19. That is correct, as was stated above.

The *Guidelines* also declare:

1 31. Freedom of religion or belief and the freedom of expression are interdependent, interrelated and mutually reinforcing rights, protecting all persons – not religions or beliefs in themselves – and protecting also the right to express opinions on any or all religions and beliefs. ... Limitations to the right to express opinions on religion or belief are a source of great vulnerability for people belonging to religion or belief minorities, but also affect majorities, not least persons holding non-traditional religious views.

2 32. In the event that violence is threatened or carried out, or restrictions are imposed in connection with an expression of opinions on religion or belief, the EU will be guided by the following principles:

a When critical comments are expressed about religions or beliefs and such expression is perceived by adherents as being so offensive that it may result in violence towards or by adherents, then:

- If there is a *prima facie* case that this expression constitutes hate speech, i.e. falls within the strict scope of article 20 paragraph 2 of the ICCPR (which prohibits any advocacy of religious hatred that constitutes incitement to discrimination, hostility or violence), the EU will denounce it, and demand that it be investigated and tried by an independent judge.
- If this expression does not rise to the level of incitement prohibited under article 20 of the ICCPR, and is thus an exercise of free speech, the EU will:

  i Resist any calls or attempts for the criminalization of such speech; ...
  ii ...
  iii Recall that the most effective way to combat a perceived offense from the exercise of freedom of expression is the use of freedom of expression itself.

b When faced with restrictions to freedom of expression in the name of religion or belief, the EU will:

- Recall that restrictions to freedom of expression shall only be such as are prescribed by law and are necessary to safeguard the rights or reputation of others, or for the protection of national security or of public order (*ordre public*) or of public health or morals, and that no national security restriction is permissible for freedom of religion and belief.
- Defend the fact that sharing information about religions or beliefs and engaging in persuasion on these matters is protected under international law, provided that such persuasion is neither coercive nor impairs the freedom of others.

These last provisions of the *Guidelines* do not cover expressions of opinions about religion or belief and religious expressions about other religions. It does not appear, it seems, to protect the religious voice who expresses a religious view on a moral issue, such as a priest teaching about homosexuality or abortion. This is an area which today needs greater legal protection, or at least the proper textual protection.

It states that 'limitations to the right to express opinions on religion or belief are a source of great vulnerability for people belonging to religion or belief minorities.' It does not specify the source of such limitations: freedom of religion or freedom of expression.

Where violence or state restrictions result from an expression of opinions on religion the EU will be guided by the enumerated policies. Where critical comments about a religion are perceived lead to violence towards or by adherents then the EU will apply the Article 20 test. Then it states in paragraph 32 that if the expressions do not rise to Article 20 severity then such expression concerning a religion is 'thus an exercise of free speech'. An 'exercise of free speech' is not the same as a manifestation of religion. They call to different restriction clauses. Here, if the speaker is a religious voice it seems to say that such expression about religion would be part of a general expression. Though it would still be protected to some degree under the expression norm, it is important that it be protected under the freedom of religion norm.

Paragraph 32b continues this problem about the legal norm to be applied, by stating:

> When faced with restrictions to *freedom of expression* ... and recall that restrictions to *freedom of expression* shall only be such as are prescribed by law and are necessary to safeguard the rights or reputation of others, or for the protection of national security or of public order (*ordre public*) or of public health or morals, and that *no national security restriction is permissible for freedom of religion and belief.* (emphasis added)

Here, in referring to the national security limitation, we finally we see a reference to the differing standards of judging religious expression. This is one of the few places in human rights law where one sees this distinction applied, though weakly. But this only applies on part of the freedom of religion norm, the restriction clause. It does not apply to the full text of that norm.

These *Guidelines* are well written, timely, and otherwise sound. They do lack a clear specific reference to religious expression about a religion or belief as constituting a manifestation of religion subject to religion norm scope and restrictions. Thus the *Guidelines* do not give the preacher or evangelist who expresses a statement or opinion or doctrine about another religion the fullest legal protection, or guidance to foresee the legal effects of his expression. That person cannot be assured that a restriction in the exercise of religious expression will be judged by the manifestation of religion norm, other than involves a government claim that a measure has as its aim protection of national security.

Conclusion

This brief look at the international legal and political community does not give us assurances that the expressions of the religious voice are adequately protected. Moreover, even the understandings of the legal advocates of religious expression cannot assure us they have the correct understanding of the *Lex Specialis* issue and the need to assert, plead, and argue the manifestation of religion standard. The juridical horizon of religious expression is therefore muddy at best.

In the meantime one more and more often hears the world calling the religious voice to be silent or at least to become more tolerant of the accepted morals and practices of the day. The world is becoming increasingly intolerant of what it sees as the intolerance of the religious voice. It is rather challenging, silencing, and punishing the religious voice for going against the spirit of the age. But the religious voice is the only voice left that can and dares to give the world a moral compass by which to guide statecraft, public policy, and law and justice. This moral voice is in jeopardy if the legal systems at both the global and local level do not actively protect as a positive obligation the freedom of the religious voice. Human rights law at present is being manipulated and misused to stifle the religious voice more than those efforts seeming to protect it. Political correctness is demanded of religion beyond what human rights law would allow.

Heiner Bielefeldt echoed our concerns for protecting the pulpit and other religious voices by juridically correct use of international human rights law:

> Apart from actual violations, freedom of religion or belief is under pressure also on the conceptual level, with a danger that its very nature as a human right may get blurred. Conceptual questions, however, are of an immediate practical relevance, since any institution-building on behalf of a more efficient implementation of freedom of religion or belief presupposes clear ideas about the right holders, content, areas of absolute protection, the scope of possible restrictions, remedies against infringements and the interrelatedness with other human rights.[39]

Bielefeldt believed it to be a part of his mandate as Special Rapporteur to 'raise awareness that conceptual clarity is needed to defend the normative basis for shaping peaceful coexistence in our religiously and philosophically pluralistic world by institutionalizing equal respect for the dignity and rights of "all members of the human family"'.[40] There continues to be, however, a lack of such conceptual clarity in international human rights discourse regarding religious freedom, particularly regarding religious expression. We must respond to this by acting to take the pressure off of this historically first of human rights, and the lynchpin of them all. If freedom of religion falls, all human rights, interdependent as they are, will fall with it. No less is at stake.

In our rush to bring about equality and non-discrimination for all, we must not throw out or even weaken the inherent, universal, and inalienable human right to freedom to manifest our religion or belief through religion-based expression. The worst lot of humankind and affront to human dignity would be to live in a world of equality and non-discrimination, but devoid of any God to make sense of it all, or even of the very right to search for God or any ultimate truth.

As Pope Benedict XVI aptly posited in a 2008 address to the United Nations,

> It is inconceivable … that believers should have to suppress a part of themselves – their faith – in order to be active citizens. It should never be necessary to deny God in order to enjoy one's rights. The rights associated with religion are all the more in need of protection if they are considered to clash with a prevailing secular ideology or with majority religious positions of an exclusive nature. The full guarantee of religious liberty cannot be limited to the free exercise of worship, but has to give due consideration to the public dimension of religion, and hence to the possibility of believers playing their part in building the social order.[41]

39 Bielefeldt, supra note 1 at 30.

40 Bielefeldt note 1 at 15.

41 Pope Benedict XVI, Address to the United Nations, New York, April 2008, http://www.vatican.va/holy_father/benedict_xvi/speeches/2008/april/documents/hf_ben-xvi_spe_20080418_un-visit_en.html.

3 The search for pluralism in Islam, Roman Catholicism, and Judaism

Iain T. Benson

Pluralism is unavoidable

Pluralism, understood as diversity, is a fact of human existence. Like belief, it can have express or hidden dimensions and, like belief, it is there whether acknowledged or not. Laws and practices can allow and encourage pluralism or they can attempt to restrict it. However such laws and practices are structured, there will be pluralism even within communities that profess homogeneity of belief. This is because human beings are in the process of interpretation, and not all interpretations agree nor do they remain static.

Being human is learning to live with pluralism either of an open or a hidden variety. The question is, will we view difference and change merely as threats or as things to be accepted and understood as part of living together in communities – not only with those who claim to believe as we do but with those who do not make the same professions of belief.

To manage the scope of what should be a longer inquiry into something more manageable, this chapter narrows 'religion' to Islam, Christianity, and Judaism, and because that is still a vast area, to a particular focus: pluralism as it is found in the works of the Muslim writer Said Nursi (1877–1960), the Catholic theologian John Courtney Murray (1904–1967), and Rabbi Lord Jonathan Sacks, the Chief Rabbi of the United Hebrew Congregations of the Commonwealth (UK) from 1991–2013. Each of these writers has taken a view of his respective religion that, while affirming the truth of his own faith, none the less allows room for others to live their own faiths with integrity in the search for truth.[1] Thus, while their religious beliefs affirm that they believe they practice 'the true faith', the writers do not claim that others must affirm that faith by force or coercion.

Quotations from each of these scholars provide a useful framework for the discussion that follows. First, from Said Nursi:

> 'O mankind! We created you from a single (pair) of male and female, and made you into nations and tribes that you may know each other.' That is, 'I created you as peoples, nations and tribes, so that you should know one another and the relations between you in social life, and assist one another; not so that you should regard each other as strangers, refusing to acknowledge one another and nurturing hostility and enmity.

1 Colin Turner and Hasan Horkuc, *Said Nursi* (I.B. Tauris 2009), 83, note that 'For Nursi, the truth is where it lies, regardless of whose hands it lies in.' Citing Hakan Yavuz, the author's comment that Nursi, unlike others such as Mawdudi, Qutb or Banna, 'did not seek a political collective movement to control the state. He stressed the formation of an individual consciousness as a precondition for a just society. He wanted to offer a new conceptual ground to Muslims to defend their inner world against the expanding ideologies of the West' (101, footnote omitted).

That is to say, being divided into groups and tribes should lead to mutual acquaintance and mutual assistance, not to antipathy and mutual hostility.'[2]

From John Courtney Murray:

> If society is to be at all a rational process, some set of principles must motivate the general participation of all religious groups, despite their dissensions, in the oneness of the community.[3]

From Rabbi Lord Sacks:

> Pluralism is a form of hope, because it is founded in the understanding that precisely because we are different, each of us has something unique to contribute to the shared project of which we are a part. In the short term, our desires and needs may clash; but the very realization that difference is a source of blessing, leads us to seek mediation, conflict resolution, conciliation and peace, the peace that is predicated on diversity, not on uniformity.[4]

Just as there are differences of interpretation within traditions about the meaning of certain terms, rules and their applications, so there are different interpretations between traditions. Terminology is always blurred at the edges meaning that it can have nuance or vagueness. This is not to be feared but recognized and it is also important because it allows for adjustment and adaptation.

In such a manner a judge in certain legal traditions argues from precedent in relation to case law. A new set of facts arises in relation to a dispute and a legal principle has to be applied to these facts. How shall this be done to ensure fairness of legal application and predictability for those in future who wish their actions to be 'according to law'? The answer is that developments must be careful, gradual and, usually, 'as little as possible' to accomplish the necessary development. If the facts are, as is said 'on all fours' with an earlier decided case of a court of comparable authority (the same level) then we say *stare decisis* – precedent is binding.

As it is with law, so with religious interpretations. These necessarily involve the faithful in applying traditional principles to the facts of change. Religious principles must remain faithful to the original teachings while the faithful wish to apply them to the changing world around them. This is not to say that religious principles must always accept what the 'world around' wishes: not at all. In fact, one of the greatest tensions in religions is when the contemporary spirit wishes to force changes that the religious tradition has weighed and rejected.

Whether and to what extent religious traditions 'develop' or change or even accept this concept is an area itself of controversy. That they do so cannot be denied and neither subject of these reflections denies such developments as I shall show below. This is how it will be with human communities. Always weighing their settled interpretations and revered truths

2 Said Nursi, 'The Letters', in *Risale-i Nur*, 1.0 CD 379–380, commenting upon the Holy Qu'ran, Sūrat al-Ḥujurāt 49:13 with Commentary from Bediuzzaman.
3 John Courtney Murray S.J., *We Hold These Truths* (Sheed and Ward 1960), x.
4 Jonathan Sacks, *The Dignity of Difference: How to Avoid the Clash of Civilizations* (Continuum 2002), 203–204.

alongside challenges and in the midst of doing so, finding or trying to find ways of explanation that allow for peaceful co-existence between those who believe one thing and those who believe another.

Colin Turner and Hasan Horkuc quote Hakan Yavuz as follows:

> Nursi's life and teaching always preach non-violence and he asks his followers to pursue civic resistance. He derives this commitment to non-violence from the tenets of Islam and the Sufi perception of human dignity. Human dignity is the key and organizing principle of Nursi's writings. Although he invites Muslims to non-violence, Nursi examines the sociological background of violence. He identifies a number of conditions that impel people to resort to violence: ignorance, poverty and the lawlessness. Nursi argues that violence exists because power is not constrained and controlled by religious teachings.[5]

Dialogue and discussion are the means of finding out how to live together and the extent of our embrace of friendship within difference – not denying the truth of our own belief systems but neither claiming exclusivity for them, is a key to living together in harmony and peace. Claims of exclusivity of belief and denial of place for others to seek the truth in their own ways, is often a cause of disharmony, disagreement, and bloodshed.

It is also a reality of terminology that it does not carry all its meanings explicitly. Many important things can be held implicitly and sometimes coming to understand these implicit or hidden meanings is important in order to understand what is being meant.

Taken together this means that when we come to examine a term such as 'pluralism' we need to be careful to make sure that what we mean by the term is clear and that if there are other meanings inconsistent with the one we mean, we make that clear at the outset.

Defining pluralism

There are many definitions of pluralism but perhaps most useful here is to define it as a philosophical and theological perspective on the world that emphasizes diversity rather than homogeneity, multiplicity rather than unity, and difference rather than sameness. Pluralism in this sense sees truth as truth wherever it is found and recognizes that the search for truth is in all human communities.[6] A further aspect of pluralism, easy to overlook, is that, properly understood, it either expressly or more often implicitly involves a useful ongoing dialogue about truth and therefore should allow for agreement and disagreement as part of this 'development'.

Structural pluralism

Pluralism may be said to be 'structural' when truth claims are maintained within specific traditions and, rather than affirming that 'truth is one' or that 'there is no truth', recognize that understandings of truth are developed within traditions and may overlap with insights from other traditions. In this case the truth being understood is shared, and a deeper insight

5 Turner and Hasan Horkuc, supra note 1 at 103.

6 This definition thus combines and revises definitions given by Calvin O. Sprag in Robert Audi, ed., *The Cambridge Dictionary of Philosophy* (Cambridge University Press 1995), 624 and in Ian S. Markham and Suendam Birinci Pirm, *An Introduction to Said Nursi* (Ashgate 2011), 194.

about the nature of truths that may be shared is not promulgated on eventual homogeneity or convergence. What is needed in social ordering are principles of modus vivendi and accommodation that allow for co-existence with disagreements and agreements about the nature of truth. Such disagreements are not denials that there is truth but merely a recognition that we disagree about its nature or extent. Emphasis in this approach can be on the necessity of freedom within and between associations with different explanations of 'the truth'. This is not, therefore, a denial of 'truth' but a recognition of practical limitations in living with others who do not believe the same thing. It places a premium on peaceful co-existence, respect, humility, and other 'civic virtues' and calls for greater understanding of their contents against a background awareness of the limitations of human interpretations of traditions – it calls, in short, for a measure of humility.

What distinguishes the various approaches to pluralism is how they approach civic ordering. If a more or less conscious and intentional 'pluralism' (or 'multi-culturalism', a variant of this that is beyond the scope of this chapter but related to it) is being undertaken then this can have policy dimensions that can be embraced and discussed. If, as is the case frequently, pluralism is left in a largely inarticulate or inchoate form, then policy will develop in a more haphazard and even chaotic manner usually divorced from debate, compromise, and well-worked out principles. How law and politics are organized in relation to the freedom of association and diversity, religious liberty, equality, and non-discrimination is key here. Also central is how the nature and limits of the State (both law and politics) are recognized and articulated. More often than not, an inchoate acceptance of a plenipotentiary state is what undergirds insufficient respect for the diversity and independence of associations – chief amongst these religious associations.

Pluralism as implying disagreement and dialogue

John Courtney Murray, the American Jesuit who did much to further ideas of pluralism in relation to the understanding of that within Roman Catholicism, in the 'Foreword' to his important collection of essays that exercised a pivotal influence on the Second Vatican Council (1963–1965), wrote this about 'pluralism':

> The term might have many meanings. By pluralism here I mean the coexistence within the one political community of groups who hold divergent and incompatible views with regard to religious questions – those ultimate questions that concern the nature and destiny of man within a universe that stands under the reign of God. *Pluralism therefore implies disagreement and dissension within the community. But it also implies a community within which there must be agreement and consensus.* There is no small political problem here. If society is to be at all a rational process, some set of principles must motivate the general participation of all religious groups, despite their dissensions, in the oneness of the community. On the other hand, these common principles must not hinder the maintenance by each group of its own different identity. The problem of pluralism is, of course, practical; as a project, its 'working out' is an exercise in civic virtue. But the problem is also theoretical; its solution is an exercise in political intelligence that will lay down, as the basis for the 'working out,' some sort of doctrine.[7]

7 Murray, supra note 3 at x (emphasis added).

Notable in this formulation is that disagreement and dissension are not signs of failure but of vitality as they imply life and the reality, as well, of agreement and consensus. The quest amidst difference is to find and describe and develop those core 'civic virtues' that make the common life possible, peaceful, and fruitful across communities of difference. The theological and political dimensions of the problem are different but inter-related depending on our conception of the relationship between religions and the state.

With respect to American religious citizens of various sorts (apart from his doctoral studies in Rome, Murray lived and wrote in America) Murray noted that:

> every church claims this freedom to define itself, and claims too the consequent right to reject definition at the hands of any secular authority. To resign this freedom or to abdicate this right would be at once the betrayal of religion and the corruption of politics.[8]

Murray noted that these questions are 'put with special sharpness to the Catholic intelligence' because:

> The Catholic may not, as others do, merge his religious and his patriotic faith, or submerge one in the other. The simplest solution is not for him. He must reckon with his own tradition of thought, which is wider and deeper than any that America has elaborated. He must also reckon with his own history, which is longer than the brief centuries that America has lived.... The conceptual equipment for dealing with the problem is by no means lacking to the Catholic intelligence ... [but he must be careful] lest the new problem be distorted or the ancient faith deformed.[9]

Murray ran into difficulty with Church authorities and was 'silenced' for a time and asked to submit his articles on theology to Rome where they were refused. Over time, however, he again emerged and became, eventually, influential on some of the key (and heavily debated) documents emerging from the Second Vatican Council.[10]

8 Murray at xi
9 Murray at xi–xii.
10 See Leon Hooper, S.J., 'John Courtney Murray', in John A Garraty and Mark C. Carnes, eds, *American National Biography* (Oxford University Press 1999). This source describes the background to Murray's controversies with the Church as follows: Murray eventually argued that Catholic teaching on church/state relations was inadequate to the moral functioning of contemporary peoples. The Anglo-American West, he claimed, had developed a fuller truth about human dignity, namely the responsibility of all citizens to assume moral control over their own religious beliefs, wresting control from paternalistic states. For Murray this truth was an 'intention of nature' or a new dictate of natural law philosophy. Murray's claim that a new moral truth had emerged outside the church led to conflict with Augustus Cardinal Ottaviani (prefect of the Vatican Holy Office) and the eventual Vatican demand, in 1954, that Murray cease writing on religious freedom and stop publication of his two latest articles on the issue. Murray continued to submit religious liberty manuscripts privately to Rome, all of which were rejected. When finally invited to the second (though not the first) session of Vatican Council II (1963), he drafted the third and fourth versions of what eventually became the conciliar endorsement of religious freedom, *Dignitatis humanae personae* (1965). After the council he continued writing on the issue, stating that the arguments offered by the final decree were inadequate, though the affirmation of religious freedom was unequivocal. At that time Murray turned to questions of how his church might arrive at new theological doctrines. He argued that, if Catholics were to arrive at new truths about God, they would have to do so in conversation 'on a footing of equality' with non-

Due to the manner in which the idea of 'development' was dealt with at the Vatican Council in the 1960s and the rigorous philosophy of religion and culture that have been developed over millennia within Catholicism, it may well be that some of the principles that will be observed in the work of Murray, and later Catholic documents, may shed light that is useful to Islam or to other traditions that must wrestle with the temptation towards monism.

Pluralism rejects exclusive claims for the state but allows them for subsidiary associations

Throughout history all religions at one time or another claim the ability and the authority to rule all aspects of the State and such claims often prove problematic. Where is the place of determination of the truth or falsity of religious truth claims? If it is the Divine who will judge then it is not for humans to make these judgments in time. Political Islam of the sort that aimed at establishing 'a near theocratic Islamic state' has been criticized by some scholars as totalitarian and 'at variance with genuine Islamic tradition'.[11]

Pluralism in world religious traditions: from the Universal Declaration of Human Rights (1948) to the South African Charter of Religious Rights and Freedoms (2010)

Variety in the idea of creation and an ordered cosmos, with a purpose, could not be more different from mere chaos lacking direction and it is the former that religions hold dear and promulgate.[12] The latter leads, not to ordered respect (and even reverence) for difference but, rather, fragmentation and perhaps even false conceptions such as 'inclusion' that does

Catholics and atheists. He suggested restructuring his church, which over the last two centuries had developed its notion of authority, according to him, at the expense of the bonds of love (secured in ongoing conversation) that more foundationally ought to define Christian living. See 'Murray Biography' at the *Woodstock Theological Library at Georgetown University*, at https://www.library.georgetown.edu/woodstock.

11 Asma Afsaruddin criticizing Pakistani thinker Abl-'Ala Mawdudi in Fred Dallmayr, *Integral Pluralism: Beyond Culture Wars* (University of Kentucky Press 2010), 88. 'What is problematic here is not the idea of divine rule as such (as a corollary of the belief in a Supreme Being) but rather its politicization and conflation with religious autocracy [and]....the slim scriptural basis for the idea.' Dallmayr is also critical of a certain 'hankering for power' amongst the so-called Christian 'Religious Right' in America (and by implication elsewhere) that results in an 'indiscriminate welding of faith and power politics' with the difference being that this 'movement', unlike political Islam, also endorses 'corporate capitalism, consumer culture, religious fervor and political ambition' driven by a 'triumphalist spirit' that lends the leadership to be receptive to 'crusading ventures' that include 'the doctrine of preemptive warfare' (at 88–89). Dallmayr also points out that other groups of Christians have opposed these tendencies. Reflection on human communities discloses that the claim not only to exclusivity of the truth and exclusion of others is as much based upon *psychological* factors as theological. In every form of human society there seem to be those who cause dissent and discord as well as those who seek peace, harmony, and cooperation. The fact that every sort of human association from sports groups to political parties to religious organizations knows these kinds of 'personalities' suggests that we need to look elsewhere than religion per se for what we might term 'the discordant personality type'. Nursi's rejection of war and 'enmity' is well known and visible throughout his works, and I shall discuss that further below.

12 George Grant, 'Natural Law' in *Philosophy in the Mass Age* (Copp Clark 1966) 28–41, and C.S. Lewis, *The Abolition of Man* (MacMillan 1947). See, for a recent view of 'natural law' within the three traditions, Anver M. Emon, Matthew Levering, and David Novak, *Natural Law: A Jewish, Christian and Islamic Trialogue* (Oxford University Press 2014).

not respect diversity or 'equality' that is vague and avoids respect for context.[13] It is no surprise that religions can, at their best, generate respect for difference as an aspect of the very idea of purposed creation and that this, in turn, may lead to co-operation across traditional lines of division. In fact, the idea of such notions as 'the dignity of the person' espoused now by signatories of the UN Declaration, speaking as it does, at Article 1 of human beings being 'born free and equal in dignity and rights' and being 'endowed with reason and conscience' alongside the obligation 'should' to 'act towards one another in a spirit of brotherhood', espouses an essentially religious conception of the person and cosmos.

Unique, so far, amongst legal or quasi-legal documents, the *South African Charter of Religious Rights and Freedoms*, takes the insights further and, in its Preamble speaks of inherent dignity emerging from an understanding that religious belief:

> may deepen our understanding of justice, love, compassion, cultural diversity, democracy, human rights and obligations, as well as our understanding of the importance of community and relationships in our lives and in society and may therefore contribute to the common good....[14]

Islam and pluralism

As one contemporary scholar, Reza Shah-Kazemi, has noted in relation to 'tolerance':

> For Muslims, tolerance of the other is integral to the practice of Islam. It is not an optional extra, a cultural luxury. The Quran sets forth an expansive vision of diversity and difference, plurality and indeed of universality. This is all the more ironic since the practice of contemporary Muslim states, not to mention extra-state groups and actors, falls lamentably short of those expectations as well as of current standards of tolerance set by the secular West.[15]

Shah-Kazemi goes on to observe that in response to this various people within and outside the Muslim world advocate a 'western approach' as a corrective to 'tradition and religiosity' but he rejects this. A 'more fruitful response' according to him is to see the development of

13 See, for example, Peter Western, 'The Empty Idea of Equality' (1982) 95 *Harvard Law Review*, 3.

14 The *South African Charter of Religious Rights and Freedoms* was signed by all the religions in South Africa in September 2010. It is best understood as a 'quasi-legal' *Charter* in so far as it was not designed nor intended to be legislated as law strictly speaking. Its status is a fascinating example of a civil society *Charter* (anticipated by Section 234 of the *Constitution of South Africa*) that is designed to influence the thinking and actions of society (including the usual legal actors) including the religions themselves: it is not, however, 'law' in the strict sense as opening it up for the formal processes of law would have destroyed its essentially 'civil society' dimensions as it would then have had to survive review within an essentially one-party state. This was deemed by the formers to be inadvisable and so the fully signed *Charter* sits as a tribute to co-operation and insight and, as indicated, a quasi-legal (but still, one hopes, influential) document. See Rassie Malherbe, 'The Background and Contents of the Proposed South African Charter of Religious Rights and Freedoms', paper presented at the Seventeenth Annual International Law and Religion Symposium, 'Religion in Contemporary Legal Systems', Brigham Young University, 4 October 2010, available at https://www.iclrs.org/content/blurb/files/Malherbe South Africa 2010.pdf (accessed 27 March 2017); and Iain T. Benson, 'South African Charter of Religious Rights and Freedoms', (2011) 4 *International Institute for Religious Freedom*, 125–134.

15 Reza Shah-Kazemi 'Tolerance' in Amyn B. Sajoo, ed., *A Companion to Muslim Ethics* (I.B. Tauris 2010), 168.

'tolerant codes of conduct as expressions of the universal principle of tolerance, and to discern this principle at the very heart of the vision of Islam itself: a vision in which the plurality of religious paths to the One is perceived as a reflection of the spiritual infinity of the One'.[16]

What this form of tolerance leading to plurality would result in, according to Shah-Kazemi, is 'tolerance of human diversity'. The framework that results involves both a duty and a right. The ethical duty is 'to permit people of different faiths to practice their own specific ways of embodying these universal values' and the spiritual right 'to benefit from the varied cultural expressions' of the universals themselves.

Many scholars have touched upon Said Nursi's thought and writings in relation to pluralism.[17] Nursi advocated the diversity of faith in the following terms:

> When you know your way and opinions to be true, you have the right to say, 'My way is right and the best.' *But you do not have the right to say, 'Only my way is right.'* According to the sense of 'the eye of contentment is too dim to perceive faults; it is the eye of anger that exhibits all vice'; your unjust view and distorted opinion cannot be the all-decisive judge and cannot condemn the belief of another as invalid.[18]

It is well known that Nursi pioneered and advocated Muslim–Christian dialogue and, similar to the passage just cited, also wrote that the reason for conflict among the people of truth 'while the misguided and worldly co-operate without rivalry' is that religious oppositions are maintained by failure to recognize the need:

> 1) To act positively, that is, out of love for one's own outlook, avoiding enmity for other outlooks, not criticizing them, interfering in their beliefs and sciences, or in any way concerning oneself with them.
> 2) To adopt a just rule of conduct that the follower of any right outlook has the right to say, 'My outlook is true, or the best,' but not that 'My outlook alone is true.' Or that 'My outlook alone is good' thus implying the falsity or repugnance of all other outlooks.[19]

Finally, further evidence of Nursi's practical pluralism was his belief that Christians and Muslims should make alliance to fight atheism and other irreligious ideologies. He wrote:

> It is even recorded in authentic traditions of the Prophet that at the end of time the truly pious among the Christians will unite with the People of the Qur'an and fight their common enemy irreligion. And at this time, too, the people of religion and truth need to unite sincerely not only with their own brothers and fellow believers, but also with the truly pious and spiritual ones the Christians, temporarily from the discussion and debate of the points of difference in order to combat their joint enemy – aggressive atheism.[20]

16 Reza Shah-Kazemi at 168.
17 See, for example, Ian Markham and Suendam Berinci Pirim, 'Nursi's Approach to Disagreement and Pluralism', in supra note 6 at 51–61.
18 Nursi, 'The Letters' in *Risale-i Nur* 1.0 CD 314, cited in Hasan Horkuc, 'New Muslim Discourses on Pluralism in the Post-Modern Age: Nursi on Religious Pluralism and Tolerance', (2002) 19 *The American Journal of Islamic Social Sciences* 2, 68–86 (emphasis added).
19 Nursi, 'The Flashes' in *Risale-i Nur*, 1.0 CD 203, cited in Horkuc, supra note 18 at 75.
20 Nursi, 'The Flashes' in *Risale-i Nur*, 1.0 CD 204 note 7, cited in Horkuc, supra note 18 at 75. See also, on dialogue among and between religions, Abdelaziz Berghout, 'Nursi's Vision for a New Universal Culture of Dialogue', in Ibrahim M. Abu-Rabi, ed., *Spiritual Dimensions of*

Clearly the dominance of contemporary cultures by atheism and agnosticism which, in often implicit ways, or by confusions as to the nature of 'secularism'[21] seeks to drive all religions out of fair public treatment (such as funding of religious schools in favour of increasingly strident agnosticism and atheism masquerading as 'neutrality') is a matter that concerns all religious citizens who have common cause, despite their religious differences, to seek justice for religions generally.[22]

Commentators on Nursi have noted his own ambivalence about and removal from active engagement with politics due to his awareness of the 'corruption' of the politics of his day. In discussing what they call 'grounded pluralism' Markham and Pirim summarize Nursi's 'attitude to pluralism' in four points as follows:

1 Said Nursi is committed to the truth of Islam and the importance of persuading others to that truth.
2 Nursi finds in his tradition several reasons why it is important to commit to constructive co-existence with other faith traditions.
3 Nursi believes that the resort to violence by Muslims against non-Muslims demonstrates a lack of self-confidence in Islam. Self-confident Muslims who are strong in their faith do not need to resort to violence.
4 Nursi believes that the state needs good citizens and pious believers make good citizens.[23]

The Roman Catholic tradition and pluralism

The Catholic Church in the Vatican II Ecumenical Council (1963–1965) recognized and encouraged a mutually beneficial cooperative relationship between Church and State and the

Bediuzzaman Said Nursi's Risale-i Nur (SUNY Press 2008), 231–258. See also the work of Ian Markham cited elsewhere in this chapter (text accompanying notes 6, 17, and 23).

21 'Secularism', if it is defined and understood as 'non-establishment of religion' by the state and law and respects the rights of all religions, is a concept consistent with pluralism. Such a definition of 'secularism' is, however, at variance with the original meaning of the word as it was coined and developed in the mid nineteenth century by English agnostic George Jacob Holyoake and the secularist movements that followed him, which were dedicated in various ways to excluding religion from the public sphere. Once non-establishment is recognized, it is a better term to use than 'secularism'. Also preferable is to understand the relation between religions and the state as one of *co-operation* between religions and the state (understood as law and politics) rather than an ideological form of 'strict *separation*' that deprives the common good of the benefits of appropriately co-operative projects such as history has shown with education and health-care to name but two. See Iain Benson, 'Considering Secularism', in Douglas Farrow, ed., *Recognizing Religion in a Secular Society* (McGill-Queen's University Press 2004), 83–98. In fact, co-operation better describes the legal situation in many countries (the UK, Canada, Australia, and South Africa to name four but there are others) than does 'separation'. The United States has made arguments over 'separation' a promised land for litigators and a bit of a nightmare for religious citizens and their projects.

22 Qutb Mustapha Sano in 'The Basis of Present Day Civilization According to the *Risale-i Nur*', in the Sixth International Symposium, Globalization, Ethics and Bediuzzaman Said Nursi's *Risale-i Nur* (Sözler 2004), 156–167 at 165 has noted that 'during the periods of supremacy of Islamic civilization in such places as Andalucia, Turkey, Iraq, and Syria, history witnesses to the mutual assistance and solidarity that were prevalent. Christians were able to live their Christianity in the shade of Islamic civilization and Jews their Judaism. Whatever people's religion, whatever their race, love, altruism and togetherness were the norm.'

23 See, Markham and Pirim, supra note 6 at 53.

limits on the role of each in various places. That there should be a distinction between the Church and the political community was set out in the following terms:

> It is highly important, especially in pluralistic societies, that proper views exist of the relation between the political community and the Church. Thus the faithful will be able to make a clear distinction between what a Christian conscience leads them to do in their own name as citizens, whether as individuals or in association, and what they do in the name of the Church and in union with her shepherds.
> The role and competence of the Church being what it is, she must in no way be confused with the political community, nor bound to any political system. For she is at once a sign and a safeguard of the transcendence of the human person.
> In their proper spheres, the political community and the Church are mutually independent and self-governing. Yet, by a different title, each serves the personal and social vocation of the same human beings. This service can be more effectively rendered for the good of all, if each works better for wholesome mutual cooperation, depending on the circumstances of time and place.[24]

The vision of the human community put forward by the Catholic Church is based on the fact that all people are called to the same end: God himself. From this comes the principle that love of neighbour is inseparable from love for God. Two 'Declarations' from the Second Council (1963–1965), *Nostra Aetate* and *Dignitatis Humanae* [25] are of particular importance in describing the Catholic conception of dialogue and collaboration with the followers of other religions.

Nostra Aetate: 'The Declaration on the Relationship of the Church to Non-Christian Religions' (28 October 1965) specifically addresses various religions in terms of the questions central to the profound human mysteries:

> What is a man? What is the meaning and the purpose of our life? What is goodness and what is sin? What gives rise to our sorrows and to what intent? Where lies the path to true happiness? What is the truth about death, judgment, and retribution beyond the grave? What, finally is that ultimate and unutterable mystery which engulfs our being, and whence we take our raise, and whither our journey leads us?[26]

Recognizing that these questions are the subject of reflection in all great world religions, the Church specifically engages (in brief) Hinduism, Buddhism, Judaism and Islam. Noting that 'the Catholic Church rejects nothing which is true and holy in these religions' (662). In the section touching on Islam, the Declaration states:

> Although in the course of the centuries many quarrels and hostilities have arisen between Christians and Moslems, this most sacred Synod urges all to forget the past and

24 Walter Abbott S.J., ed, *The Documents of Vatican II* (Guild Press 1966), 287–288, quoting *Gaudium et Spes*, 'The Pastoral Constitution on the Church in the Modern World', para. 76 (emphasis added).

25 See Abbott, supra note 24, '*Dignitatus Humanae*' (675–700); '*Nostra Aetate*' (660–671). A further declaration, '*Unitatis Redintegratio*' ('The Decree on Ecumenism' 1964), dealt with ecumenism and the re-integration of unity amongst Christians. Its approach might well set out principles of interest within Islam as well.

26 Abbott, '*Nostra Aetate*' at 661.

> to strive sincerely for mutual understanding. On behalf of all mankind, let them make common cause of safeguarding and fostering social justice, moral values, peace and freedom.[27]

Much could be said about *Dignitatus Humanae*: 'The Declaration on Religious Freedom: On the Right of the Person and of Communities to Social and Civil Freedom in Matters Religious' (7 December 1965), a most important and controversial document.[28] Two paragraphs, however, will serve here, as they focus directly on the developed Catholic understanding of 'pluralism.' The first focuses on what governments should do:

> [G]overnment is to assume the safeguard of the religious freedom of all its citizens, in an effective manner, by just laws and by other appropriate means. Government is also to help create conditions favourable to the fostering of religious life, in order that the people may be truly enabled to exercise their religious rights and to fulfill their religious duties, and also in order that society itself may profit by the moral qualities of justice and peace which have their origin in men's faithfulness to God and to His holy will.[29]

The second focuses on what governments must not do in the name of religion:

> It follows that a wrong is done when government imposes upon its people, by force or fear or other means, the profession or repudiation of any religion, or when it hinders men from joining or leaving a religious body. All the more is it a violation of the will of God and of the sacred rights of the person and the family of nations, when force is brought to bear in any way in order to destroy or repress religion, either in the whole of mankind or in a particular country or in a specific community.[30]

The Declaration had to deal with the idea of 'development' within Catholic theology as well as overcome a long-standing ambiguity in Church teaching relating to the relationship between Catholic and non-Catholic citizens. According to John Courtney Murray's notes to the *Declaration*:

> The Church does not deal with the secular order in terms of a double standard – freedom for the Church when Catholics are a minority, privilege for the Church and

27 Abbott, '*Nostra Aetate*' paras 2–3 at 662–663, footnotes omitted except at the end of the first sentence (fn 13, on 663), which reads: 'Students of the history of relations between Christians and Moslems will find this section a remarkable change in the Church's approach. One thinks invariably of the Crusades (but note that there were Moslem crusaders as well as Christian). Those were ideological wars. This Council, as it also makes clear in the Pastoral Constitution on the Church in the Modern World, wants to disassociate itself from war.'

28 A very useful overview of the document is from F. Russell Hittinger, 'Political Pluralism and Religious Liberty: The Teaching of *Dignitatus Humanae*', in Mary Ann Glendon and Hans F. Zacher, eds, 'The Proceedings of the 17th Plenary Session on Universal Rights in a World of Diversity: The Case for Religious Freedom', *The Pontifical Academy of Social Sciences Acta 17* (Pontifical Academy of Social Sciences 2012), 39–55. The controversy, which related in essence to the notion of 'development of doctrine' within the Catholic tradition is well discussed by John Courtney Murray S.J. in his introductory note to the Abbott edition of *The Documents of Vatican II*, supra note 24 at 672–674.

29 Abbott, *Dignitatis Humanae* at 685.

30 Abbott, *Dignitatis Humanae* at 685.

> intolerance for others when Catholics are a majority. The Declaration has opened the way toward new confidence in ecumenical relationships, and a new straightforwardness in relationships between the Church and the world.[31]

In other words, the Church now embraces a principled pluralism in all situations, for the religious rights of other religions as well whether they are the minority or the majority.

In his Encyclical, *Caritas in Veritate* (2009 para. 9) former Pope Benedict XVI cited a variety of earlier Encyclicals and the *Compendium of the Social Doctrine of the Church* (2004, para. 76), shedding light 'upon humanity's journey towards unity' (para. 8) and the importance of truth 'wherever it is manifested' as the only possibility of 'integral human development'. He stated that:

> This mission of truth is something that the Church can never renounce. Her social doctrine is a particular dimension of this proclamation: it is a service to the truth which sets us free. Open to the truth, from whichever branch of knowledge it comes, the Church's social doctrine receives it, assembles into a unity the fragments in which it is often found, and mediates it within the constantly changing life-patterns of the society of people and nations.[32]

The Catholic Church's vision, thus expressed, does not view its insights as limited to Catholics nor the journey to 'truth' as reaching a homogeneous end as is the case with 'civic totalist' or 'convergent' theories; here, diversity is recognized. It views the description of the architecture of society as part of a human journey involving all religions across communities, nations, and time.[33]

The most recent articulation of the Catholic understanding of diversity and the limits of the state is to be found in the *Compendium of the Social Doctrine of the Church* (2004) in which the foundation and purpose of the political community, and the law, are set out. Here we observe that 'a political community is established to be of service to civil society from which it originates'. The Catholic Church sets out its commitment 'on behalf of social pluralism' to 'bring about a more fitting attainment of the common good and democracy itself according to the principles of solidarity, subsidiarity and justice'.[34]

Two points should be made in closing. First, the Church recognizes that 'the separation of Christian faith and daily life is one of the most serious errors of our day':[35]

> Without a metaphysical perspective, the loss of a longing for God in self-serving narcissism and the varied means found in a consumerist lifestyle; the primacy given to technology and scientific research as ends in themselves; the emphasis placed on appearance, the quest for image, communication techniques: all of these phenomena must be

31 Abbott, *Dignitatis Humanae* at 673.

32 *Caritas in Veritate*, para. 9, citing *Compendium of the Social Doctrine of the Church* (para. 76).

33 Most Encyclicals are directed to the Church but also beyond it. Thus, the 'address' at the front of *Caritas in Veritate* of Benedict XVI (2009) is addressed to: 'The Bishops, Priests and Deacons, Men and Women Religious, the Lay Faithful and *All People of Good Will*' (emphasis added). The Encyclical deals with 'Integral Human Development in Charity and Truth'. The attempt is integrative yet respectful of diversity.

34 Pontifical Council for Justice and Peace, *Compendium of the Social Doctrine of the Church* (Libreria editrice Vaticana 2004), para. 417.

35 Pontifical Council at para. 554.

> understood in their cultural aspects and placed in relation to the central issue of the human person...[36]

Thus the Church understands her role to be metaphysical, moral, and practical. The Church understands her role to be in a dialogical relationship with contemporary politics. The Church rejects the 'autonomy' of the state if that is understood to be an independence of the state from the moral law.[37] The question is, therefore, how is moral law to be mediated?

The *Compendium* sets out a second and indispensable aspect of the Catholic position in relation to the political order. The *Compendium* states that 'because truth is one':

> A sincere quest for the truth, using legitimate means to promote and defend the moral truths concerning social life – justice, freedom, respect for life and for human rights – is a right and duty of all members of the social and political community.[38]

The moral obligation of the political order extends not just to the Catholic Church but in fact to all 'communities of believers'. A 'pluralistic society' is expressly recognized and 'secularity' is identified as providing 'a place for communication for different spiritual traditions and the nation'.[39] Thus, an expressly pluralistic conception of society has been developed through Roman Catholic thought, but it is a pluralism connected to a wider moral vision that includes moral mediation through human communities. Connected to this is the recognition that democratic societies may not, in fact, extend the same courtesy of moral recognition to the Church because 'secularism' seeks to dominate just as surely as 'theocracies' did in earlier ages:

> Unfortunately, even in democratic societies there still remains expressions of secular intolerance that are hostile to granting any kind of political or cultural relevance to religious faiths. Such intolerance seeks to exclude the activity of Christians from the social and political spheres because Christians strive to uphold the truths taught by the Church and are obedient to the moral duty to act in accordance with their conscience. These attitudes even go so far, and radically so, as to deny the basis of a natural morality. This denial, which is the harbinger of a moral anarchy with the obvious consequence of the stronger prevailing over the weaker, cannot be accepted in any form by legitimate pluralism, since it undermines the very foundations of human society. In the light of this state of affairs, the marginalization of Christianity ... would not bode well for the future of society or for consensus among people; indeed, it would threaten the very spiritual and cultural foundations of civilization.[40]

We know from history that the eventual realization of peaceful co-existence allowing for difference has not always been honoured. The concept of 'pluralism' and its nature and scope plays an important role in these developments.

36 Pontifical Council at para. 554.
37 Pontifical Council at para. 571.
38 Pontifical Council at para. 571.
39 Pontifical Council at para. 572.
40 Pontifical Council at para. 572 (footnotes omitted).

Judaism and pluralism

Writing on dignity and difference, Jonathan Sacks, the Chief Rabbi of the United Kingdom, has considered the importance of the idea of 'covenant' between God and man within Judaism and noted that such a notion posits a strong recognition of the limits of government and law:

> Members and citizens alone cannot sustain themselves, let alone establish a framework of collaborative action and collective grace. Covenants exist because we are different and seek to preserve that difference, even as we come together to bring our several gifts to the common good.[41]

This good, while it is 'common', is not uniform. Sacks, therefore, endorses the conception of 'a community of communities' that undergirds a developed religious insight about pluralism. For Sacks:

> Pluralism is a form of hope, because it is founded in the understanding that precisely because we are different, each of us has something unique to contribute to the shared project of which we are a part. In the short term, our desires and needs may clash; but the very realization that difference is a source of blessing, leads us to seek mediation, conflict resolution, conciliation and peace, the peace that is predicated on diversity, not on uniformity. Covenant tells me that my faith is a form of relationship with God - and that one relationship does not exclude any other, any more than parenthood excludes a love for all ones' children.[42]

Sacks calls not for a global government, nor a global civil religion, but for something more subtle and more profound. He calls for a 'global covenant'. Such a covenant would need to frame 'our shared vision for the future of humanity'. Hope, which requires courage, '... is the faith that, together, we can make things better'.[43] Such a covenant would be expressed through the shared and differing insights of the world's religions.

41 Jonathan Sacks, *The Dignity of Difference: How to Avoid the Clash of Civilizations* (Continuum 2002), 203. David Novak in *Covenantal Rights: A Study in Jewish Political Theory* (Princeton University Press 2000) has also written about re-understanding 'rights talk' in the context of what he argues is the richer ground of 'covenant' and notes, citing Maimonides, *Guide to the Perplexed* (3.27) that 'political life is pluralistic because we are embodied' (75 fn 95) which echoes the passage from the Qu'ran cited at the head of this chapter. Thus our nature as embodied persons in community and the natural limitations on society so that it does not become a 'superperson' rather than 'a communion of separate persons' ensure that individual rights are a limit on the power of society 'because the life of the human person as the image of God points to a transcendent dimension beyond the grasp and thus beyond the authority of any human society' (217). 'No individual or society itself can claim to be the exclusive conduit of divine authority in the world. God's authority is revealed, instead, in the limiting interaction of these two domains [what is human and what is divine]' (217). Novak concludes by noting that: 'the renewed government of Jewish law in civil society, of which the institution of individual human rights must be developed, can only come when there is a true renewal of the covenant by the vast majority of the Jewish people with their God' (218). Thus spiritual renewal outside of government is key to government but the two realms must not be conflated into one. This seems to echo in a powerful way the insights of both Said Nursi and John Courtney Murray (as well as the Catholic understandings set out above).

42 Sacks, supra note 41 at 203–204.

43 Sacks at 206.

Hope differs from optimism in that optimism is a passive virtue whereas hope requires us to be involved in change. Setting this religious insight about covenant and hope and the global possibilities for covenant in juxtaposition to alternative explanations for the human situation, Sacks notes that 'in the midst of our hypermodernity' there is an old–new call to 'a global covenant of human responsibility and hope' that will require the following:

> Only when we realize the danger of wishing that everyone should be the same – the same faith on the one hand, the same McWorld on the other – will we prevent the clash of civilizations, born of the sense of threat and fear. We will learn to live with diversity once we understand the God-given, world-enhancing dignity of difference.[44]

Alan Mittleman, however, writing from a Jewish perspective and discussing how history has brought religious claims in Judaism and Catholicism (but not Islam) into line with 'the normative authority of the regime of liberty as the organizing principle of the modern state' asks, rather poignantly, whether Islam, if invited into the same concordat with modern democratic citizenship, 'could take the final step towards religious liberty without giving political latitude to the uneasy scepticism that has come to define the public culture of the West'.[45] He reminds us at the conclusion of his thoughtful essay that 'the goods of liberty and pluralism are ill at ease with the good of religious truth'.

There is an *a fortiori* here: should a form of pluralism arise that purports to transfer the terms of peaceful co-existence into a simplistic formula for 'inclusion' without respect for genuine associational diversity understood as *difference*, then what has arisen is not a respectful 'liberal' state but, rather, a new form of tutelary power as theocratic in its own way as the theocracies it sought to replace.

Avoiding monisms of the atheistic, agnostic, or religious form

It is clear that Sacks and Mittleman, like Nursi and Murray, articulate an essentially religious vision of the world that can co-exist with democratic liberalism of a non-convergence form. In this world dignity and respect are rooted in belief in God and his religious framework. This framework requires recognition of the dignity of 'the other' as an obligation of the self-in-relation, not as a chance 'feeling' or obligation about which one cannot form an explanation. These writers recognize that respect and an appropriate form of tolerance are what is required of 'the other'.

Said Nursi and John Courtney Murray both suffered and suffered suppression and exclusion (and in Nursi's case long periods of exile, torture, and imprisonment) for their views, as so many have been over the centuries of human history for challenging the settled 'orthodoxies' of the day. Yet in both cases the positions that each advocated are coming to be more and more influential and widely accepted within traditions that, for a time at least, seemed to reject initially what each writer offered. Monism in our own time has resurfaced in a variety of forms. The hypertrophy of law and politics puts continued pressures on the regulation of associational life. Frequently articulated views of 'secular' or 'public' that are impliedly stripped of religion when, in fact, open societies are made up of citizens some of whom are religious believers, *but all of which are believers*, gives the whip hand to agnosticism and atheistic domination of cultures.

44 Ibid. at 206.
45 Alan Mittleman, 'Toleration, Liberty and Truth: A Parable', (2002) 94 *Harvard Theological Review* 4, 353–372.

Can civic totalism (as discussed by Stephen Macedo and William Galston)[46] come to recognize itself as a species of atheistic or agnostic theocracy as far away from fair treatment of other belief systems as the religious theocracies in earlier times? Can we see political theology or constitutional theocracy or civil religions as concepts that elevate law and politics beyond their competence? Time will tell. One thing, however, is sure. Liberal legal and political cultures that pay lip service to diversity but deny it in practice will slowly have to find new terms, other than 'equality' and 'non-discrimination' to define their acts of cultural domination. They will need to speak about 'deep equality' or some similar thing, and will reject explicitly, or more likely implicitly, toleration and accommodation in the process. It is this we should look for and recognize the early signs of this new monism, which are already around us.[47]

46 William Galston, referring to Macedo in 'Religion and the Limits of Liberal Democracy' in Farrow, ed., supra note 21 at 43–44, 49.

47 See, for an example of what seems to be a rejection of 'accommodation' and 'religious tolerance' in preference to a concept (rather confusingly laid out it has to be said) of 'deep equality' see a recent collection of essays in Canada. Lori Beaman, ed., ***Reasonable Accommodation: Managing Religious Diversity*** (UBC Press 2012). Thus, Beaman writes of 'a solution that begins with or is framed in deep equality, ***rather than accommodation....***' (213, emphasis added). Tolerance and accommodation are seen as establishing 'hierarchies of difference' (213). While purporting to respect difference, the introduction and conclusion to this volume seem to suggest, as we see with the notion of '*a* solution' (note the singular) above, that we embrace a 'cohesive' solution to the problems of 'hierarchies' and 'diversity'. Needless to say, this approach ought to give concern to genuine pluralists who view modus vivendi and irreconcilable differences as unavoidable aspects of human society and 'convergence' or 'totalist' conceptions of ordering as posing significant threats to diversity, freedom, and constitutional legal principles and traditions. See, also, the unanimous approach of the Canadian Law Deans opposing, in the name of a highly selective reading of 'equality', one that ignores religious diversity entirely, the establishment of what would be Canada's first law school taught 'from a Christian perspective'. Iain T. Benson, 'Law Deans, Legal Coercion and the Freedoms of Association and Religion in Canada', (2013) 71 *The Advocate*, 5, 671–675.

4 Religious freedom and pluralism

A Judaic perspective

Asher Maoz

While the idea of equality between people has deep philosophical roots in Judaism,[1] the notion of religious tolerance seems problematic. If you know that truth lies with you, why should you tolerate contrary teachings? Why should you sanction the freedom to practice a religion that you know is false?

The term 'freedom of religion' is a modern one. It does not appear in Jewish classical texts. This term may convey two different messages: the freedom of 'the other' to adhere to a different religion, and the tolerance towards different streams within one's own faith as well as towards non-religious members of one's community. In Judaism this dilemma is further complicated by the fact that Judaism is a nation-religion.[2] By belonging to the Jewish people one belongs to the Jewish faith. By converting to Judaism one also becomes a daughter, or a son, of the Jewish people.

To summarize the Jewish attitude, it may be correct to state that while Jewish religion is non-missionary outward, it is missionary indeed inward.

This chapter deals with the Jewish attitude towards other religions. It is wise at the outset to add a word of caution. It would be wrong to look for monolithic answers in Judaism. The Jewish faith is ancient. It hardly speaks with one voice. Historical not less than theological aspects have influenced attitudes.[3] This chapter seeks to describe the attitude of mainstream contemporary Judaism, but the assertions here might be questioned.

The statement, for example, that Jewish religion is not a proselytizing one might be challenged. Indeed, in ancient times we may trace periods of massive, even forced, conversion to Judaism. What signifies in those episodes is that they were carried out for political, rather than religious, reasons and were not welcomed by the Sages.[4] Even nowadays, we may witness rather esoteric movements that advocate conversion in order to strengthen the Jewish people.

It would be accurate to state that from a Jewish point of view the option of conversion exists. However, there is an ostensible reluctance to individual conversion let alone massive conversion.

1 'And you shall love your neighbor as yourself.' Leviticus 19:18.

2 See Asher Maoz, 'State and Religion in Israel', in Menachem Mor, ed., *International Perspectives on Church and State* (Creighton University Press 1993), 239, 243

3 See Asher Maoz, 'Can Judaism Serve as a Source of Human Rights?', (2004) 64 *Heidelberg Journal of International Law* 677, 714–718.

4 Chazal (an acronym for the Hebrew 'Ḥakhameinu Zikhronam Liv'rakha' ('Our Sages, may their memory be blessed')), is a general term that refers to all Jewish sages of the Mishna, Tosefta, and Talmud eras, spanning from the times of the final 300 years of the Second Temple of Jerusalem until the sixth century CE (250 BCE – c. 625 CE).

The Jewish attitude towards other faiths might be discussed in terms of past, present, and future.

The attitude of the past is defined, as explained in the Genesis narrative, by a covenant God made with humankind after the Great Flood, when the people, who were all descendants of Noah, were 'one', and had 'all one language'.[5] With these people God made 'the Covenant of the Rainbow'. According to Judaic sources this covenant included the seven Noahide laws or commandments that are binding upon all mankind.[6] Though known as Noahide laws, the *Talmud* tells us that six of these seven commandments had been given in the beginning to Adam and Eve.[7] As these laws concern basic moral character, they are described by some philosophers as rules of natural law. However, one of the commandments, prohibiting the cursing of God as well as the worship of other gods, might be described as of religious flavor or even as advocating monotheism, as it includes the prohibition against blasphemy and the prohibition against idol worship.[8]

Certainly Maimonides states the laws in religious terms: 'Whoever among the Nations fulfills the Seven Commandments to serve God belongs to the Righteous among the Nations, and has his share in the World to Come.'[9] Arguably this statement implies that the Noahide commandments are optional, as only those who wish to be regarded as righteous must follow them. Yet, according to most Jewish authorities, these commandments are obligatory upon all descendants of Noah.[10] Maimonides teaches, moreover, that a share in the World to Come is earned only if a person follows the Noahide laws specifically because the person considers them to be of divine origin (through the Torah). One who simply considers the laws to be recommendations for a good way to live would merely be considered wise.[11] Not all authorities follow Maimonides' distinction, but in any case what is important to understand is that in this world view universal freedom of religion lies only beyond these laws that apply to all humankind alike.

The second stage, the present, begins with the appearance of the Jewish people and the revelation of God to Moses on Mt. Sinai. In order to fully understand the meaning of this stage in Jewish thought it might be useful first to consider the third stage – the end of the days. In the words of the prophet Micah:

> In the last days the mountain of the Lord's temple will be established as chief among the mountains; it will be raised above the hills, and peoples will stream to it.

5 Genesis 11:6.

6 On the Noahide Laws, *see* Aaron Lichtenstein, *The Seven Laws of Noah* (Rabbi Jacob Joseph School Press/Z. Berman Books, 2nd edn, 1986).

7 *Babylonian Talmud,* tractate *Sanhedrin* 56a/b, quoting *Tosefta* (a compilation of oral law from the period of the Mishnah) *Sanhedrin* 9:4. These commandments are based on exegesis of Genesis 2:16 and 9:4–6.

8 Note, however, David Novak's reservation that these laws do not impose a positive obligation to worship God. See Novak's book *The Image of the Non-Jew in Judaism: An Historical and Constructive Study of the Noahide Laws* (Edwin Mellen 1983), 126 ff.

9 Maimonides, *Mishneh Torah* [verb., Repetition of the Law], known also as *Code of Maimonides, Hilkhot Melakhim u'Milhamot* [Laws of Kings and Wars] 8:14. Maimonides (Moshe ben Maimon, known as the Rambam), twelfth-century Spain, Pez, and Egypt, is regarded as the greatest post-Talmudic codifier.

10 See Michael J. Broyde, 'Jewish Law and the Obligation to Enforce Secular Law', in David Shatz and Chaim I. Waxman, eds, *The Orthodox Forum Proceedings VI: Jewish Responsibilities to Society,* (1997) 103–143 ch. II, sec. 1, reprinted in http://www.jlaw.com/Articles/noach2.html (accessed 9 July 2018).

11 Maimonides, supra note 9.

> Many nations will come and say, 'Come, let us go up to the mountain of the LORD, to the house of the God of Jacob. He will teach us his ways, so that we may walk in his paths.' The law will go out from Zion, the word of the LORD from Jerusalem.[12]

There is much debate as to which law will go out of Zion and what will be the paths that the peoples will follow. Is this a reference to the Torah of Israel? Or does it mean the ultimate word of the Lord, what may be referred to as scriptural truth? The following verse of Micah's prophecy states: 'All the nations may walk in the name of their gods; we will walk in the name of the Lord our God for ever and ever.' It is obvious that by this Micah refers to a future reality, the 'last days', when all the peoples will walk in the paths of the Lord.

This phrase, then, might be understood as laying the ground for the contemporary attitude towards what could be called, in present terminology, freedom of religion of the non-Jews. For until the last days it is only the Children of Israel who must walk in the name of the Lord, while all others are free to walk in the name of their gods. Until then the Lord is both the God of Israel and at the same time Lord of the Universe.

Maimonides notes that Moses bequeathed the *Torah* and commandments 'to Israel only and to whomever wishes to proselyte from the other nations, but whoever does not wish, we do not coerce him to accept *Torah* and commandments.'[13] He continues, 'Moses our Master ordered, in the name of the Lord, to enforce all creatures on earth to accept all the commandments that were ordered to Noah, and whoever does not accept them will be put to death.'[14] Then he adds that a gentile must not observe the commandments given to the Israelites but only those given to Noah, and summarizes:

> The general rule is: They are not permitted to innovate into religion and devise new commandments for themselves out of their own mind, but either he becomes a proselyte and accepts all the commandments, or adhere to his own religion, neither adding to it nor subtracting anything from it.[15]

The attitude towards other religions is not unequivocal. From the passage in Micah we may infer the legitimacy of those religions. Yet it is obvious that these religions are of lower status, since in the Messianic days, when the earth shall be full of the knowledge of the Lord, as the waters cover the sea,[16] they will be elevated to the utmost stage of walking in the paths of the Lord.[17] We may find in both the Bible and Judaic classic teachings harsh statements regarding idolatry,[18] associating paganism with moral corruption. It is essential to note, in this context, that according to Halakhic authorities this does not apply to monotheistic faiths. In this regard a distinction was drawn between Islam and Christianity. Maimonides, and his disciples, while regarding Islam as pure monotheism, viewed the Christian

12 Micah 4:1–3.
13 *Code of Maimonides, Hilkhot Melakhim u'Milhamo*t, 8:10.
14 *Code of Maimonides, Hilkhot Melakhim u'Milhamo*t 8:13.
15 *Code of Maimonides, Hilkhot Melakhim u'Milhamo*t 10:12.
16 *Isaiah* 11:9.
17 Moreover, a gentile who converts to Judaism may not renounce it and return to the status of a son of Noah. *Code of Maimonides, Hilkhot Melakhim u'Milhamo*t 10:3.
18 The Hebrew term for idolatry is *avodah zarah* (foreign worship) or *avodat kochavim umazalot* (worship of planets and constellations).

Trinity to be idolatrous.[19] On the other hand, rabbis that lived in Christian countries ruled that 'though they utter the name of an alien divinity, their intention is to the creator of heaven and earth'.[20]

Nowadays there is full agreement that the rules regarding idolatrous religions apply neither to Muslims nor to Christians. Rabbi Menachem haMeiri regarded both Muslims and Christians 'nations bound by the way of religion', different from the pagan societies of ancient times, that were not restricted by religious laws and norms.[21] Thus both Christians and Muslims were regarded as 'assemblies for the sake of Heaven, destined to endure; their intentions are for the sake of Heaven and their reward will not be withheld'.[22] Rabbi Joseph Albo even admitted the existence of 'two divine Torahs, at the same time, for different nations'.[23] Christianity and Islam were not only regarded as legitimate religions but were even praised for removing the idols and subordinating their nations to the Noahide laws, thus giving them 'moral attributes' far beyond what was demanded of them by the Torah of Moses.[24]

In concluding his essay 'Judaism Views Other Religions',[25] Aviezer Ravitzky deals with the transition from coexistence or tolerance to religious pluralism, requiring welcoming the existence of the other religion. He points out the difficulties involved in such a move and suggests the need to 'support the minimalist conception of the "Seven Noahide Laws," which requires us to rest content with the basic decency of the other as the controlling criterion and not to look to the other faiths' special contribution to divine truth or make any positive doctrinal demands.'[26]

There is no doubt that Jewish sources over the ages contain harsh statements regarding non-Jews. We might bear in mind, however, that for the Jew the 'relationship between Jews and Gentiles is at all times a reciprocal one. The behaviour of the Jews towards their neighbours is conditioned by the behaviour of the latter towards them, and vice versa.' In

19 See *Code of Maimonides, Hilkhot Akkum* [Laws Concerning Idolatry and the Ordinances of the Heathens] 9:4. See, further, David Novak, 'The Treatment of Islam and Muslims in the Legal Writings of Maimonides', in William M. Brinner and Stephen D. Ricks, eds, *Studies in Islamic and Jewish Traditions* 2 vols. (Scholars Press 1986), Vol. I, 233–350, and David Novak, *Maimonides on Judaism and Other Religions* (Hebrew Union College 1977).

20 Rema on *Shulhan Arukh, Orah Hayyim,* sec. 156. The Rema [Rabbi Moshe Isserles], of the sixteenth century, Poland, wrote glosses to the *Shulhan Arukh*, [lit.: Set Table] a code of *halakha*, composed by Rabbi Joseph Caro, of the sixteenth century in *Eretz Israel* [Palestine], considered the most authoritative compilation of Jewish Law since the *Talmud*. The *Shulhan Arukh* is divided into four books, the first of which is *Orah Hayyim* [ways of life]. See also Rabbeinu Tam (Rabbi Jacob ben Meir, twelfth century, France), *Tosafot* [Critical and explanatory glosses on the *Talmud*], *Sanhedrin* 63b.

21 See Rabbi Menachem haMeiri, thirteenth-century Provence, *Beit haBechira* [the Temple, Novellae on the *Talmud*], Tractate *Avodah Zarah* [Idolatry], 2b, 22a, 26a.

22 Rabbi Jacob Emden, of seventeenth-century Germany, see: David Rozen, 'Esau – Jacob's Brother: The Christian World Changes its Attitude Towards Judaism', *De'ot* 9 (October 2001), 16. (Hebrew).

23 Joseph Albo, *Sefer HaIkkarim* [Book of Fundamentals] (Jerusalem: Mahbarot le'Sifrut, 1951), 155. See Novak, supra note 8 at 336–340. Rabbi Albo lived in fifteenth-century Spain.

24 Jacob Emden, *Letter at the Conclusion of Seder Olam Zuta ve-Rabbah* [Small and Large Order of the World] (chronicle in Hebrew and Aramaic, starting with Adam and concluding with Mar Zutra IV of the sixth century).

25 Aviezer Ravitzky, 'Judaism Views other Religions', in J. D. Gort, Henry Jansen, and H. M. Vroom, eds, *Religions View Religions: Explorations in Pursuit of Understanding* (Rodopi 2006), 75–107.

26 Ravitzky at 97.

this regard attention must be paid to the Christian theology under which '[n]either Jewish residence, both settled and temporary, in Christian countries, nor even the very existence of the Jew was taken for granted.'[27]

Already in ancient times it was ruled that 'the poor amongst the non-Jews are supported together with the poor of Israel, and the sick amongst the non-Jews are visited together with the sick of Israel and the dead of the non-Jews are buried together with the dead of Israel',[28] and eulogies are said over their dead and their mourners are comforted.[29] Moreover, it was ruled that 'cheating a non-Jew is worse than cheating a Jew'.[30] It is moreover stressed that rules regarding the gentiles were imposed 'for the sake of peace' or even to avoid 'desecration of the Divine Name'.

As to the deep philosophical roots in Judaism of the idea of equality between peoples, we find the following in our sources:

> 'And you shall love your neighbour as yourself' – Rabbi Akiba says: 'This is a great Biblical law.' Ben Azzai said: 'This is the book of the generations of Adam – it is an even greater principle.'[31]

Rabbi Goren's resolution of this tannaitic dispute is interesting:

> According to Rabbi Akiba, the principle applies only to the Israelites, because it refers to 'your neighbour', but according to Ben Azzai, the principle refers to universal fraternity, and fraternity applies not only amongst the Jewish people themselves, but to love of mankind in general, 'for in the image of God made He man' (Genesis 9, 6). Of course, this great principle can only be achieved gradually and by stages. First we must achieve love of Israel, which is the intermediate stage to universal fraternity. In any case, the final goal, according to Ben Azzai, is love of all mankind when they have accepted upon themselves the Kingdom of Heaven. And therefore Ben Azzai said that 'This is the book of the generations of Adam' constitutes a greater and more purposeful principle in the Torah than, 'and you shall love your neighbour as yourself.'[32]

It should be pointed out that Rabbi Goren's response is not merely theoretical. As founder of the Israel Defense Force (IDF) chaplaincy and as chief chaplain he gave the response following requests by soldiers and officers.

> Indeed, elsewhere Rabbi Akiba himself says: 'Beloved is the person who was created in the image. Great love is the lot of the one who is created in the image, as it says: "In the image of God He created man."'[33]

27 Jacob Katz, *Exclusiveness and Tolerance: Studies in Jewish-Gentile Relations in Medieval and Modern Times* (Oxford University Press 1961), 3–4. See further Shlomo Simonson, *The Apostolic See and the Jews* (Dvir Publishing House 1994), 8 (Hebrew): 'The Jewish People never attempted to force Judaism upon the Christians, and did not persecute Catholics. The Jewish People is not commanded to seek the pardon of the Church: quite the contrary.'

28 *Babylonial Talmud, Tractate Gittin* 61a.

29 *Mishna, Gittin* 5:5.

30 *Tosefta* (Zuckermandel) *Bava Kamma* 10:15.

31 *Sifra Weiss, Kedoshim* 4:12; *Jerusalemite Talmud, Nedarim* 9:4.

32 Shlomo Goren, 'Ethics of Combat According to *Halakha*', in his book *Meshiv Milxamah: Responsa on Matters of the Military, War, and Security* (1983), Vol. I, 5–6 (Hebrew).

33 *Mishnah Avot* 3:14.

Moreover, supposedly harsh statements against gentiles are no more than a misconception. Thus we come across what seems a shocking statement by Rabbi Simeon bar Yoxai: 'You are called man but the nations of the world are not called man.'[34] This statement was incidental to a halakhic discussion on the question of whether the graves of non-Jews cause impurity; the Rabbis were strict in their ruling and Rabbi Simeon bar Yoxai was lenient. The discussion revolved around the verse 'When a man dies in the tent.'[35] According to Rabbi Simeon bar Yoxai, 'man' refers only to an Israelite, but not a gentile.[36] It would appear that Rabbi Simeon bar Yoxai's words must be interpreted semantically, that is wherever Scripture uses the term 'the man', it is referring to all humankind, whereas the word 'man' refers only to an Israelite.[37] Indeed, it is said of Moses: 'Now the man Moses was exceedingly humble, above all the men on the face of the earth.'[38] There is no doubt that this means that Moses was more humble than all mankind, and not just of the Israelites.

We can cite the words of many other Tannaim[39] who interpret 'the man' as applying to the non-Jew and comparing his status to that of the greatest of Israel. Thus, for example, in explaining the verse, 'Ye shall therefore keep my statutes, and my judgments: which if the man do, he shall live in them,'[40] Rabbi Meir says: 'It does not say Priests and Levites and Israelites, but man. From this we learn that even a gentile who occupies himself with the study of the Torah equals the High Priest.'[41]

Some may perceive seeming discrimination against the gentile in the halakhah. Although many sources explain that the reason for discrimination against the gentile, for example with respect to compensation for the ox who gored and in relation to the commandment of returning lost items, is the fact that the gentile to whom it refers does not observe the seven Noahide laws.[42] These laws reflect, in principle, a minimal moral standard in a civilized society.

34 *Yevamot* 61a.

35 Numbers 19:14.

36 In interpreting *Ezekiel* 34:31: 'And you are my sheep, the sheep of my pasture, you are Man and I am your God.'

37 This is the view of Rabbenu Tam, cited in *Tosafot on Yevamot* 61a, *s.v.* 'And the Gentiles are not called Man.'

38 Numbers 12:3.

39 Sages whose views are recorded in the Mishnah, from approximately 10–220 CE.

40 Leviticus 18:5.

41 *Bava Kamma* 38a. This saying is cited in *Sifra, Axarei Mot* 13:13, in the name of R. Yirmia. Cf. Maimonides, *Iggrot Harambam* 23:2: 'Thus said the true Sages our Rabbis of Blessed Memory: The Righteous Gentiles have a place in the world to come.' Even if Rabbi Simeon b. Yoxai's tone was derisive, we must note the circumstances in which the words were uttered. Bar Yoxai lived at the time of the Hadrianic persecutions, when Jews were forbidden to learn Torah and observe the commandments, and the great Sages of Israel were executed, including Rabbi Akiba, the teacher of Rabbi Simeon b. Yoxai: see Asher Bar-Tanna, *Basic Topics in Judaism* (Tel-Aviv University 1993), 211 (Hebrew). Bar-Tanna stresses the deep hatred of the Romans for the Jews: they regarded Judaism as a 'vile plague upon the whole of humanity' and the Jews as 'sub-humans, worse at times than domesticated animals'; Moshe D. Herr, 'Hatred of Jews in the Roman Empire in the Light of Rabbinic Literature', in Menahem Stern ed., *Jews and Judaism in the Eyes of the Hellenistic World – Collection of Essays* (Jerusalem: The Zalman Shazar Center for Jewish History, 1984), 33, 43 (Hebrew). Compare Abba Hillel Silver, *Where Judaism Differed: An Inquiry into the Distinctiveness of Judaism* (Macmillan 1956), 236: 'At times, in some occasional saying of a Rabbi, we become startlingly aware of some bitter, intolerant judgment clearly struck out of the tense emotion of the hour. We hear the cry wrung out of a hurt and wounded spirit by the cruel wrongs visited upon the people by the oppressors of Israel. These have been preserved as the sad records of a tragic national experience. They are neither precept nor norm.'

42 See R. Avahu in *Bava Kamma* 31a, and see *Bava Kamma* 113b.

They include the prohibitions against bloodshed, incest, theft, tearing the flesh from a living animal, and the positive commandment to set up courts of law, as well as two prohibitions from the religious sphere – the prohibitions against idolatry and against cursing God.[43] Even the exemption of an Israelite from the obligation of protecting property of a gentile can be seen as deriving from the fact that the particular gentile exempts himself from the prohibition against theft.[44] At the same time, Israelites were not permitted to steal from the gentiles, and according to Maimonides:

> The prohibition against any form of theft is scriptural law. Even the idolater: it is forbidden to steal from him or to oppress him, and if one has stolen from him or oppressed him, he must return [what he has taken].[45]

Rabbi Jacob Avigdor, Chief Rabbi of Mexico City, discusses the basis of the reciprocity in the approach of the halakhah to the non-Jewish world.[46] He says that the fact that the commandments which were given to Israel do not apply in their relations with the gentiles 'is a very simple matter … all the laws concerning man and his fellow-man are based on obligations which bind both.'[47] Rabbi Avigdor illustrates the idea with the explanation of the author of *Havot Yair* of the seventeenth century, as to why the Israelites were commanded concerning the prohibition against taking interest from a Jew, but not in relation to a gentile.[48]

43 Maimonides, *Mishneh Torah: Laws of Judges, Kings and their Wars* 9:1. See text to note 8.

44 Compare Maimonides' explanation (*Mishneh Torah, Nizkei Mamon* 8:5) of the law relating to the ox that gored: 'The ox of an Israelite who gored the ox of a gentile – whether for the first time or a persistent gorer – is exempt, since the gentiles do not hold a person liable for his animal that caused damage, and we judge them according to their laws. The ox of a gentile that gored the ox of an Israelite – whether for the first time or a persistent gorer – pays full damages. This fine is imposed upon gentiles since they do not observe the commandments and do not remove the risk, and if we would not hold them liable for damage caused by their animals, they would not take care of the animals and people would suffer financial loss.' It appears that already at the time that this *halakhah* was formulated, the Sages were not comfortable with it. It is related in *Bava Kamma* 38a: 'The Rabbis said: The Roman Government long ago sent two commissioners to the Sages of Israel with a request to teach them the Torah. It was accordingly read to them once, twice and thrice. Before taking their leave they made the following remark: We have gone carefully through your Torah, and found it correct with the exception of this point, *viz*, your saying that if an ox of an Israelite gores an ox of a Canaanite there is no liability, whereas if the ox of a Canaanite gores the ox of an Israelite, whether for the first time or a persistent gorer, compensation has to be paid in full. In no case can this be right. For if the implication of "his neighbor" has not to be insisted upon, why then even in the case of an ox of an Israelite goring an ox of a Canaanite should there not be liability? We will, however, not report this matter to our Government.'

45 Maimonides, *Mishneh Torah, Hilkhot Gezela ve'Aveda*1:2. See, in general, Avraham Sherman, 'The Principles of the Basic Law: Human Rights in the Light of the Principles of the Torah of Israel and its Laws', in G. Freishtak, ed., *Human Rights in Judaism* (1992), 285 (Hebrew).

46 Jacob Avigdor, 'Between Israel and the Nations', in Avraham Bick (Shauli), ed., *Contemporary Problems in the Light of the Halakhah – The Great Scholars of Israel Reply to R. Shlomo Zalman Shragai* (Rabbi Kook Institute 1993), 1 (Hebrew).

47 Avigdor, 1–2.

48 See Deuteronomy 23:20–21: 'You shall not lend upon interest to your brother: interest of money, interest of victuals, interest of any thing that is lent on interest. To a foreigner you may lend upon interest; but to your brother you shall not lend upon interest, that the Lord your God may bless you in all that you put your hand unto, in the land where you go in to possess it.'

> The Torah laid down this law because it is based on justice and integrity. See for yourself: the gentiles do not have the Torah,[49] and they are not commanded not to lend on interest. Therefore if the gentile should lend money to an Israelite, he will lend to him on interest, because he is permitted to do so. Thus, if an Israelite who lends to a gentile were not to take interest, this would be a perversion of justice. Every law and every obligation between people is reciprocal, and privileges cannot be granted to one side only. Since it is permitted for the non-Jew to take interest from an Israelite, we learn that the prohibition against taking interest applies only in relation to an Israelite [borrower], because today's borrower may be tomorrow's lender, and then he too will not charge interest, for he too is bound by the prohibition. If the gentile is a lender, however, he will charge interest; but if he is the borrower [from the Jew] he will not pay interest. This is not just.[50]

Similarly, Rabbi Avigdor explains the obligation upon a Jew to save another Jew, but not a gentile. The origin of this obligation is in the prohibition, 'You shall not stand by your brother's blood.'[51] This prohibition is unique to biblical law, and it does not appear in the legal codes of other nations, for whom there is no legal prohibition, but rather a moral one:

> It is well known that no nation in the world, even in our modern and cultured society, which may claim that it has a law and obligation, a rule of law that obligates individuals not to stand by when another is in danger. This is a matter of virtue only, the straight path in life, commendable conduct, but there is no law or obligation in this world to require a person not to stand by when another is in danger, or else stand to be convicted as a criminal.[52]

Accordingly, if a Jew would be required not to stand by when a non-Jew is in danger, the law would be lopsided:

> The Jew seeing the non-Jew in danger would be obligated to save him, and would be liable to punishment if he did not do so. The non-Jew who stood by when the Jew was in danger would be exempt from saving him, which would be merely a matter of virtuous conduct and integrity. Therefore the Torah was precise in specifying 'brother', that is only with respect to your brother do you have an obligation and are liable to punishment on this matter, but with respect to the non-Jew it is a matter of virtuous conduct and integrity, just as it is for him with respect to you.[53]

49 That is, they are not bound by the laws of the Torah, as opposed to the Seven Noahide Laws.

50 Avigdor, supra note 46 at 2. Thus R. Avigdor understands Rashi on the verse, 'And if you lend money to any of My people, even to the poorest of them, you shall not be to him as a creditor; neither shall you charge him interest.' Exodus 22:24: 'You should regard yourself as if you are poor.' R. Avigdor explains: 'In other words, today you are the creditor and tomorrow you might be the borrower, and therefore you must not charge interest, and tomorrow your brother will not charge you interest.'

51 Leviticus 19:16. See Maimonides, *Hilkhot Nizke Mamon* 1:14, and see Aaron Kirschenbaum, 'The 'Good Samaritan' and Jewish Law', *Dine Israel* 7 (1976), 7.

52 Avigdor, supra note 46 at 2.

53 Avigdor at 3.

Rabbi Avigdor sums up:

> This seems to be so very simple, so much so that I am amazed that anyone questions it. The matter has become complicated because it is thought that a Jew must not save the gentile, but this is a lie. Saving the non-Jew is not a scriptural obligation, but a moral and human obligation, just as the non-Jew is not obligated to save a Jew by virtue of a law or statute, but rather because of his humanity, which demands that he saves the person in danger, and nothing more.[54]

The logic underlying various laws in relation to pagans indicates why the sources stipulated that they do not apply to the members of the monotheistic religions.[55] Thus Rabbi Menachem HaMeiri limited the exemption from returning a lost object to the non-Jew to 'idol-worshippers who are not bound by the ways of religion':

> Finding a lost object is a partial acquisition, and its return is a measure of piety, and a person who has no religion is not subject to piety ... every person from a nation which is bound by the ways of religion and the service of God in any form whatsoever, even though their beliefs may be distant from ours, are not included in this; but rather they are absolutely like Jews concerning these matters – both with regard to lost objects and with regard to mistake and all other such matters.[56]

In a similar vein, in the context of saving a gentile, Rabbi Judah Loew son of Bezalel distinguishes between 'the idol worshippers who lived in the time [of our Sages] who would worship the stars and the signs, and they did not believe in the exodus from Egypt and in the creation of the world; but those gentiles in whose shadow we, the Jewish people, live and amongst whom we are dispersed – they believe in the creation of the world and in the exodus from Egypt and in the principles of religion, and they worship the Creator of Heaven and earth – not only is it not prohibited to save them, but we are even obligated to pray for their wellbeing'.[57]

Rabbi Yehonatan even states unequivocally: 'To the claims of the heretics we can answer that the Mishna was referring only to the seven nations of antiquity.'[58]

The Mishna already contains a halakhic development in a field close to this subject – even if the reasons are allegedly technical. The question arose whether it was permitted for an Ammonite proselyte to come into the community and marry an Israelite woman. The Mishna relates:

> Rabbi Joshua said: 'You are permitted to enter the congregation.' Rabban Gamliel said to him: 'Does it not say, "An Ammonite and a Moabite will not enter the assembly of

54 Avigdor at 3.

55 See Naxmanides, *Sefer Hamitzvot* 16; *Resp. Ribash* 119; *Bet Yosef, Tur, -oshen Mishpat* 266.

56 HaMeiri, *Bet Habexirah, Bava Kamma* 113b; nevertheless, 'You may not steal from the idol-worshippers and the heathens, and if he sold to an Israelite, you may not take it without payment, and you may not default on a debt to him.'

57 *Be'er Hagola*, ['The Well of the Diaspora'] *-Hoshen Mishpat* 425:300; for additional sources see Katz, supra note 27, Chapter 13, 156–168.

58 *Shittah Mekubetset, Bava Kamma* 38a. For additional sources and for a critical analysis, see Jacob Katz, 'The Peregrinations of Three Apologetic Statements', in his *Halakhah and Kabbalah: Studies in the History of the Religion of Israel* (The Magness Press 1994), 270–290 (Hebrew).

> the Lord."' Rabbi Joshua said to him: 'Do Ammon and Moab still reside in their original homes? Sennacherib king of Assyria long ago went up and mixed up all the nations.'[59]

Rabbi Joxanan ruled, as far back as the third century, that 'the daughter of an Ammonite proselyte is fit for the priesthood [that is, she may marry someone from the priestly caste].'[60]

Throughout history, Jews have been prosecuted in countries where they lived. Some outstanding examples include the Crusades, the Inquisition, blood libels and pogroms, and above all, the Holocaust.[61] Even the Scroll of Esther, allegedly contains 'a permit for the eradication of the non-Jews'.[62] We should not forget, however, that this followed a plot 'to kill, to destroy and wipe out all the Jews, from young to old, children and women.'[63] Moreover, the extent of the historical veracity of this text may reasonably be doubted. It may be presumed that the Jews, who suffered under the yokes of various Hamans, paid back in literary form what they could not do in reality. It is not for nothing that there are those who dubbed the Scroll of Esther as 'the Scroll of the Exile'.[64] Not surprisingly, the Festival of Purim became the one day in the year on which the Jews, who all year long were subject to the persecutions of hooligans, were able to 'take revenge' on those who persecute them. One historian writes as follows:

> Over many generations, the 'contrary' nature of the festival expressed itself in belligerent acts, usually derisive, towards ancient and less ancient enemies ... there is evidence of mockery of Christianity and its symbols as part of the festivities; the crucified Jesus and the hanged Haman have merged in their eyes into the one despicable image.[65]

It may be no coincidence that in the State of Israel, where Jews confront their enemies with weapons and not in fancy-dress, Purim has lost this character.[66]

59 *Berakhot* 28a.
60 *Yevamot* 77a.
61 One should not overlook the fact that 'Despite its teachings, the Christian Church has been used in the two millennia since the life of Christ to support some of the most repressive, intolerant regimes on earth. At times the Church itself has been party to some of the worst crimes against humanity.' Howard O. Hunter, 'International Conference on Christianity and Democracy - Introductory Remarks' (1992) 6 *Emory Int'l L. Rev.* 19.
62 Avigdor Levontin, 'Judaism and Democracy: Personal Reflections', (1994–95) 13 *Tel-Aviv University Law Review* 521, 530 (Hebrew).
63 Esther 3:13.
64 Abraham Kariv, *The Seven Pillars of the Bible – Essays of Biblical People and Biblical Ideas* (Am Oved Publishers 1968), 151 (Hebrew).
65 Elimelech Horowitz, 'Quite the Reverse: The Jews Against their Enemies in the Purim Celebrations', (1994) 49 *Zion* 129 (Hebrew).
66 Kariv, supra note 64 at 166, conjectures that despite the cancellation of Haman's decree, the 'vilifiers' had begun its implementation, and the Jews were defending themselves. Kariv bases himself on the language of the Scroll: 'they gathered to preserve their souls'. Indeed, when Esther enjoined the King 'to reverse the letters devised by Haman the son of Hamedatha the Agagite, which he wrote to destroy the Jews that are in all the king's provinces', Ahasuerus had to refuse the request, for 'the writing which is written in the king's name and sealed with the king's ring, may no man reverse' (Esther 8:5–6). All that the King could do was to 'grant the Jews that were in every city to gather themselves together and to stand for their life' (Esther 8:11).

The war of conquest of the Land of Israel in the time of Joshua, and the commandment to wipe out all the inhabitants of the land.[67] must be seen in the context of those days with their special circumstances, and conclusions regarding other wars should not be drawn from it. Rabbi Goren wrote on this matter:

> Despite the explicit Biblical commandment regarding warfare, we are commanded to have mercy even on our enemies and not to kill, even in times of war, except when this is necessary for the purpose of self defence, for conquest and victory, but not to harm the non-belligerent population, and it is certainly forbidden to harm women and children who are not participating in the battle. Apart from those wars in ancient times in relation to which there is an express Biblical commandment 'not to leave anyone alive', since the enemy acted with cruelty, and therefore the Torah was harsh towards them ... We must not, Heaven forfend, draw conclusions from them in relation to other wars and to our times, when we have seen the extent to which the Lord, Blessed be He, has mercy even on idol worshippers, and He does not rejoice in their downfall and suffers when they are lost. We are commanded to walk in His ways and to have mercy on His creatures, as is written, 'His mercy extends to all his creatures' (Psalm 145).[68]

We may learn about the attitude of Judaism towards non-Jews from the laws relating to the various pilgrim festivals. The sources pose the question: why were the Jewish people commanded three times concerning rejoicing on the Festival of Tabernacles,[69] 'but in relation to Passover rejoicing is not mentioned even once'. They answer: 'Because the Egyptians died'.[70] For the same reason, the full Hallel (Prayer of Rejoicing) is recited only on the first day of Passover and not on the rest of the week, 'for you shall not rejoice in the downfall of your enemy and your heart will not be made glad by his failure'.[71]

Throughout the entire seven days of the Festival of Tabernacles, seventy bullocks were sacrificed in the Temple 'for the seventy nations'. In this context, the statement of Rabbi Joxanan is interesting: 'Woe to the idol-worshippers who have suffered a loss but do not know what they have lost. When the Temple was standing – the altar could atone for them; and now – who will atone for them?'[72]

The author of Midrash Tanxuma protests: 'One finds that on the Festival, Israel sacrificed seventy bullocks for the seventy nations ... therefore they too should have loved us – not only do they not love us but they hate us.'[73]

Much criticism has been leveled against the Jews for regarding themselves as 'The Chosen People'. However, the feeling of being 'chosen' characterizes every nation and every religion; otherwise, what is it that causes member of groups to belong to them? This does not necessarily lead to derision of all other nations. The real question is, what is the source of this election and what are its manifestations? According to Abba Hillel Silver:

67 Levontin, supra note 62 at 530.
68 Goren, supra note 32 at 14.
69 'And you shall rejoice in your feast ... and you shall be altogether joyful': Deuteronomy 16:13–15; 'And you shall rejoice before the Lord your God seven days': Leviticus 23:40.
70 *Yalkut Shimoni, Amar* 5674.
71 *Yalkut Shimoni, Amar* 5674, on the verses from Deuteronomy 16:13,15. See also *Pesikta deRav Kahana*.
72 *Sukkah* 45b.
73 *Tanxuma, Pinxas* 14.

> Judaism regarded Israel as a 'chosen people', a 'holy people', not because every member was assumed to be holy and morally immaculate, or because the race itself was regarded as divine ... Judaism opposed the race myth ... It tolerated no doctrine of racial superiority or exclusiveness ... Israel was a 'holy people' in respect to the object which it was to serve – to increase holiness in the world ... 'Holiness' is not an accolade of self-glorification but a hard discipline of self-purification ... It is only in the sense of consecration to the service of divine purposes that the term 'holy' has any validity, whether applied to a people or to a non-national religious community.[74]

The implication of the idea of the choice can be learned from the midrash on the verse, 'Judges and officers shall you appoint ....'[75]

> Rabbi Levy said: To what may this be compared? To a king who had many sons, and he loved the youngest best. He had one orchard which he loved more than all his other possessions. The King said: I will give this orchard, which I love best of all that I have, to my youngest son, whom I love more than all my sons. So did the Holy One Blessed Be He say: of all the nations I created I love only Israel. Of all my creations, I love only the Law. I give what I love to the nation that I love.[76]

It was an orchard in the sense of neither material goods, nor even privilege that was given to the Chosen People; rather, the burden of the law was laid upon them. This idea emerges clearly in a passage from the Mishnah of Rabbi Eliezer:

> The[re is a] difference between righteous Jews and righteous Gentiles: the Jews are not called righteous unless they observe the entire Torah. The righteous Gentiles, however, are called righteous because they observe the seven Noahide laws scrupulously. In what way? When they observe them they say: Because our father Noah commanded us ... And if they do so, they will inherit the World to Come like the Israelite.[77]

The concept of election appears in various sources, one of which is the Additional Prayer Service for the Festivals:

> You have chosen us from all the peoples; You loved us and found favour in us; You exalted us above all the tongues and You sanctified us with your commandments. You drew us close, our King, to Your service and proclaimed Your great and Holy Name upon us.[78]

The motif of the parable of the orchard returns once more: the election of the Jewish people means the imposition of the yoke of the commandments and the service of the Lord upon them. True, there is holiness in observing the commandments and serving the Creator;

74 Silver, *Where Judaism Differed* ..., supra note 41 at 228–230. On the other hand the Catholic Church, which took the idea of a chosen people from Judaism, 'came to speak of itself as the "Holy Church" and claimed for its members an especial grace'; Silver at 229.

75 Deuteronomy 16:18.

76 *Deuteronomy Rabbah* 5.

77 *Mishnat Rabbi Eliezer* 121; cited by Katz, supra note 27 at 271.

78 For manifestations of the concept of Election in the prayers and blessings, see Ephraim E. Urbach, *The Sages: Their Concepts and Beliefs* (The Magnes Press 975), Vol. I, 453–454 (Hebrew).

nevertheless, it is a burden, rather than a privilege, which was laid upon the Chosen People. This can be seen in the continuation of the prayer: 'Because of our sins we were exiled from our land and sent far from our soil.'

Had God not chosen the Jewish people from all the nations and sanctified them with His commandments, they would not be punished by exile, for in the absence of the burden of the commandments, there would be nothing to transgress. Moreover, these words contain recognition of the exalted value of the election that confers upon the Jewish people the obligation of serving the Creator. At the same time, these words contain a form of frank admission of the fact that the People is not up to the enormity of the task, for it is not superior to other nations, and it too is afflicted with the human quality of sinning. As opposed to other nations, in respect of which such conduct does not lead to devastation, this is not the case with Israel. Does this smack of arrogance in any way?[79] Maybe. In any case, the purpose of this 'arrogance' is important, just as the manifestations of the idea of election are important.

A related subject that may be problematic for Jewish–Gentile relations is that of differentiation. Our sources contain prohibitions, such as the prohibitions on 'gentile' bread and wine, which are intended to distance the Jews from their gentile neighbors. These prohibitions, which are seemingly incompatible with the idea of the brotherhood of man, are not derived from hatred of the non-Jew, and were intended to preserve Jewish society from non-Jewish influence. It even fits in with the attitude of the gentile world to the Jews.[80]

Finally, in discussing the concept of election and differentiation from the non-Jews, we must not ignore the institution of conversion. Maimonides writes as follows concerning the nature of conversion:

> Each and every convert who converted and accepted all the commandments of the Torah, and the slaves when they are freed, are as Israelites for all purposes, as it is said: 'The one decree shall be for you,'[81] and they may enter the congregation of the Lord immediately, and this is the case when the proselyte or the freed slave marries an Israelite woman, or the Israelite marries a female proselyte or freed slave.[82]

The entry gates to the Jewish people and the religion of Israel are open to all, irrespective of race or nationality.[83] Even if there is nothing new about joining a religion, in joining a

79 Possibly in the sense of 'over-righteousness' to which Levontin refers, supra note 62 at 539.
80 See Katz, supra note 27.
81 Numbers 15:15.
82 Maimonides, *The Book of Holiness, Issurei Bi'ah* [Laws of Forbidden Intercourse] 12:17. Further on Maimonides explains that this law does not apply to the four nations (Ammon, Moab, Egypt, and Edom, which were forbidden in the Torah from entering into the congregation of the Lord, either eternally or for three generations (Deut. 23:4–9)), but 'when one of their members converts, he is an Israelite in every respect, other than for the purpose of marrying into the community'. But this is only in theory. In practice, Maimonides rules: 'When Sennacherib the King of Assyria arose he mixed up all the nations with each other and exiled them from their place. And the Egyptians who are now in the Land of Egypt are different people, and the Edomites in the Field of Edom. And because the four forbidden nations were mixed up with all the other nations who are permitted, all were permitted … therefore when a person converts in our time in any place, whether an Edomite or an Egyptian, whether an Ammonite or a Moabite, whether a Cushite or from the other nations, whether male or female – they are admitted to the congregation immediately' (*halakhah* 25).
83 It may not be superfluous to point out in this context the report of Scripture concerning Moses, that he 'married a Cushite woman': Numbers 12:1.

people Judaism has something exclusive, indeed, an exclusivity that derives from the identity between these two components. Moreover, even though the gates of conversion are open to 'all the nations', nevertheless, unlike other religions – Christianity above all – the Judaism of today is not a missionary religion and does not preach to non-Jews to leave the religion of their parents and their people in order to become Jewish.[84]

It may be true that 'it is not only on the level of race that there may be discrimination.'[85] But what is the meaning of the argument that 'Judaism advocates discrimination, and even segregation, on the religious level'?[86] True, Judaism does advocate segregation, there is confusion of segregation with discrimination. Indeed, in its treatment of minorities, a State ought to reject the 'equal but separate' approach,[87] but this does not apply to relations between religions themselves.

We may conclude our survey by returning to Micah's prophecy, which genuinely encapsulates the Judaic approach to other religions: 'For let all the people walk each one in the name of its god, But we will walk in the name of the Lord our God for ever and ever.'[88] It is noteworthy that the President of the State of Israel, Zalman Shazar, chose this verse as a motto for his words of greeting upon receiving Pope Paul VI during his visit to Israel in 1964.[89]

84 The law is: 'They are told [those seeking to convert] about the burden of Torah and the hardship in its performance … so that they will withdraw. If they accept and do not withdraw, and they … come back with love, they are accepted': *Shulxan Arukh, Yoreh De'ah* 268:12. Maimonides, *Issurei Bi'ah* 14:1 rules: 'How are righteous converts accepted? When one of the gentiles seeks to convert and he is checked and no cause is found [not to convert], he is asked: What have you seen that has made you convert? Do you not know that Israel at this time is downtrodden and oppressed and subject to tribulations? If he says: I know and I am not worthy, he is accepted immediately.' See also *Yevamot* 47b. The origin of this formulation derives from the time of the Hadrianic persecutions: see Urbach, supra note 78 at 486–487.

85 Levontin, supra note 62 at 534.

86 Levontin even proclaims this conclusion to be 'obvious'.

87 *Brown v. Board of Education* 347 U.S. 483 (1954); *Johnson v. Virginia* 373 U.S. 61 (1963): '[It] is no longer open to question that a State may not constitutionally require segregation of public facilities.' See also Herbert Wechsler, 'Toward Neutral Principles of Constitutional Law', (1959) 73 *Harvard Law Review* 1.

88 Micah 4:5.

89 'Texts of the Greetings by Pontiff and Israeli President, and Host's Farewell', *The New York Times*, 6 January 1964, at https://www.nytimes.com/1964/01/06/archives/texts-of-the-greetings-by-pontiff-and-israeli-president-and-hosts.html (accessed 9 June 2018).

5 Western 'civic totalism', sovereignty of the people, and the need for limited government

Hans-Martien ten Napel

Expressive liberty and value pluralism

In a fascinating, comparative philosophical article, Sungmoon Kim attempts 'to revamp Confucian democracy, which is originally presented as the communitarian corrective and cultural alternative to liberal democracy, into a robust democratic political theory and practice that is plausible in the societal context of pluralism'.[1] The same source of inspiration that Kim uses to reconstruct Confucian democracy – William Galston's notion of liberal pluralism – can be used to critically appraise the current state of Western liberal democracy, to consider, more specifically, the extent to which Western liberal democracy still manages to realize the principle of expressive liberty, defined by Galston as 'the absence of constraints, imposed by some individuals on others, that make it impossible (or significantly more difficult) for the affected individuals to live their lives in ways that express their deepest beliefs about what gives meaning or value to life'.[2]

In the light of the principle of expressive liberty, the right to freedom of religion or belief is naturally of particular relevance. Kim rightly points out that, paradoxically, religious freedom is often in fact 'grounded in the radical unavailability of freedom of choice for a person who is radically situated in a particular religious and/or cultural community as a member'.[3] Just as it is threatened by the ethically monistic character of certain theorizations of Confucian democracy, expressive liberty is threatened by a Western 'civic totalism' that – as Galston puts it – 'tacitly views public institutions as plenipotentiary and civil society as a political construction possessing only those liberties that the polity chooses to grant and modify or revoke at will'.[4]

This chapter argues that the West may well have to come to terms with the fact that its ideal of liberal democracy will remain fundamentally flawed as long as the sovereignty of the people on which its political legitimacy is ultimately based hinders instead of advances a true sort of value pluralism. A source of inspiration for this argument is *A Confucian Constitutional Order. How China's Ancient Past Can Shape Its Political Future* by Jiang Qing.[5] In his introduction to this book, Daniel A. Bell calls Jiang 'the most prominent Confucian

1 Sungmoon Kim, 'A Pluralist Reconstruction of Confucian Democracy', (2012) 11 *Dao*, 315.
2 William A. Galston, *Liberal Pluralism. The Implications of Value Pluralism for Political Theory and Practice* (Cambridge University Press 2002), 28.
3 Kim, supra note 1 at 319.
4 William A. Galston, *The Practice of Liberal Pluralism* (Cambridge University Press 2005), 23.
5 Jiang Qing, *A Confucian Constitutional Order. How China's Ancient Past Can Shape Its Political Future* (edited by Daniel A. Bell and Ruiping Fan, translated by Edmund Ryden, Princeton University Press 2013).

political thinker of our day' and this particular book 'Jiang's most detailed and systematic work on Confucian constitutionalism'.[6]

One of the goals of comparative constitutional studies can be to develop a better understanding of a different constitutional system.[7] In this case, however, the study of Jiang's book on Confucian constitutionalism serves primarily to reflect on some of the problems that lie at the root of the West's own weakening consensus behind the right to freedom of religion or belief.

Finally, this chapter points to the notion of limited government as a possible means to better guarantee the principle of expressive liberty. In doing so, the legitimacy of liberal democracies can also more generally be enhanced. At the same time, the partly Christian roots of this notion raise at least some doubts with respect to the question of how realistic this suggestion really is in an arguably (post-) secular age.[8]

'Civic totalism'

As Sungmoon Kim notes, Galston's liberal pluralism represents 'the most sophisticated philosophical engagement with value pluralism by giving full attention to the intrinsic value of diversity and human plurality particularly in the modern democratic context', notwithstanding the fact that Galston's political pluralism can be regarded as 'characteristically liberal'.[9] According to Galston, liberalism presupposes 'a robust though rebuttable presumption in favor of individuals and groups leading their lives as they see fit, within a broad range of legitimate variation, in accordance with their own understanding of what gives life meaning and value'.[10] This requirement, which Galston calls the principle of expressive liberty, 'implies a corresponding presumption (also rebuttable) against external interference with individual and group endeavors'.[11]

Practically speaking, Galston's liberal pluralism has, as Kim rightly notes, two main consequences.[12] The first is 'multiple sovereignties', that is, the notion that 'our social life comprises multiple sources of authority and sovereignty – individuals, parents, associations, churches, and state institutions, among others – no one of which is dominant for all purposes and on all occasions'.[13] Second, 'public institutions must be cautious and restrained in their dealings with voluntary associations, and there is no presumption that a state may intervene in such associations just because they conduct their internal affairs in ways that diverge from general public principles.'[14]

This position differs from the position of civic liberals such as John Rawls, who tend to believe that the principle of expressive liberty poses certain risks for social cooperation.[15] In fact, civic liberals are tempted by a form of 'civic totalism' that as we have seen insists that 'politics enjoys general authority over subordinate activities and institutions because it aims

6 Daniel A. Bell, 'Introduction', Jiang, supra note 5 at 1, 2.
7 Vicky C. Jackson, 'Methodological Challenges in Comparative Constitutional Law', (2010) 28 *Penn State International Law Review*, 319, 320.
8 Charles Taylor, *A Secular Age* (The Belknap Press of Harvard University Press 2007).
9 Kim, supra note 1 at 317.
10 Galston, supra note 4 at 3.
11 Galston at 3.
12 Kim at 321.
13 Galston at 36.
14 Galston at 9.
15 Kim at 320.

at the highest and most comprehensive good for human beings.'[16]As a result of this tendency, contemporary liberalism, as Michael W. Connell has put it, runs the risk of degenerating from 'a set of political arrangements by which persons of widely differing views can live together in relative harmony', into 'a narrow and sectarian program enforcing its dogmas by force'.[17]

As I have argued elsewhere,[18] a contemporary influential Western conception of the right to freedom of religion or belief starts from the ideal of individual autonomy. According to this conception, every person should be able to choose the life they want in general and, as a result, should also be able to choose their beliefs. Although initially this seems plausible, it turns out that the conception encounters a number of severe difficulties, both in theory and in practice. First, the notion of individual autonomy rests to a large extent on a particular conception of the good life, namely that only the self-chosen life is a good life. As a result, the relationship between the autonomy principle and many religions becomes strained. Many religions contain not only individual, but also social and communal aspects, in ways that make their conceptions of the good life at least partly incompatible with the concept of autonomy. Further, the autonomy principle is usually combined with a conception of the state as the holder of what is ultimately unfettered, legitimate sovereign executive power.

The first point, that a conception of religious freedom starting from the ideal of individual autonomy is currently influential, was as far as the United States is concerned argued by Mary Ann Glendon and Raul F. Yanes in a 1991 article. After a comprehensive survey of the US Supreme Court's modern Religion Clause jurisprudence, Glendon and Yanes observed that 'in retrospect (...) the Court was fairly consistent in pursuing an individualistic, secularist, and separationist approach to religion cases.'[19]

In a lecture delivered exactly 20 years after this article was published, Glendon conceded that the right to freedom of religion or belief in the West was 'at heightened risk from, inter alia, the erosion of conscience protection for religious individuals and institutions, restrictions on the autonomy of religious institutions, and inroads on the rights of parents regarding the education of their children'.[20] Indeed, according to Glendon,

> Our legal system's neglect of the associational and institutional dimensions of religious freedom, though punctuated with some notable exceptions, seems to be accelerating. As freedom of religion comes into conflict with claims based on nondiscrimination norms, abortion rights, and various lifestyle liberties, the freedom of religious entities to choose their own personnel, and even to publicly teach and defend their positions on controversial issues, is coming under increased attack.'[21]

16 Galston at 23.

17 Michael W. McConnell, 'Why is Religious Liberty the "First Freedom"?' (2000) 21 *Cardozo Law Review* 4, 1259.

18 Jaco van den Brink and Hans-Martien ten Napel, 'The State, Civil Society and Religious Freedom', (2013) 2 *Oxford Journal of Law and Religion* 2, 354–370.

19 Mary Ann Glendon and Raul F. Yanes, 'Structural Free Exercise', (1991) 90 *Michigan Law Review* 477–550 at 536. Compare Mary Ann Glendon, *Rights Talk: The Impoverishment of Political Discourse* (The Free Press 1991).

20 Mary Ann Glendon, 'The Harold J. Berman Lecture. Religious Freedom – Second-Class Right?' (2012) 61 *Emory Law Journal*, 975.

21 Glendon, 'Berman Lecture' at 978. The exceptions obviously include *Hosanna-Tabor Evangelical Lutheran Church and School v. EEOC*, 565 US__ (2012); *Sindicatul 'Pastoral Cel Bun' v. Romania*, Application No. 2330/09 (ECtHR, 9 July 2013).

Paul Horwitz equally discerns as 'a common thread' in the First Amendment's literature and jurisprudence that 'they routinely emphasize the individual and deemphasize the institutional.'[22]

As far as the second point is concerned – the fact that the autonomy principle is usually combined with a conception of the state as the holder of what is ultimately unfettered, legitimate sovereign executive power – Roger Trigg has pointed out that '[t]he more the role of the individual is extolled, the more powerful the state has to become, since the role of any protective institutions, even that of the family, to act as buffers between the state and the individual is eroded.'[23] This applies at present perhaps in particular with respect to equality. The paradox at work here is that, the more the importance of equality and individual freedom are being emphasized, the more government interference and regulation become necessary to realize these ideals. As a result, freedom is diminished, to the extent that all are now required to subscribe to these ideals, even if this was not the case before the state became involved.[24]

How can the development within liberalism described above, and the ensuing rise of 'civic totalism', be explained? This chapter undertakes, by means of hypothesis, to point to one possible explanation: the fact that the legitimacy of Western liberal democracies has come to rest more and more exclusively on popular sovereignty. This at least has been argued in recent literature on Confucian constitutionalism.

Sovereignty of the people

A well-known lemma on the concept of political legitimacy at one point asks the question what exactly it is that grounds its normativity.[25] It then concludes that since the seventeenth century, at least in the West, consent has replaced natural law and divine authority theories as the ultimate source of political legitimacy. This constitutes an example of a monistic conception of political legitimacy.[26] Yet, as the lemma rightly notes, non-monistic or mixed conceptions of political legitimacy are also feasible.

Jiang similarly distinguishes between legitimation and implementation as far as Confucian constitutionalism is concerned. According to him, the so-called 'Way of the Humane Authority' is primarily about 'legitimizing the Way', legitimacy being 'the deciding factor in determining whether a ruler has the right to rule'.[27] This is of more importance than, and also prior to, 'implementing the Way', that is, the exact way in which legitimate political authority is actually exercised. Jiang calls the legitimacy of the constitutional order 'the biggest and most urgent question' that Chinese politics faces today.[28]

Confucian constitutionalism holds in this regard that the notion of equilibrium is not just of relevance in implementation, but also when it comes to legitimizing the Way. Such legitimacy will preferably have to be balanced, so that the different sources of political

22 Paul Horwitz, *First Amendment Institutions* (Harvard University Press 2013), 27.

23 Roger Trigg, *Equality, Freedom & Religion* (Oxford University Press 2012), 12.

24 Trigg at 51.

25 Fabienne Peter, 'Political Legitimacy', in Edward N. Zalta, ed., *The Stanford Encyclopedia of Philosophy* (Summer 2016 edition), http://plato.stanford.edu/archives/sum2010/entries/legitimacy, section 3.

26 Peter defines a monistic conception of political legitimacy as one that 'reduces the normativity of political legitimacy to a single dimension' ('Political Legitimacy', section 4).

27 Jiang, supra note 5 at 27–28.

28 Jiang at 29.

legitimacy work together in a harmonious manner. More specifically, in order to be legal and justified political power needs the legitimacy of heaven, earth, and the human. As Jiang explains,

> The legitimacy of 'heaven' refers to transcendent, sacred legitimacy. In Chinese culture 'heaven' has both the character of a ruling will, personal yet hidden, and a transcendent, sacred sense of natural morality. The legitimacy of 'earth' refers to the legitimacy that comes from history and culture because cultures are formed through history in particular places. The legitimacy of the 'human' refers to the legitimacy of the will of the people because conformity to the will of the people directly determines whether or not people will obey political authorities ... Despite the desired equilibrium between them, the three sources of political legitimacy are not fully equal, in the sense that the sacred legitimacy is 'sovereign'.[29]

The contrast with contemporary Western constitutionalism is clear. In the West, political legitimacy is based on the notion of the sovereignty of the people, which is widely considered to be 'unique, supreme, absolute, exclusive, and inalienable. From a political point of view there is nothing that can keep it in check.'[30] As a result, the sovereignty of the people resembles medieval theories of divine authority, both being examples of thinking in absolutes rather than in terms of equilibrium and harmony: 'In fact, the sovereignty of the people is simply the secular equivalent of the sovereignty of God.'[31]

This thoroughly monistic conception of political legitimacy, according to Jiang, results in 'extreme secularization, contractualism, utilitarianism, selfishness, commercialism, capitalization, vulgarization, hedonism, mediocritization, this-worldliness, lack of ecology, lack of history, and lack of morality'.[32] Later on in his book, while responding to Li Chenyang's criticism of Confucian constitutionalism, Jiang adds that especially taking part in mass elections leads to 'secularism, pursuit of interests, agitation, demagogy, self-projection, performance, fawning, hypocrisy, pretence, pandering to the populace, including even absurdities, farce, and a great waste of money'.[33]

Going through this list, many in the West will no doubt be inclined to point to the central role that fundamental rights play – in particular since World War II – in Western constitutions. Jiang admits that rights have indeed become 'the transcendent moral foundations of Western constitutionalism'. Yet, for him, rights and morality are of a very different order. While morality is about one's responsibility towards others, rights concern duties that others have towards oneself. Compared to morality, rights are therefore 'very selfish and very low-down'.[34]

Jiang adds that it is only since the seventeenth century that Western constitutionalism is morally based on rights. As the lemma referred to above pointed out already, around that time social contract theory replaced traditional religious morality. In the eyes of Jiang, together with philosophers such as Hobbes, Locke, and Rousseau, the West has taken 'a great, false turn backward': 'constitutionalism no longer made the goodness of sacred morality the basis of its legitimacy. In its place came a selfish, secularist, legal power

29 Jiang at 28, 29–30.
30 Jiang at 29.
31 Jiang at 30.
32 Jiang at 33.
33 Jiang at 195.
34 Jiang at 53. See also Glendon, *Rights Talk*, supra note 19.

masquerading as sacred values.'[35] With the idea of a social contract, political legitimacy has become 'a product of pure reason and speculation that lacks an authentic historical background'.[36]

Yet, Jiang does not go so far as to deny that Western constitutionalism has any historical and cultural legitimacy at all. On the contrary, although for example the United States is formally characterized by a certain separation of church and state, the leading values in American society still predominantly stem from Protestant Christianity. This includes the very idea of constitutional democracy itself, the Western version of which has deep roots in Christian theology in general and Protestantism in particular.[37]

What has subsequently happened, however, is that these originally Protestant values have been transformed into abstract, philosophical principles. It is thanks to this transformation, that 'the one rule over the many is achieved in the West.'[38] The price that has to be paid for this is high, however, in that '[t]he rational form in which liberal-democratic values are promoted has led to an erosion of religious, moral values and to a valuing of relativism, even nihilism.'[39] Although the West more or less desperately tries to export its liberal-democratic values, it stands in fact for 'a politics with no values at all'. Or, to put it differently, its secular version of originally Protestant values is little more than 'a value of no values, based on reason, autonomy, enlightenment, equality, and pluralism'.[40]

As a result, it is not so much the historical and cultural legitimacy which is missing in Western constitutionalism, but the dimension of sacred legitimacy. The problem is not that the sovereignty of the people is among the sources of political legitimacy, but that because of the separation of church and state the will of the people is no longer checked by moral considerations.[41] This stands in sharp contrast to Confucian constitutionalism, which regards sacred legitimacy as sovereign.

It might perhaps be thought that the above criticisms of Western constitutionalism are rather harsh and will therefore not easily also be found outside the realm of Confucianism. In their recent book on *Intelligent Governance in the 21st Century*, however, Nicolas Berggruen and Nathan Gardels – after convening a host of academics and political practitioners – voice some of the same profound concerns. Thus, as they point out, like China's current regime, Western democracy is 'headed for terminal political decay unless it reforms': 'Dysfunction and decay aptly describe governance across much of the democratic West today, which is in crisis from its ancient birthplace in Greece to its most advanced outpost in California.'[42] In their view, the United States in particular has turned into a 'consumer democracy' focused on immediate gratification. As a result, 'a guiding societal ethos of short-term self-interest inevitably tends to eclipse any perspective of the long-term and common

35 Jiang at 53–54. See also Robert P. Kraynak, *Christian Faith and Modern Democracy. God and Politics in the Fallen World* (University of Notre Dame Press 2001), Chapter 1 ('Why Modern Liberal Democracy Needs God').

36 Jiang at 31.

37 Jiang at 164–165. See also Jan Willem Sap, *Paving the Way for Revolution. Calvinism and the Struggle for a Democratic Constitutional State* (Damon 2001) and Hans-Martien ten Napel, 'Protestantism, Globalisation, and the Democratic Constitutional State', in Volker Küster, ed., *Reshaping Protestantism in a Global Context* (Lit Verlag 2009), 155–163.

38 Jiang at 168.

39 Jiang at 168.

40 Jiang at 168.

41 Jiang at 34.

42 Nicolas Berggruen and Nathan Gardels, *Intelligent Governance for the 21st Century: A Middle Way Between West and East* (Polity Press 2013), 9–10.

good.'[43] The ideology of consumerism is so strong, that according to Bergguen and Gardels 'clearly an evolution in democracy itself is required to temper its excesses with a new set of checks and balances.'[44]

Is it too far-fetched to hypothesize that one explanation for the fact that the principle of expressive liberty has come under increasing pressure in Western liberal democracies is precisely that, as far as popular sovereignty is concerned, '[f]rom a political point of view there is nothing that can keep it in check'?

Limited government

If the legitimization of Western liberal democracy is not as strong as it may seem, how can political legitimacy be reinforced? For China, Jiang's Confucian constitutionalism recommends the adoption of the worldview of Confucianism as the foundation for the constitutional order.[45] The question is how realistic this proposal is, given the fact that contemporary China is an increasingly pluralistic society.[46] It is even more unrealistic for the West, however.

It is contended in this chapter that there is a more realistic way to strengthen the legitimacy of liberal democracies: by taking a closer look at the sources of Western constitutionalism itself, notably the notion of limited government. A sound, justifying, and guiding conception of religious freedom presupposes an answer to the question why the state must assign freedom to civil society organizations and individual citizens to live out their deepest convictions. And indeed an answer to the question how the state can realize this. If we only try to account for the meaning of religion for autonomous subjects, we examine only one side of the coin. Religious freedom determines to a certain extent the relationship between state and religion. In order to fully appreciate this complex relationship, we should not focus only on individual religious rights. We also need to reflect on the state and, more specifically, on its proper place within society.

Glendon and Yanes have pleaded in this context for an alternative, more holistic approach to religion cases that they termed 'structural free exercise'. They use the term 'structural', as they explain in their 1991 article, 'to refer to the relations within and among texts, and between legal and social institutions'.[47] Their approach attempts to take into account the role religion has played culturally and historically in the American democratic experiment. In doing so, it almost automatically comprises both the individual and the associational and institutional dimensions of religious freedom.[48] At the time they wrote their article, Glendon

43 Berggruen and Gardels at 30.
44 Berggruen and Gardels at 34.
45 Joseph Chan, 'On the Legitimacy of Confucian Constitutionalism', in Jiang, supra note 5, 99–112, at 104. Using the term 'worldview' is an attempt to stay away from the debate over whether Confucianism should be regarded as a religion or as a philosophical tradition. Nor do I want to enter the discussion whether Confucianism is (exclusively) an ethical doctrine or has also something to say on constitutional matters. Apparently, Jiang believes the latter to be the case.
46 Chan at 103.
47 Glendon and Yanes, supra note 19 at 537.
48 Johann Van der Vyver helpfully describes the associational dimension of religious freedom as '[t]he right to self-determination of religious communities, which is a collective group right (it vests in individuals as members of the religious community) and includes (i) the right to practice one's religion, in association with other members of the religious community, and (ii) the right to form, join and maintain religious associations'. He defines the institutional dimension, on the contrary, as 'sphere sovereignty of religious institutions, which is an institutional group right (the right vests

and Yanes prophetically foresaw that the major challenge ahead would become 'to accord as much scope as possible to the constitutional guarantee of free exercise in its personal, associational, and institutional dimensions, while respecting the freedom of conscience of nonbelievers and without preferring one religion to another'.[49]

In a similar vein, Richard W. Garnett has warned against 'overenthusiastic or insufficiently deliberate' attempts to enforce the inherently political ideal of equality, as these form a potential threat to the even more fundamental idea of constitutional, that is, limited, government.[50] As Garnett puts it, 'sound application of the antidiscrimination norm requires equally clear thinking about when and why discrimination is wrongful, and about when and why constitutionally limited government may or should regulate, discourage, or condemn it.'[51]

There is a striking resemblance between Galston's theory of liberal pluralism, Glendon's and Yanes's holistic approach, and Garnett's defense of limited constitutionalism on the one hand and what the Catholic political scientist Robert P. Kraynak has called 'constitutionalism without liberalism' on the other, 'according to which democracy is not an absolute but a conditional good – a political and social order that is not just in itself but is legitimate insofar as it serves a higher order of perfection and reflects its transcendent glory, however dimly'.[52] In his book on *Christian Faith and Modern Democracy* (2001), Kraynak points out that 'Christianity is not inherently a liberal or democratic religion, nor does it make the support of a political order its highest priority.'[53] In fact, according to Kraynak, one 'startling conclusion' of his book is precisely that Christianity 'has been rather illiberal and undemocratic for much of its history'.[54]

More specifically, Kraynak in this context refers to 'the weaknesses and anxieties that underlie the liberal democracies of the modern Western world'. Perhaps the central weakness is that it is not considered possible or even desirable to develop any meaningful sense of direction for liberal democracy:

> Surely it is a sign of confusion and loss of purpose when the most common argument that one hears today in defense of liberal democracy derives from moral relativism – from the denial of objective truth about good and evil which seems to suggest that liberal democracy is preferable because it permits any kind of behavior within the limits of the law.[55]

in a religious institution as such) and which requires of the State not to interfere in the internal affairs of religious institutions'. Johan D. van der Vyver, 'Constitutional Protection and Limits to Religious Freedom', in W. Cole Durham, Jr., Silvio Ferrari, Cristiana Cianitto, and Donlu Thayer, eds, *Law, Religion, Constitution: Freedom of Religion, Equal Treatment, and the Law* (Routledge 2013), 105. See also Iain Benson's articulation of 'structural pluralism' in Chapter 3 of the present volume.

49 Glendon and Yanes at 549.

50 Richard W. Garnett, 'Religious Freedom and the Nondiscrimination Norm', in Austin Sarat, ed., *Matters of Faith: Religious Experiences and Legal Response* (Cambridge University Press 2012), 198.

51 Garnett at 205.

52 Robert P. Kraynak, *Christian Faith and Modern Democracy* (University of Notre Dame Press 2001), 245.

53 Kraynak at xii.

54 Kraynak at 3.

55 Kraynak at 10.

On the other hand, this agnosticism and skeptical relativism 'are actually a form of modesty that disguise a rigid and stultifying dogmatism. (…) [T]he fact remains that modern liberal democracies have been shaped by philosophical doctrines in a way that previous regimes never were; and the decisive doctrine is the philosophy of liberalism.'[56] As Kraynak points out, modern liberal democracy elevates 'politics to a metaphysical, cosmological, or quasi-religious level. (…) Modern liberal democracy, therefore, is more than a political system: it is a philosophy of freedom and a theoretical doctrine of human dignity translated into practical action.'[57] In particular the welfare state as it has developed since the mid-twentieth century 'is highly intrusive in the imposition of secular liberal values'.[58] While the currently prevailing type of liberalism pretends to be neutral, it is in fact a distinct ideology with a particular vision on what the good life comprises. Whatever one may otherwise think of (moral) autonomy, free market capitalism, or secular democracy, they are certainly not objective and unprejudiced.[59] Kraynak points out that this 'secular humanism' is now widely promoted and inculcated in young people.[60]

Interestingly, just like Confucian constitutionalism, Kraynak criticizes not just democracy but also human rights. He even goes so far as to speak of 'a deep resistance to the concept of human rights' that historically characterizes Christianity:

> As shocking as it may sound today, there are numerous and profound reasons why this is so. (…) Ultimately, of course, Christians cannot accept the premise of human autonomy or the natural freedom of the autonomous self that underlies most doctrines of rights.[61]

The resemblance between Galston's aversion to a civic totalism, Glendon's and Yanes's holistic approach, Garnet's defense of limited constitutionalism, and Kraynak's ideal of constitutionalism without at least the currently prevailing type of liberalism can hardly come as a complete surprise. After all according to Galston, although he himself is a liberal, the 'most useful point of departure for the reconsideration of politics' he urges 'is found in the writings of the British political pluralists and thinkers working in the Calvinist tradition'.[62] Glendon is, among other things, a former United States ambassador to the Holy See, while Garnett consults regularly with the Alliance for Catholic Education. For Kraynak, his 'deepest inspiration is the notion of "sphere sovereignty" developed by the Dutch Calvinist Abraham Kuyper and the Catholic doctrine of "subsidiarity", both of which try to articulate the appropriate associations for each level of political authority'.[63] As he notes, 'When brought together into a coherent theory of two realms, the diverse spheres make up a hierarchy of being that is the metaphysical basis of Christian constitutionalism.'[64]

56 Kraynak at 201, 221.
57 Kraynak at 25.
58 Kraynak at 224.
59 See Michel Rosenfeld, 'Recasting Secularism as One Conception of the Good Among Many in a Post-Secular Constitutional Polity', in Susanne Mancini and Michel Rosenfeld, eds, *Constitutional Secularism in an Age of Religious Revival* (Oxford University Press 2014), 79–109.
60 Kraynak, supra note 52 at 124.
61 Kraynak at 153.
62 Galston, *The Practice of Liberal Pluralism*, supra note 4 at 23.
63 Galston, *The Practice of Liberal Pluralism* at 207.
64 Galston, *The Practice of Liberal Pluralism* at 207.

In terms of this chapter, one could say that such Christian or pluralist constitutionalism is more limited than Confucianism as a possible foundation for the constitutional order, yet it mitigates the Western monistic conception of political legitimacy by (implicitly) adding a certain sacred as well as cultural and historical legitimacy to it. In this sense, not just a pluralist reconstruction of Confucian democracy may be needed, but also a reconsideration of Western liberal democracy from the perspective of limited government.

A broader relevance

This chapter has argued that the legitimization of Western liberal democracy is not as strong as it may seem, as long as the sovereignty of the people on which its political legitimacy is ultimately based hinders instead of advances a true sort of value pluralism. The chapter has also contended that there is a way to strengthen the legitimacy of liberal democracies by taking a closer look at the sources of Western constitutionalism itself, notably liberal pluralism and its accompanying notion of truly limited government.

The fact that this notion, at least in part, has its roots in Christianity, does perhaps not make it seem overly realistic, however, to propose such a pluralist reconstruction of Western democracy at this point in time. Trigg is among those who have also more generally raised the question of what sorts of consequences the decay of (institutional) Christianity will eventually turn out to have for the development of democracy and human rights in the West. Given the fact that these concepts have until recently been relatively strongly bound up with Christianity in general and Protestantism in particular, 'the contemporary question must be how far they will survive in any country once their traditional grounding is repudiated.'[65]

Admittedly, the exact relationship between freedom of religion and other civil liberties and social outcomes still needs to be studied in more detail.[66] Yet, recent empirical research clearly suggests 'that religious freedom is embedded within a much larger bundle of civil liberties',[67] in that there exists a correlation between the degree to which the right to freedom of religion or belief is restricted with restrictions on the freedom of expression and the freedom of association, and indeed on democracy as a whole. Against this background, the topic of 'civic totalism', sovereignty of the people, and the need for limited government acquires an even broader relevance.

65 Trigg, *Equality, Freedom, and Religion*, supra note 23 at 155.

66 Brian J. Grim, 'Restrictions on Religion in the World', in Allen D. Hertzke, ed., *The Future of Religious Freedom. Global Challenges* (Oxford University Press 2013), 102.

67 Grim at 101.

6 From Rabat to Istanbul

Combating advocacy of religious hatred that constitutes incitement to discrimination, hostility or violence[1]

Mohamed Saeed M. Eltayeb

The Rabat Plan of Action and the Istanbul Process: an overview

This chapter aims at examining the *Rabat Plan of Action on the Prohibition of Advocacy of National, Racial or Religious Hatred that Constitutes Incitement to Discrimination, Hostility or Violence* (Rabat Plan of Action) and the *Istanbul Process on the Follow-up and Implementation of the Human Rights Council Resolution 16/18 entitled 'Combating Intolerance, Negative Stereotyping and Stigmatization of, and Discrimination, Incitement to Violence and Violence against, Persons Based on Religion or Belief'* (Istanbul Process), and the extent to which both processes are effectively contributing to combating advocacy of religious hatred that constitutes incitement to discrimination, hostility, and violence. The chapter contends that the two processes should be analyzed and examined in the light of the quest for wider implementation strategies for combating religious hatred. Hence, the two processes can be seen as complementary and mutually reinforcing.

The Rabat Plan of Action

The Rabat Plan of Action[2] resulted from several workshops organized by the UN Office of the High Commissioner for Human Rights (OHCHR) in various regions of the world on the prohibition of incitement to national, racial, and religious hatred between 2008 and 2011.[3] In her opening statement on the launching of the Rabat Plan of Action in February 2013, the former UN High Commissioner for Human Rights, Navanethem Pilly, stated:

1 The views expressed in this chapter are strictly of a personal nature and are not necessarily shared by the Qatari Ministry of Foreign Affairs.
2 See *Rabat Plan of Action on the Prohibition of Advocacy of National, Racial or Religious Hatred that Constitutes Incitement to Discrimination, Hostility or Violence* at www.ohchr.org/Documents/Issues/Opinion/SeminarRabat/Rabat_draft_outcome.
3 The Office of the High Commissioner for Human Rights (OHCHR) has been working for many years on subject of combating the advocacy of religious hatred. After a first expert seminar on the links between articles 19 and 20 of the International Covenant on Civil and Political Rights (ICCPR), held in Geneva in October 2008, the OHCHR launched in 2011 a series of expert workshops on the prohibition of advocacy of national, racial, or religious hatred which constitutes incitement to discrimination, hostility, or violence. These workshops were held in various regions and served to study national practices, in terms of legislation, public policies, and jurisprudence. In total, four workshops took place, which brought together 45 experts, including special procedures mandate holders and treaty body members, representing different legal and cultural traditions. The Kingdom of Morocco subsequently, in October 2012, hosted a wrap-up workshop in Rabat, and on the basis of the findings of four regional workshops, produced the Rabat of Action, for more information on those workshops, see http://www.ohchr.org/english/issues/opinion/articles1920_iccpr/docs/compilation_conference_room_papers.pdf,

> The remarkable collection of experts who have worked together on this issue over the past two years have fulfilled our hopes by reaching a consensus on how to effectively address the issue of incitement, and have devised a clear pathway to help us identify where to draw the demarcation line between freedom of expression and incitement.[4]

The Rabat Plan of Action presents a set of practical recommendations to states, the UN system, political and religious leaders, civil society, and the media. The Plan of Action recommends, *inter alia*, the adoption of comprehensive anti-discrimination national legislation with preventive and punitive action to effectively combat incitement to hatred; the empowerment of minorities and vulnerable groups; the collective responsibility of public officials, religious, and community leaders, the media, and individuals in preventing incitement to hatred, and the need to nurture social consciousness, tolerance, mutual respect, and intercultural dialogue.[5] Furthermore, the Plan of Action underlines the key role to be played by education to change mindsets and advocates that education on pluralism can also contribute to preventing incitement to hatred, intolerance, negative stereotyping, stigmatization, and discrimination on the basis of nationality, ethnicity, religion, or belief.[6]

The Rabat Plan of Action contains conclusions and recommendations in the area of legislation, judicial infrastructure, and policy that aim for guiding all stakeholders in implementing the international prohibition of any advocacy of national, racial, or religious hatred that constitutes incitement to discrimination, hostility, or violence. Despite the fact that the Rabat Plan of Action provides recommendations to all stakeholders, it nevertheless emphasizes the crucial role of the states as central in implementing the Plan's conclusions and recommendations in the area of legislation, judiciary, and policy. Thus, the Rabat Plan represents an important step in clarifying state obligations to prohibit incitement to hatred, while providing coherent protection to the rights to freedom of expression and freedom of religion.

In this context, the Plan of Action provides that states should be guided by express references to Article 20(2) of the UN's International Covenant for Civil and Political Rights (ICCPR, entry into force March 1976) in their domestic legislation. Such legislation should include robust definitions of key terms like hatred, discrimination, violence, and hostility, as suggested by the Camden Principles.[7] States should repeal blasphemy laws because these laws have a stifling impact on the enjoyment of freedom of religion or belief, and inhibit healthy dialogue and debate about religion.[8] The Plan of Action further stresses the crucial

4 For the text of the High Commissioner's statement see www.ohchr.org/RU/NewsEvents/Pages/.

5 See the Rabat Plan of Action, supra note 1, at paras 23, 26.

6 Rabat Plan para. 25.

7 ARTICLE 19 is a British human rights organization, founded in 1987, which takes its objectives from Article 19 of the United Nation's 1948 Universal Declaration of Human Rights, which states: 'Everyone has the right to freedom of opinion and expression; the right includes freedom to hold opinions without interference and to seek, receive and impart information and ideas through any media regardless of frontiers.' See https://www.article19.org/. The Camden Principles were prepared by ARTICLE 19 on the basis of multi-stakeholder discussions involving experts in international human rights law on freedom of expression and equality issues. The principles represent a progressive interpretation of international law standards, accepted state practice (as reflected, *inter alia*, in national laws and the judgments of national courts), and the general principles of law recognized by the community of nations. The *Camden Principles on Freedom of Expression and Equality* (London 2009), available at http://www.article19.org/data/files/pdfs/standards/the-camden-principles-on-freedom-of-expression-and-equality.pdf

8 See generally Mohamed S. M. Eltayeb, 'The Prohibition of Incitement to National, Racial or Religious Hatred: The case of West Asian Arab Countries', (2012) 7 *Religion and Human Rights*, 95–108.

importance of an independent judiciary that ensures consistent interpretation of incitement to hatred cases, including assessing them through a comprehensive threshold test in accordance with the ARTICLE 19 six-part incitement test.[9] The Plan of Action states that criminal sanctions should be applied only in the most severe cases, and states should apply a broad set of measures to sanction and prevent incitement to hatred. These include policies that promote intercultural dialogue, pluralism, and diversity, and positive measures for the protection of minorities and vulnerable groups.

In implementing the above-mentioned recommendations, states are encouraged to benefit from the broad, inclusive, and joint consultative process that led to the adoption of the Rabat Plan of Action; set priorities and time bound framework for the implementation process; and strengthen cooperation among themselves at sub regional, regional, and international levels in implementing the Rabat recommendations as well as benefiting from best practices. Moreover, the crucial role of states in implementing the Rabat Plan of Action is to reinforce, complement, and supplement by strengthening the UN special procedures and the treaty mechanisms that work on the protection of freedom of expression, freedom of religion, preventing incitement to hatred, and preventing discrimination, as well as enhancing stronger cooperation between various entities of the United Nations system including the Office of the High Commissioner for Human Rights (OHCHR), the UN Alliance of Civilizations, and the Office of the Special Advisor on the Prevention of Genocide, and between various regional and cross-regional mechanisms such as the Council of Europe, the Organization for Security and Cooperation in Europe (OSCE), the European Union, the Organization of American States (OAS), the African Union, ASEAN, and the Organization of Islamic Cooperation (OIC).

With special reference to hate speech, the Rabat Plan of Action has stressed that freedom of expression and freedom of religion or belief are mutually dependent and reinforcing. The freedom to exercise or not to exercise one's religion or belief cannot exist if the freedom of expression is not respected, as free public discourse depends on respect for the diversity of deep convictions which people may have. Likewise, freedom of expression is essential to creating an environment in which a constructive discussion about religious matters could be held. Indeed, free and critical thinking in open debate is the soundest way to probe whether religious interpretations adhere to or instead distort the original values that underpin religious belief convictions which people may have.[10] Under international human rights standards, which are to guide legislation at the national level, expression labeled as 'hate speech' can be restricted under Articles 18 and 19 of the ICCPR on different grounds, including respect for the rights of others, public order, or even sometimes national security. States are also obliged to 'prohibit' expression that amounts to 'incitement' to discrimination, hostility, or violence (under Article 20.2 of the ICCPR and, under some different conditions, also under Article 4 of the ICERD).[11]

9 ARTICLE 19, *Prohibiting Incitement to Discrimination, Hostility or Violence* (Policy Brief) (Free World Centre 2012), 29–40, available at https://www.article19.org/data/files/medialibrary/3548/ARTICLE-19-policy-on-prohibition-to-incitement.pdf.

10 Rabat Plan para 10. See also Mohamed S. M. Eltayeb, 'The Limitations on Critical Thinking on Religious Issues under Article 20 of ICCPR and its Relation to Freedom of Expression', (2010) 5 *Religion and Human Rights*, 119–135 and Abdullahi An-Na'im, 'Freedoms of Speech and Religion in the Islamic Context', in David Marshall, ed, *Tradition and Modernity: Christian and Muslim Perspectives* (Georgetown University Press 2013), 57–66.

11 Rabat Plan para 14. See Mohamed S. M. Eltayeb, 'The Quest for Permissible Limitations on Freedom of Expression: Public Order and Public Morality Exceptions', (Spring 2015) 13 *The*

The Plan of Action has pointed out that Article 20 of the ICCPR requires a high threshold because, as a matter of fundamental principle, limitation of speech must remain an exception. Such a threshold needs to be read in consonance with Article 19 of the ICCPR. Indeed the three-part test for restrictions (legality, proportionality, and necessity) also applies to incitement cases; that is, such restrictions must be provided by law, be narrowly defined to serve a legitimate interest, and be necessary in a democratic society to protect that interest. This implies, among other things, that restrictions are clearly and narrowly defined and respond to a pressing social need; are the least intrusive measures available; are not overly broad, in that they do not restrict speech in a wide or untargeted way; and are proportionate in the sense that the benefit to the protected interest outweighs the harm to freedom of expression, including in respect to the sanctions they authorize.[12]

The Plan of Action has further contended that blasphemy laws are counter-productive, since they may result in the de facto censure of all inter-religious belief and intra-religious belief dialogue, debate, and also criticism, most of which could be constructive, healthy, and needed. In addition, many of these blasphemy laws afford different levels of protection to different religions and have often proved to be applied in a discriminatory manner. There are numerous examples of persecution of religious minorities or dissenters, but also of atheists and non-theists, as a result of legislation on religious offences of various laws that use a neutral language. Moreover, the right to freedom of religion or belief, as enshrined in relevant international legal standards, does not include the right to have a religion or a belief that is free from criticism or ridicule.[13]

The Istanbul Process

The Istanbul Process on the Follow-up and Implementation of the Human Rights Resolution 16/18 entitled 'Combating Intolerance, Negative Stereotyping and Stigmatization of, and Discrimination, Incitement to Violence and Violence against, Persons Based on Religion or Belief' (Resolution 16/18) was initiated by former OIC Secretary General Prof. Ekmeleddin Ihsanoglu, former US Secretary of State Hilary Clinton, and the EU High Representative for Foreign Affairs and Security Policy Catherine Ashton in order to explore and ensure ways of implementing Resolution 16/18. To date, six experts meetings have been held under the framework of the Istanbul Process.

The first two meetings were hosted by the United States (in Washington DC in December 2011) and by the United Kingdom, in association with Canada (at Wilton Park in December 2012).[14] These meetings addressed, among other things, strategies to engage religious minorities, training government officials on religious and cultural awareness, and building networks with civil society to promote religious freedom.

The third meeting was hosted by OIC and held in Geneva in June 2013. Three topics were on the agenda: speaking out against intolerance, including advocacy of religious hatred

Review of Faith & International Affairs, 69–74; see also H. Victor Condé, 'Human Rights and the Protection of Religious Expression: Manifestation of Religion as *Lex Specialis* of Freedom of Expression', Chapter 2 of the present volume.

12 Rabat Plan para. 18.

13 Rabat Plan para. 19.

14 See US Department of State, 'Report of the United States on the First Meeting of Experts to Promote Implementation of United Nations Human Rights Council Resolution 16/18', Washington DC, December 2011.

that constitutes incitement to discrimination, hostility, or violence; adopting measures to criminalize incitement to imminent violence based on religion or belief; and recognizing that open, constructive, and respectful debate of ideas, as well as interfaith and intercultural dialogue at local, national, and international levels can play a positive role in combating religious hatred, incitement, and violence.[15]

The fourth meeting, hosted by the State of Qatar and held in Doha in March 2014, focused on 'Advancing Religious Freedom through Interfaith Collaboration'.[16] It has to be noted that the fourth meeting was the first Istanbul process meeting to be held in the Muslim World and the first where few NGOs and non-state actors were invited.

The fifth meeting, hosted by the General Secretariat of the OIC, was held in Jeddah in June 2015 under the title 'From Resolution to Realization – How to Promote Effective Implementation of the HRC Res 16/18'.[17]

The sixth meeting, hosted by the Government of Singapore, was held in Singapore in July 2016 and entitled 'A Cross-Regional Perspective on the Best Practices and Policies for Promoting Religious Tolerance and Strengthening Resilience'. This was the first Istanbul process meeting to be held in Southeast Asia.[18]

HRC Resolution 16/18, which was adopted in March 2011,[19] came as an initiative of OIC, and it has codified the eight points contained in the address of the OIC Secretary-General to the 15th Session of the Human Rights Council in September 2010. Resolution 16/18 has been considered as a breakthrough. It moved away from the controversial phrase 'defamation of religions' and reflected a clear commitment to combating religious hatred and religious intolerance.[20] Resolution 16/18 has the following characteristics:

15 See 'Istanbul Process for Combating Intolerance, Discrimination and Incitement to Hatred and/ or Violence on the Basis of Religion or Belief', Report of the 3rd International Expert Meeting on the Follow-up of Implementation of HRC Resolution 16/18, Geneva, 19–21 June 2013, published by the Organization of Islamic Cooperation.

16 See 'Collaborative Interfaith Report on Istanbul Process – Doha Meeting: Advancing Religious Freedom', Report of the 4th Istanbul Process (Doha, 24–25 March 2014), published by the Doha International Centre for Interfaith Dialogue (DICID).

17 See '5th Meeting of the Istanbul Process, in Jeddah: Another step towards a full and effective implementation of HRC Resolution 16/18', *Geneva Center for Human Rights Advancement and Global Dialogue*, https://www.gchragd.org/5th-meeting-of-the-istanbul-process-in-jeddah-another-step-towards-a-full-and-effective-implementation-of-hrc-resolution-1618/.

18 For a detailed account of the Sixth Meeting see Universal Rights Group (URG), '6th Meeting of the Istanbul Process: A Cross-Regional Perspective on the Best Practices and Policies for Promoting Religious Tolerance and Strengthening Resilience, 20–21 July – Singapore'.

19 For the text of the resolution see A/HRC/RES/16/18 at www.ohchr.org/EN/HRBodies/HRC/RegularSessions. For a detailed analysis of Istanbul Process see Marc Limon, Nazila Ghanea, and Hilary Power, 'Combating Global Religious Intolerance: The Implementation of Human Rights Council 16/18', Policy Report published by Universal Rights Group (December 1014), Caka A. Awal, 'A way forward for the 16/18 process', in *URG Insights*, Universal Rights Group New York (16 February 2016), at http://www.universal-rights.org/blog/a-way-forward-for-the-1618-process/; Marc Limon, 'The road to Istanbul passes through Rabat', in ibid. (9 June 2015), at http://www.universal-rights.org/blog/road-istanbul-passes-rabat/; Andrew Smith, 'Implementing Resolution 16/18: the role of Rabat and the importance of civil society space', in ibid. (18 February 2016), at http://www.universal-rights.org/blog/implementing-resolution-1618-the-role-of-rabat-and-the-importance-of-civil-society-space/; Marghoob Saleem Butt, 'How to move forward with the implementation of resolution 16/18 and with global efforts to combat religious intolerance and discrimination', in ibid. (5 April 2016), at http://www.universal-rights.org/blog/3231/.

20 In this way resolution 16/18 endorses the view of the former UN Special Rapporteur on Contemporary Forms of Racism, Racial Discrimination, Xenophobia and Related Intolerance, Mr.

- It is a consensual, trans-regional resolution with a global ownership, and these characteristics strengthen its legitimacy.
- It avoided the controversial phrase 'defamation of religions' and reflected a clear commitment to combating religious intolerance within the framework of international human rights law, and hence shifted the debate from defamation of religion to incitement to religious hatred.[21]
- It situates itself within mainstream international human rights discourse by specifically promoting freedom of expression, freedom of religion, and non-discrimination.
- The operative part of Resolution 16/18 is based on the 8-point plan generated by the OIC Secretary General at 15th Session of the Human Rights Council.
- Resolution 16/18 moves us from standard-settings to implementation, or in other words, it is an action-oriented resolution.
- As the OIC Secretary-General stated in his opening speech during the third expert meeting of the Istanbul process,[22] Resolution 16/18 is not an end in itself, but rather it is a means to an end.
- Resolution 16/18 contains important features crucial for its successful implementation. It formulates a list of pragmatic action oriented points taken, and encourages member states to include information on their implementation efforts in their regular reporting to OHCHR. This places the responsibility for implementation where it should principally rest, namely at the national level. The practical introspective nature of Resolution 16/18 is what the Istanbul Process seeks to enhance.[23]

The quest for wider implementation strategies

Both the Rabat Plan of Action and the Istanbul Process endorse the importance of having wider and multi-layered tools and strategies for combating incitement to religious hatred, and hence, they call for various administrative, political, and legislative actions to be taken at both national and international levels. Thus they uphold that legal measures should be seen as part of wider strategies for combating advocacy of religious hatred that constitutes incitement to discrimination, hostility, or violence. In this regard, education and both inter-

Githu Muigai, who has suggested that the debate should be shifted from the 'sociological notion of defamation of religions' to the established 'human rights concept of incitement to racial and religious hatred', thus coming closer to an appropriate balance between freedom of expression and the need to eliminate hate speech. See the Report of UN Special Rapporteur on Contemporary Forms of Racism, Racial Discrimination, Xenophobia and Related Intolerance, Mr., Githu Muigai UN Doc. A/HRC/12/38.

21 For discussion on defamation of religions, see Maxim Grinberg, 'Defamation of Religions v. Freedom of Expression: Finding the Balance in a Democratic Society', (July 2006) 18 *Sri Lanka Journal of International Law*, 1–22, and Allison G. Belnap, 'Defamation of Religions: A Vague and Overbroad Theory that Threatens Basic Human Rights', (2010) *Brigham Young University Law Review*, 635–686.

22 See the Opening Speech of HE Prof. Ekmeleddin Ihsanoglu, Secretary General of the Organization of Islamic Cooperation, at the 3rd International Expert Meeting on the Follow-up and Implementation of HRC Resolution 16/18, Geneva, 19 June 2013.

23 See the Opening Remarks by Bacre Waly Ndiaye, Director, Human Rights Council and Special Procedures Division (OHCHR) at the 3rd International Expert Meeting on the Follow-up and Implementation of HRC Resolution 16/18, Geneva, 19 June 2013.

religious and intra-religious dialogues are indispensable strategies in supporting legal measures.

The Istanbul Process for the Follow-up and Implementation of Resolution 16/18 is a member-states-driven process, while the Rabat Plan of Action is an expert document, which resulted from several workshops organized by the OHCHR between 2008 and 2011 in various regions of the world on the prohibition of incitement to national, racial and religious hatred. Nevertheless, the Istanbul Process and the Rabat Plan of Action are complementary and mutually reinforcing. The Rabat Plan of Action provides the normative content on how to effectively address the issue of incitement and clearly clarifies states' international obligations to prohibit incitement to hatred, while providing coherent protection to the rights both to freedom of expression and freedom of religion.[24] The Istanbul Process aims at combating religious intolerance, and in that endeavor the Rabat Plan of Action can pave the way and effectively contribute to the implementation of the Istanbul Process. Paragraph (29) of the Rabat Plan of Action states that the adoption of Resolution 16/18 constitutes a promising platform for effective, integrated, and inclusive action by the international community.[25] Moreover, Resolution 16/18 requires implementation and constant follow-up by states at the national level, including through the Rabat Plan of Action, which contributes to its fulfillment.[26] However, the question of complementarity and reinforcement is dependent to a large extent on the actions that would be taken by the states which are supporting the Istanbul Process in so far as the process would endorse the Rabat Plan of Action and accommodate other stakeholders, namely civil society organizations at the national, regional, and international levels. It is to be seen how the future Istanbul meetings would make use of the conclusions and recommendations of the Rabat Plan of Action in the area of legislation, judicial infrastructure, and policy.

24 Building on the 2012 Rabat Plan of Action that laid out religious leaders' core responsibilities in countering incitement to hatred, the Beirut Declaration, which was recently adopted as part of a 'Faith for Rights' initiative launched by faith-based and civil society actors from around the world, expands those responsibilities to the full spectrum of human rights. It calls on believers of all faiths to join hands and hearts in articulating ways in which they can stand together in defending fundamental rights against discrimination and violence. For the text of Beirut Declaration and the 18 Faith for Rights Commitments, which are linked to it, see 'Beirut Declaration enhances role of religions in promoting human rights', United Nations Human Rights Office of the High Commissioner, at http://www.ohchr.org/EN/NewsEvents/Pages/FaithforRights.aspx.

25 Rabat Plan para. 29.

26 Rabat Plan para. 29.

7 The prohibition of advocacy of religious hatred that constitutes incitement to discrimination, hostility or violence

A taxonomy

Jeroen Temperman

The incitement clause as an oddity

Article 20(2) of the UN International Covenant on Civil and Political Rights (ICCPR) is a weird species.[1] It provides that '[a]ny advocacy of national, racial or religious hatred that constitutes incitement to discrimination, hostility or violence shall be prohibited by law.'[2] Accordingly, this provision does not appear to codify a fundamental right but rather a *sui generis* state obligation. Moreover, this norm may very well be construed as a special limit on other fundamental rights, notably on the right to freedom of expression, but also for instance on the right to freedom of association. This quality can be considered, in the words of Manfred Nowak, an 'alien element in the system of the Covenant'.[3]

To be sure, there are other examples of norms enshrined in international human rights treaties that do not read like an individual right, but that are nevertheless very much interpreted as and accepted to be fundamental, 'invocable' rights. Accordingly, 'No one shall be subjected to torture or to cruel, inhuman or degrading treatment or punishment' certainly embodies a right to be free from torture.[4] 'All persons are equal before the law' indisputably contains an autonomous right to equality.[5] And, to provide an example from the regional (European) level, the duty for the 'High Contracting Parties' to 'hold free elections at

1 International Covenant on Civil and Political Rights, GA. res. 2200A (XXI), 21 UN GAOR Supp. (No. 16) at 52, UN Doc. A/6316 (1966), 999 UNTS 171, entered into force 23 March 1976, Article 20(2). See for a detailed analysis Jeroen Temperman, *Religious Hatred and International Law* (Cambridge University Press 2016).

2 ICCPR, Article 20, second paragraph.

3 Manfred Nowak, *U.N. Covenant on Civil and Political Rights: CCPR Commentary* (Engel Publishing, 2nd rev edn, 2005), 468.

4 ICCPR, Article 7. The Human Rights Committee has no difficulty in construing this norm as a freedom from torture. For example, Human Rights Committee, General Comment 20: Article 7 (Forty-fourth session, 1992), Compilation of General Comments and General Recommendations Adopted by Human Rights Treaty Bodies, UN Doc. HRI/GEN/1/Rev.1 at 30 (1994), para. 15 ('freedom from').

5 Certainly since the Dutch social security cases. Human Rights Committee, *S.W.M. Broeks v. the Netherlands*, Communication No. 172/1984, UN Doc. Supp. No. 40 (A/42/40) at 139 (1987), of 9 April 1987; Human Rights Committee, *F.H. Zwaan-de Vries v. The Netherlands*, Communication No. 182/1984, UN Doc. CCPR/C/OP/2 at 209 (1990), of 9 April 1987, which line of jurisprudence has been continued in subsequent cases concerning Article 26 of the ICCPR. See for example. Human Rights Committee, *A.P. Johannes Vos v. The Netherlands*, Communication No. 786/1997, UN Doc. CCPR/C/66/D/786/1997, of 29 July 1999; Human Rights Committee, *Mr. Michael Andreas Müller and Imke Engelhard v. Namibia*, Communication No. 919/2000, UN Doc. CCPR/C/74/D/919/2000 [2002], of 26 March 2002.

reasonable intervals by secret ballots' evidently incorporates an individual right to vote according to the jurisprudence of the European Court of Human Rights.

The question, then, is whether Article 20(2) ICCPR, despite is peculiar formulation, similarly contains an individual right as a corollary to the expressly stated obligation – the prohibition of incitement. And if so, what does such a right mean in terms of state obligations and in terms of legal standing for alleged incitement victims?[6]

The incitement clause as a prohibition

The text of the incitement clause suggests that it is intended as a prohibition – nothing more, nothing less. Specifically, Article 20(2) ICCPR is formulated as an *international order to prohibit* incitement. State parties to the ICCPR 'shall' prohibit by law any advocacy of national, racial, or religious hatred that constitutes incitement to discrimination, hostility, or violence. The fact that implementation laws are required at the national level seems to suggest that the provision cannot be self-executing. From the area of fundamental economic, social, and cultural rights we, however, know that standards that are not self-executing can nevertheless be considered human rights.

From the manner in which the incitement provision was crafted and especially from its position in the overall Covenant, we can distill that the incitement prohibition is more than just a ground for restricting speech. This becomes strikingly clear when one compares Article 20(2) ICCPR with the way 'incitement' is dealt with by for instance the UN Migrant Workers Rights Convention.[7] Article 13 of the latter Convention lists the purpose of preventing advocacy of religious and other hatred that constitutes incitement as one of the grounds on the basis of which speech may legitimately be restricted. The drafters of the ICCPR could have merged the incitement prohibition with the limitations on freedom of expression contained in Article 19 of the Covenant, but decided to reserve a separate provision for the purposes of tackling incitement. As a result an autonomous incitement provision forms part of Part II of the Covenant, the part that lists the fundamental civil and political rights individuals are entitled to. By contrast, Article 5 containing the general abuse of rights doctrine (holding that no-one may use his or her rights with a view towards destroying the freedoms of others) is included in a miscellaneous part (Part II) on state obligations. The question remains, however, whether these peculiarities elevate Article 20(2) to the level of fundamental right and, if so, what would be the ramifications of that status.

The incitement clause as a 'right of others'

To date only a handful of cases have been decided in which Article 20(2) plays a direct or indirect role. The meager output notwithstanding, these cases do show an interesting development as to the taxonomy of this provision. In this section it is argued that the UN Human Rights Committee has gradually developed a 'right to be free from incitement'; however, this same Committee does not yet accept all the legal ramifications that typically come with such status.

The early case of *J. R. T. and the W. G. Party v. Canada* is inconclusive on the question whether Article 20(2) ICCPR contains a right, which was importantly due to the fact that

6 The investigation into these questions draws on Temperman, supra note 1, particularly chapter 5.

7 International Convention on the Protection of the Rights of All Migrant Workers and Members of Their Families, adopted by General Assembly Resolution 45/158 of 18 December 1990.

this complaint was brought by a convicted inciter who telephonically spread hateful messages, not by alleged hate speech victims. That is, in that case there was no need for the Committee to infer any 'right' from the incitement provision, rather it sought in this provision additional reasons for restriction of extreme speech – reasons it did indeed find.[8] The first traces of a 'right to be free from incitement' can be found in *Faurisson v. France*, even though this case was also brought by the inciter.[9] This case revolved around Robert Faurisson, a British-French literature professor, who was convicted in France under the Gayssot Act.[10] He had publicly cast doubt as to the existence of gas chambers for extermination purposes at Auschwitz and in other Nazi concentration camps in various writings and statements. The Human Rights Committee argued that the restrictions on Faurisson's free speech were permitted and necessary for the sake of ensuring 'respect of the rights or reputations of others' (Article 19, paragraph 3(a) ICCPR). Crucially, in that respect the Committee reiterated that this ground for restriction may relate to individuals but also to a 'community as a whole'.[11] The Committee concluded that '[s]ince the statements made by the author, read in their full context, were of a nature as to raise or strengthen anti-Semitic feelings, the restriction served the respect of the Jewish community *to live free from fear of an atmosphere of anti-semitism*.'[12]

Thus, under the Covenant, there is a community right to live free from fear of discrimination. Remarkably, the Committee did not at this stage directly reference Article 20 (2) to augment the existence and significance of such a right; indeed, the plenary Committee altogether omits this provision in its reasoning, to the dismay of some of the individual Committee members.

From the appended individual (concurring) opinions to this case it transpires that a number – yet apparently short of a majority – of Committee members would have liked to apply Article 20(2) directly and outspokenly to the merits of this case. These individual opinions are also much more clear and specific as to which 'rights of others' are at stake here. Emphasizing both Article 7 of the Universal Declaration of Human Rights ('protection against any incitement to discrimination') and Article 20(2) ICCPR, members Elizabeth Evatt and David Kretzmer, for instance, argued that '[e]very individual has the right to be free not only from discrimination on grounds of race, religion and national origins, but also from incitement to such discrimination.'[13] This 'right to be free from racial, national or religious incitement'[14] features a number of times in their opinion. It is also referred to as the 'right of a person to be free from incitement to discrimination on grounds of race,

8 *J.R.T. and the W.G. Party v. Canada*, Communication No. 104/1981, decision of 6 April 1983, para. 8(b): 'the opinions which Mr. T. seeks to disseminate through the telephone system clearly constitute the advocacy of racial or religious hatred which Canada has an obligation under article 20 (2) of the Covenant to prohibit.'

9 *Robert Faurisson v. France*, Communication No. 550/1993, decision of 8 November 1996.

10 Loi no 90–615 du 13 juillet 1990 tendant à réprimer tout acte raciste, antisémite ou xénophobe.

11 *Faurisson*, para. 9.6. Something accepted as early as in (the now replaced) General Comment No. 10 of 1983: 'Paragraph 3 expressly stresses that the exercise of the right to freedom of expression carries with it special duties and responsibilities and for this reason certain restrictions on the right are permitted which may relate either to the interests of other persons or to those of the community as a whole.' Human Rights Committee, General Comment 10, Article 19 (Nineteenth session, 1983), para. 4.

12 *Faurisson*, para. 9.6 (emphasis added).

13 Individual opinion by Elizabeth Evatt and David Kretzmer, co-signed by Eckart Klein, para.4. Cecilia Medina Quiroga in her opinion expresses her support for this opinion.

14 *Faurisson*, para. 7.

religion or national origins';[15] a 'right to be free from incitement to anti-semitism';[16] and 'the right to be free from incitement to racism or anti-semitism'.[17] Occasionally it is referred to as a group right ('right of the Jewish community in France to live free from fear of incitement to anti-semitism'[18]) rather than an individual right, indicating that these individual Committee members had not yet resolved the issue of whether we are dealing with a classic individual right or some type of group, collective, or perhaps minority right. Committee member Bhagwati, similarly, posits that the crucial question in such a case is 'whether the restriction can be said to be necessary for respect of the rights and reputations of others so as to be justifiable under paragraph 3 (a)'.[19] He indeed concludes that the restrictive law served the 'purpose of respect for the right and interest of the Jewish community to live free from fear of an atmosphere of anti-semitism, hostility or contempt'.[20]

Accordingly, in *Faurisson* the *right to freedom from religious (and other) incitement* for the first time saw the light of day, albeit in the individual opinions of Committee members rather than in the actual decision. Given the specifics of this case, the main function of this freedom is to be construed as a 'right of others' so as to be applied, in turn, as a ground to legitimately restrict the freedom of expression of the inciter. Whether or not this freedom from incitement may be independently invoked by alleged hate speech victims was for the time being left unanswered. Granted, that would have been beyond the legal questions raised by the specifics of the *Faurisson* case. In any event, the majority opinion for the first time supported a community right 'to live free from fear of an atmosphere of discrimination' (in this case anti-Semitism), while individual members moreover fleshed out a 'right to be free from racial, national or religious incitement'.

In *Malcolm Ross v. Canada*, revolving around an anti-Semitic school teacher, the Committee further developed the notion of a right against incitement.[21] It stated that 'as held in *Faurisson v. France*, restrictions may be permitted on statements which are of a nature as to raise or strengthen anti-Semitic feeling, in order to uphold the Jewish communities' right to be protected from religious hatred. Such restrictions also derive support from the principles reflected in Article 20(2) of the Covenant.'[22] Though suggesting it had considered the exact same in *Faurisson*, actually two important new steps are made in the Committee's argument. First, the accepted ground for restricting the freedom of expression is now called a 'right' to be protected from religious hatred rather than an 'interest', making clearer than before what particular 'rights of others' are at stake in this type of case.[23] Second, so as to substantiate the existence of this right explicit reference is made this time to Article 20(2) of the Covenant. All in all this makes the *Ross* case the first Human Rights Committee case where the majority of Committee members (i.e. as part of their adopted Views) recognize a *right to be protected from religious hatred*, distilling this notion expressly from Article 20(2) ICCPR. Somewhat confusing is the fact that in the same paragraph of this case the Committee

15 *Faurisson*, para. 4.
16 *Faurisson*, para. 9.
17 *Faurisson*, para. 10.
18 *Faurisson*, para. 7
19 Individual opinion by Prafullachandra Bhagwati.
20 Bhagwati. Furthermore referring to 'respect for the rights and interests of the Jewish community to live in society with full human dignity and free from an atmosphere of anti-semitism'.
21 *Malcolm Ross v. Canada*, Communication No. 736/1997, views of 18 October 2000, para. 2.1 and para. 4.2.
22 *Malcolm Ross*, para. 11.5.
23 As was still the case in *Faurisson*, para. 9.6.

comes up with a dissimilar type of 'rights and reputations of others' when it concludes 'that the restrictions imposed on him were for the purpose of protecting the "rights or reputations" of persons of Jewish faith, including the *right to have an education in the public school system free from bias, prejudice and intolerance.*'[24]

Such a right cannot as such be found in the Covenant;[25] though perhaps this notion could be considered a species of the more general norms on equality before the law (Article 26) and protection against hatred (Article 20) when taken into conjunction. In any event, the formulation appears to have been copied from the domestic proceedings and should be considered a Canadian legal notion.[26] The Committee could have geared that ground more towards the language of Article 20(2) of the Covenant and stick to its newly adopted general 'right to be protected from religious hatred'.

Throughout the *Ross* decision the Committee shifts between a group right and an individual right when it addresses this right to be protected against hatred. When it speaks of the 'Jewish communities' right' clearly it alludes to a collective right. Then again, in the second reference to this right in the case mention is made of 'persons of Jewish faith' as rights holders, more or less individualizing the same notion. At this place the Committee appears to adopt the language of minority rights as codified by Article 27 ('persons belonging to such minorities shall not be denied the right...'). Though the general rationale of those rights is to protect minorities, it is strictly speaking 'persons', i.e. individuals, belonging to such minorities that are the beneficiary of these rights.

In sum, the plenary Committee for the first time unambiguously recognized the right to be protected from religious hatred, inferring this fundamental right directly from the principles laid down in Article 20(2) ICCPR. This right's main function in the *Ross* case was again to function as recognized 'rights of others' (the Jewish community in Canada, or individuals belonging to the Jewish minority), which in turn meant that the impugned extreme speech could be legitimately limited. Now that a right to be protected from religious hatred was finally recognized by the Committee as a whole, it would be all the more interesting to learn whether alleged hate speech *victims* are in a position to invoke that right before the Committee.

The incitement clause as a right invoked by incitement victims

The *Maria Vassilari et al. v. Greece* case does not deal with religious hatred, but instead with racist incitement against Roma, yet is certainly unique and important for our purposes as it is one of the first cases to be brought by an alleged *victim* of hate speech and as such one of the very few instances in which Article 20(2) was invoked by the applicant as the norm on which the human rights complaint is based.[27] Again, typically in the jurisprudence hitherto this provision was invoked by the responding state, so as to persuade the Committee to deny

24 *Faurisson*, para. 11.5 (emphasis added).

25 The ICCPR does not deal with education other than in the context of so-called parental rights as formulated by Article 18(4).

26 It is based on the equal access to public service principle and on equality before the law as codified by Article 5 of the Canadian Human Rights Act, R.S.C., 1985, c. H-6 and Article 15 of the Canadian Charter of Rights and Freedoms, which is part of the Constitution Act, 1982 (80), 1982, c. 11 (UK), Schedule B. A 'right to be educated in a school system that is free from bias, prejudice and intolerance' is distilled from those norms in paras. 80, 83, 85 of *Ross v. New Brunswick School District No. 15*, [1996] 1 SCR. 825.

27 *Maria Vassilari et al. v. Greece*, Communication No. 1570/2007, views of 19 March 2009.

standing to a convicted inciter or so as to underscore that the state was not only permitted but actually obliged under international law to limit the speech act at hand.

Accordingly, in *Vassilari* we are not dealing with a convicted inciter who claims his or her freedom of expression was illegitimately restricted; instead the case concerns alleged incitement victims who claim that the state *did not do enough to restrict the inciter's free speech.* Indeed, this scenario raises the crucial question whether it is possible that a state breaches international human rights law *by not sufficiently combating incitement*, thus by not limiting someone's speech act for instance by way of ex post (criminal) penalties?

The Human Rights Committee did not reach that conclusion in this particular case. In fact, it altogether dodged the question whether Article 20, second paragraph, can be 'invoked' by an applicant. The precise formulation used to establish the inadmissibility of the relevant part of the complaint is very telling: '*Without determining whether article 20 may be invoked under the Optional Protocol*, the Committee considers that the authors have insufficiently substantiated the facts for the purposes of admissibility. Thus, this part of the communication is inadmissible under article 2 of the Optional Protocol.'[28]

The case revolved around a published newspaper letter signed by a number of local residents calling for 'militant action' against a group of Roma people living near a Greek town. These particulars surely minimally substantiated a *prima facie* case. This makes one wonder whether the reluctance on the part of the Committee members to decide the question '*whether article 20 may be invoked under the Optional Protocol*' is in fact what clouded their overall admissibility judgement. The content of the inciteful letter and the vulnerable position of the verbally attacked minority in this case seemed such to at least warrant discussion of the merits, which is not the same, clearly, as saying that a violation should have been determined by the Committee.[29] But for a discussion on the merits, a discussion (and resolution) of the question as to the precise legal nature of Article 20(2) would have been necessary. The Committee's decision literally states that it wishes, for the time being, not to resolve that very discussion.

One Committee member, Mr. Abdelfattah Amor, joined by two others (Mr. Ahmad Amin Fathalla and Mr. Bouzid Lazhari),[30] similarly criticized the Committee in relation to this non-committal approach. In relation to the nature of Article 20(2), and particularly the question whether it can be invoked by individuals, he argues:

> The Committee has not ventured an opinion on the applicability of article 20, paragraph 2, to individual cases. While it may, of course, decide to do so in the future, the reasons for evading the question are puzzling. There is no logical or objective reason to do this. In stating that 'any advocacy of national, racial or religious hatred that constitutes incitement to discrimination, hostility or violence shall be prohibited by law', article 20, paragraph 2, provides protection for individuals and groups against this type of discrimination. Article 20 is not an invitation to add another law to the legal arsenal merely for form's sake. Even if this was the purpose, which is not the case in Greece, such a law would be ineffective without procedures for complaints and penalties. In fact,

28 *Maria Vassilari*, para. 6.5 (emphasis added).

29 As the Committee itself reasoned further on in relation to the Article 26 claims (the only part deemed admissible), '[a]n acquittal in itself does not amount to a violation' (ibid., para. 7.2.). After assessment of the domestic enforcement of the relevant hate speech legislation it may have very well come to such a conclusion in theory. The point is that such an assessment was necessary.

30 See individual opinion of Committee members Mr. Ahmad Amin Fathalla and Mr. Bouzid Lazhari, indicating they associate themselves with the views of Mr. Amor.

> the invocation of article 20, paragraph 2, by individuals who feel they have been wronged follows the logic of protection that underlies the entire Covenant and consequently affords protection to individuals and groups. It would be neither logical nor legally sound to consider excluding its applicability under the Optional Protocol. By declining to give an opinion on this aspect of the communication, the Committee allows uncertainty to persist on the scope of article 20, paragraph 2, particularly as, given the points raised, discussion was needed at the very least with regard to the question of admissibility.[31]

Moreover, Greece had not objected to the admissibility of the communication either on the grounds of the applicability of Article 20, paragraph 2, or any other grounds. Amor elaborates on this point, contending that '[t]he Committee's settled jurisprudence holds that, when the State party raises no objection to admissibility, the Committee declares the communication admissible unless the allegations are manifestly groundless or not serious or do not meet the other requirements set out in the Protocol.'[32] He further points out that the Greek courts did rule on the merits without raising questions of admissibility.[33] Turning to the particulars of the case at hand and the threshold question as to whether the facts presented by the applicants satisfied the admissibility criteria, he goes on arguing rather convincingly:

> To say that, in the case in point, the authors have insufficiently substantiated the facts for the purposes of admissibility relies on an assessment that cannot be confirmed or justified by the contents of the file. While the facts may be discussed on the merits, they are sufficiently serious not to present an obstacle to admissibility under article 2 of the Optional Protocol. The case in point concerns a letter signed by 1,200 non-Roma individuals, entitled 'Objection against the Gypsies: Residents gathered signatures for their removal'. The letter accuses the Roma, as a group, of physical assault, battery and arson. The signatories demand that the Roma be 'evicted' – 'removed' according to the State party – from their settlement and threatened to take 'militant action' ... The authors took their case to the Committee, claiming to be the victims of a violation by the State party of article 20, paragraph 2, read in conjunction with article 2, paragraph 1, of the Covenant, because the [Greek] court 'failed to appreciate the racist nature of the impugned letter and to effectively implement the Anti-Racism Law 927/1979 aimed at prohibiting dissemination of racist speech'. This allegedly 'discloses a violation of the State party's obligation to ensure prohibition of the advocacy of racial hatred that constitutes incitement to discrimination, hatred or violence'. *Was it advocacy of racial hatred or just words? Was a racist offence committed or not? Was there the intention to offend, and who must prove this? These are questions that should be discussed, analysed and assessed on the merits.* To say, subsequently, that the facts have been insufficiently substantiated for the purposes of admissibility is indefensible both legally and factually. Sometimes there are reasons which the legal mind knows nothing of![34]

31 Individual opinion of Committee member Mr. Abdelfattah Amor (dissenting), para. (1).

32 Amor, para. (2).

33 Amor, para. (3)

34 Amor, para. (4) (emphasis added).

In sum, it is clear that the Committee – deliberately or not – missed out on the ideal opportunity to provide certainty as to the precise nature of the rights enshrined by Article 20(2). It could and arguably should have seized upon this case to pronounce on the legal nature of Article 20(2) ICCPR: does it contain an *invocable* fundamental right or not? Is there a right to be protected against incitement? In 2009 there was no majority in the Committee for that course of action, with three of the participating 15 Committee members dissenting and essentially deeming Article 20(2) applicable to and invocable by incitement victims. In 2011, by implication, there was still no majority let alone a consensus, as General Comment No. 34 is altogether silent on the question of invocability of Article 20(2). Likewise, the 2012 *Rabat Plan of Action* on conceptualization and implementation of Article 20(2) is silent on the question whether this provision can be invoked by incitement victims.[35]

The future of the incitement clause

Whereas in *Vassilari* the Committee still saw ways to evade this question, in *Mohamed Rabbae, A.B.S. and N.A v. the Netherlands* [36] finally for once and for all held that persons alleging a breach of Article 20(2) ICCPR have standing before the Human Rights Committee, indicating that this provision despite its odd formulation encapsulates a justiciable right. This case in a sense flows from the domestic (Netherlands) Geert Wilders case that revolved around the question whether this Dutch rightist politician had incited discrimination against Muslims, amongst other charges.[37] Particularly Wilders' statements about Muslims in various media and his anti-Quran film *Fitna* were subject of the domestic criminal proceedings against him. Ultimately, on 23 June 2011,[38] Wilders was fully acquitted of

35 *Rabat Plan of Action on the Prohibition of Advocacy of National, Racial or Religious Hatred that Constitutes Incitement to Discrimination, Hostility or Violence.* Conclusions and recommendations emanating from the four regional expert workshops organized by OHCHR, in 2011, and adopted by experts in Rabat, Morocco on 5 October 2012. In four regional workshops – Europe (Vienna, 9 and 10 February 2011); Africa (Nairobi, 6 and 7 April 2011); Asia and the Pacific (Bangkok, 6 and 7 July 2011); and the Americas (Santiago de Chile, 12 and 13 October 2011) – some 50 experts and more than 200 observers and other stakeholders have reflected on the question of incitement in the meaning of Article 20(2) ICCPR. This has led to a wealth of comparative information on virtually all ICCPR States parties, but also to background studies, legal and other expert papers, ultimately cumulating in this Rabat Plan of Action. The Plan has been welcomed by leading human rights and freedom of expression NGOs, notably by ARTICLE 19. For more on the Rabat Plan, see Mohamed Saeed M. Eltayeb, 'From Rabat to Istanbul: Combating Advocacy of Religious Hatred that Constitutes Incitement to Discrimination, Hostility, or Violence', Chapter 6 of this volume.

36 *Mohamad Rabbae, A.B.S. and N.A. v. The Netherlands*, Communication No. 2124/2011, Views adopted on 14 July 2016. For the precise complaint ('Communication') as originally filed with the Human Rights Committee by the applicants and their lawyers, see *M.R., A.B.S. and N.A v. the Netherlands*, CCPR Communication, 15 November 2011, available at http://www.bohler.eu/nl/nieuws-overzicht/klacht-tegen-vrijspraak-wilders-ingediend/, 5.

37 The case also revolved around counts of incitement to discrimination of Moroccans and other non-Western immigrants, an aspect which is further ignored here. This section partly draws on Jeroen Temperman, 'A Right to be Free from Religious Hatred?: The Wilders Case in the Netherlands and Beyond', in Peter Molnar, ed., *Turning Points in Free Speech and Censorship Around the Globe* (Central European University Press 2014), 509–530.

38 An English summary of the Amsterdam District Court Decision is available at http://www.rechtspraak.nl/SiteCollectionDocuments/Translation%20verdict%20Wilders%20230611.pdf.

the chargers of inciting hatred against Muslims and inciting discrimination against Muslims.[39]

Subsequently, a group of alleged victims brought this complaint against the Netherlands requesting the UN Human Rights Committee to determine a violation of Article 20(2) ICCPR. It is logical that these stakeholders brought the case to Geneva and not to Strasbourg.[40] The European Convention on Human Rights does not contain a hate speech prohibition, let alone a right to be free from incitement. That said, the recent case of *Aksu v. Turkey* shows that alleged hate speech victims could attempt to persuade the Strasbourg court to determine a violation of Article 8 on private life.[41] Although in *Aksu* the European Court of Human Rights ultimately did not find a violation of this right, it did grant Mr. Aksu standing to voice his complaint about two allegedly anti-Roma publications. That is, the fact that the case was not immediately declared inadmissible is in its own right an important step for future incitement victims. Moreover, from the even more recent judgement in *Karaahmed v. Bulgaria*, concerning acts of hooliganism and intimidation during Friday prayer at a mosque in Sofia, a right to be protected against incitement on anti-religious grounds could arguably be directly distilled from Article 9 of the Convention on freedom of religion.[42]

Be that as it may, the two Dutch lawyers of the international law-oriented Dutch firm Böhler Advocaten,[43] acting for the three anonymous applicants M.R., A.B.S. and N.A, lodged the case against the Netherlands with the UN Human Rights Committee. The latter three are Dutch citizens of Moroccan descent, and all claimed to have personally experienced the negative impact triggered by Mr. Wilders' statements, ranging from more general feelings of anxiety, to increasingly feeling threatened and marginalized, to very concrete incidents of hatred and discrimination.[44] In addition to other claims,[45] the applicants' principal claim was a breach of Article 20(2) ICCPR, taken in conjunction with the equality principle of Article 26 and minority right codified by Article 27. In

39 Article 137d of the Dutch Criminal Code: '1. He who publicly, verbally or in writing or in an image, incites hatred against or discrimination of people or violent behaviour against person or property of people because of their race, their religion or belief, their gender or hetero- or homosexual nature or their physical, mental, or intellectual disabilities, will be punished with a prison sentence of at the most one year or a fine of third category. 2. If the offence is committed by a person who makes it his profession or habit, or by two or more people in association, a prison sentence of at the most two years or a fine of fourth category will be imposed.'

40 Had Wilders lost his domestic case he would likely have brought a complaint about freedom of expression to Strasbourg. It is not at all self-evident that he would have won that case there: one may recall the somewhat comparable cases of European politicians being fined for hate speech offences and not being successful in Strasbourg, such as *Mark Anthony Norwood v. the United Kingdom*, App. No. 23131/03 (ECtHR admissibility decision, 16 November 2004); *Le Pen v. France*, App. No. 18788/09 (ECtHR admissibility decision, 7 May 2010); and *Féret v. Belgium*, App. No. 15615/07 (ECtHR, 16 July 2009). See also, *Glimmerveen and Hagenbeek v. the Netherlands*, App. Nos. 8348/78 and 8406/78 (ECmHR admissibility decision, 11 October 1979).

41 *Aksu v. Turkey*, App. Nos. 4149/04 and 41029/04 (ECtHR Grand Chamber, 15 March 2012).

42 *Karaahmed v. Bulgaria*, App. No. 30587/13 (ECtHR, 24 February 2015).

43 The same lawyers and law firm that assisted the victims in the domestic 'Article-12 Sv procedure', the procedure whereby stakeholders urge a Court to overrule a prosecutorial dismissal (a procedure, also, that may permit a degree of involvement, as witnesses, in the trial).

44 See CCPR Communication, 15 November 2011, supra note 36 at 3–4, narrating the background of the complainants and these personal experiences. A witness statement made by N.A. during the domestic proceedings is appended to the Communication (Annex 4).

45 Other complaints invoke Article 2 and Article 14 of the ICCPR.

sum, the applicants claimed before the Committee that The Netherlands failed to (appropriately) apply its anti-incitement legislation, that is, the Dutch legislation giving effect to the Covenant's standards on incitement.

To that effect, the lawyers acting for the alleged victims submitted that while Article 20 ICCPR is formulated 'in terms of obligations of the state rather than in rights of individuals, this does not imply that these are matters to be left to the internal jurisdiction of state parties and as such immune from review under the individual communication procedure. If such were the case, the protection regime established by the Covenant would be weakened significantly.'[46] The Communication hence posited that '[a]s a consequence of the acquittal, the complainants are not only victims of the hate speech of Wilders but also victims of a violation of article 20 CCPR by the State of the Netherlands.'[47]

The applicants explained that they complained not because they felt insulted; they have lodged their complaint because they feel threatened – a real threat, according to them, that the Dutch state does not sufficiently seek to combat.[48] Further, the applicants do not claim that the Netherlands breached the Covenant merely because Wilders was acquitted; what is claimed is more specifically that (i) the Dutch judge did not interpret advocacy of hatred in accordance with international standards; and (ii) that there was very solid evidence that successful advocacy of religious hatred constituting discrimination, hostility or violence was available but not adequately valued by the Dutch judiciary.[49] The applicants argued more specifically that the Dutch judge failed to appreciate the *context* enough, and concentrated overly on the *content* of the individual berated statements. The relevant statements were, moreover, scrutinized by the Dutch judiciary in too much isolation rather than in conjunction. Specifically, it was argued that the Dutch court ought to have assessed the *cumulative effect* of all Wilders' statements on Dutch society.[50] The applicants further presented data on discrimination and hate crimes with a view towards linking up what they experienced as systematic incitement and a discernible poisoned atmosphere.[51]

Ultimately, the Human Rights Committee rejected the complaint, emphasizing that the reasoned acquittal by the Dutch judiciary did not amount to a breach of Article 20 (2). In this case it was clear, the Committee argued, that the Netherlands complied with the clause's obligation that incitement shall be prohibited by law; after all, so it was reasoned, a law to that effect was in place and this anti-incitement law even led to actual criminal proceedings. In other words, there is no right to see another person convicted.

While short of a first Article 20(2) violation, the decision is highly significant in that it explicitly rendered standing to alleged incitement victims under the Covenant. It remains to be seen whether other alleged incitement victims will pick up on this and file complaints against states over allegations of not sufficiently implementing Article 20(2) ICCPR.

46 CCPR Communication, 15 November 2011, supra note 36 at 2.
47 CCPR Communication at 2.
48 CCPR Communication at 5.
49 CCPR Communication at 5.
50 CCPR Communication at 9–10.
51 CCPR Communication at 20–22.

Part III

Perspectives

8 Religious pluralism

The Argentine experience

Norberto Padilla

Religious pluralism in a national context

When considering religious pluralism in the context of any particular country, we may start by examining the diversity of creeds and the way they coexist with each other and in the greater society. We can consider the degree of freedom each creed or belief system has for sharing ideas and cultural space, and for developing as a coherent community within the larger society. We can look at the existence of legal protections and provisions for individual and group manifestation of religious belief and practice, as well as at societal attitudes and traditions that foster harmony among a diversity of religious believers.

It is useful to consider these notions in the context of such a country as Argentina, where the historical predominance of a single religion, Roman Catholicism, has not meant a society lacking in religious harmony.

Argentina had its beginning as a nation, like most countries of South America, in colonization by Catholic Spain during the sixteenth century. Although national census data does not track religious affiliation, and estimates from other sources vary, a credible 2015 estimate is that even now, after centuries of immigration, approximately 71% of Argentina's 44.3 million people are Roman Catholic.[1]

It is true that Argentine history records harsh times of political intolerance and divisions, fragile democratic institutions, and bloodshed in internal conflicts. However, state, creeds, and society have learned, in fidelity to their constitutional foundations, to live and grow in religious pluralism.

Professor Brett Scharffs has noted that Catholic-majority countries in South America, as well as Italy, Portugal, and Spain (the South American 'mother countries'), and in fact almost all of the world's nations where Catholic majorities exceed 70 percent of the population, show consistently low levels of both government restrictions on religion and social hostilities concerning religion. Scharffs has suggested that this phenomenon may be explained in part by the 'dramatic recalibration' of the attitude toward religious freedom in the Catholic Church as a result of the Second Vatican Council, as reflected in the declaration *Dignitatis Humanae: On the Right of the Person and of Communities to Social and Civil Freedom in Matters Religious*, promulgated by Pope Paul VI in December 1965.[2]

For Argentina in particular, it is proposed in this chapter that the nation's own religious, social, and political history have created a society capable of great solidarity in matters of religious and social harmony.

1 See United States Department of State, *International Religious Freedom Report 2017 – Argentina*.
2 Brett G. Scharffs, 'Religious Majorities and Restrictions on Religion', (2016) 91 *Notre Dame Law Review* (4), 1419–1443.

The program of the Argentine Constitution

The Argentine Constitution, first written in 1853, has gone through a number of reforms, the latest in 1994. Throughout all of these reforms, however, the foundational principles have remained, following what might be called 'the program of the Constitution', which gave impulse to Argentine as a country outstanding for its promise at the beginning of the twentieth century. The basic principles of this program might be summarized in five constitutional provisions:

1 *The theistic principle:* The Preamble of the Constitution invokes God as 'the source of all reason and justice' and in the Article 19 states that any judgment concerning private actions of people, as long as they do not affect the moral or public order and the rights concerning third parties, are reserved only to God and exempted from courts.
2 *The principle of in-migration*: The Constitution has the aspiration, written in its Preamble, of being a nation open to securing 'the blessings of liberty to … all [people] of the world who wish to dwell on argentine soil'.[3] This was the aim that moved the 'founding fathers': to attract a useful immigration and that immigrants would not feel excluded or limited because of religious beliefs that might be different from those of the majority profession, and that they would enrich the nation with their work and their contributions to the arts and to science.
3 *The relationship of Church and State.* Section 2 of the Constitution presents a compromise concerning the relationship between the State and the Catholic Church. Some drafters desired that Catholicism would be recognized as the State Religion; some even wanted to go so far as to insert into the text a proclamation that Roman Catholicism is the 'only true' religion. Certainly none of the drafters was against some kind of recognition. So Section 2 determines that 'The Federal Government supports the Roman Catholic Apostolic religion', which means not only granting a situation of preeminence, but also providing economic aid. This preeminence is tempered, however, by the provisions of Sections 14 and 20.
4 *The right to religious freedom.* Among the rights granted to all the inhabitants of the Nation in Section 14 of the Argentina Constitution is the right to 'profess freely their religion'. In Section 20 it is further clarified that 'Foreigners enjoy within the territory of the Nation all the civil rights of citizens; they may … practice freely their religion ….'
5 *Public office, patronage, and promoting conversion.* The 1853 Constitution set no religious limitations on the rights of non-Catholics to hold public office, except in the case of the president and vice-president of the Nation. This requirement was abolished in the 1994 constitutional revision. Also eliminated from the constitutional text in 1994 was Patronage, an interference of the State in the autonomy of the Catholic Church, though in fact this practice had ended in 1966 with an Agreement between the Argentine Republic and the Holy See. The 1994 reform also deleted reference to the goal 'to keep a pacific relationship with the Indians and promote their conversion to Catholicism'.
6 *The status of international human rights treaties.* Section 31 of the 1994 Constitutional provides that 'treaties with foreign powers' (including of course all clauses regarding freedom of religion that may be contained in them), along with the Constitution and law enacted by Congress, have status as 'the supreme law of the Nation; and the

3 From the Constitution of the Argentine Nation (1994), official English translation available at http://www.biblioteca.jus.gov.ar/argentina-constitution.pdf (accessed 26 June 2018).

authorities of each province are bound thereby, notwithstanding any provision to the contrary included in the provincial laws or constitutions....'

Certainly, God was not an abstraction for drafters of the Argentine Constitution. They believed in God revealed in fullness through Jesus Christ, as confessed in the Catholic Communion. However, religious faith did not prevent these legislators from freely opening the doors of the Nation to all men and women of the most diverse origins. To quote Argentina's seventh president, Domingo Faustino Sarmiento, 'The Argentine Republic is a piece of the Earth's surface which has been given to humankind as a dwelling.'[4]

A country of immigration

In fulfillment of the dreams of its founders, Argentina received in the late nineteenth and early twentieth centuries a flow of immigrants. These groups significantly changed the appearance and composition of the population. According to the census carried out in 1869, Argentina had a population of 1,736,400, 12 percent of whom were foreign. By 1895 the population was 3,956,060, and in 1914 the number had reached 7,885,237 inhabitants, 30 percent of which were foreign.

Men and women from around the world from different religious traditions found in Argentina their space and freedom for personal development. Most of the population continued to belong to the Roman Catholic Church because of the fact that Spanish and Italian immigrants were the largest groups, but there also were immigrants from France, Germany, and other parts of Europe, from the Middle East and many other parts of the world. An important Jewish immigration came from the Russian Empire, where they had been subjected to pogroms and discrimination; these immigrants settled in Buenos Aires and in agricultural colonies in the provinces of Santa Fe and Entre Ríos.

For this reason, in a 'melting pot' of different cultures and races the offspring of the immigrants who were arriving, and those of the '*criollo*' (the early Spaniards to arrive on Argentine soil), and of the original native population were brought up together, receiving the same education. Public schools represented a very important tool for integration, surpassing any religious or ethnic barriers. The immigrant groups shared the life of small towns, cities, and neighborhoods, together in sometimes precarious housing ('*conventillos*') but with the hope of better conditions for them and their children. They mingled through marriage, commerce, sport, and social clubs, in the universities, factories, and military service. Conflicts in Europe brought new waves of immigrants, such as Armenians fleeing persecution in what was the late Ottoman Empire and the early Turkish Republic. Immigrants coming from the Middle East (Sephardic Jews, Christians, and Muslims) shared the same social groups during half a century.

As time went by, children of immigrants became the heads of the most important posts in the State, the Army, the Catholic Church, and in Argentine economic and social life, taking the place of the traditional families that had ruled the country until that point.[5]

4 Norberto Padilla, 'Ciento cincuenta años después', in Roberto Bosca, comp., *La Libertad Religiosa en Argentina. Aportes para una Legislación* (CALIR–Konrad Adenauer Stiflung 2003), 31, http://www.calir.org.ar/libro/04.pdf (accesssed 26 June 2018).

5 A classic and fundamental study of this fascinating subject is José Luis de Imaz, *Los Que Mandan* (Eudeba, 1st edn, 1 1964). An English translation by Carlos A. Astiz, with updated information, was published by the State University of New York and Albany in 1970.

Confrontation and integration

During the nineteenth century the liberal[6] governments in Argentina were more than once in conflict with the Catholic Church, although not violently, as in some other countries. In particular, as the Congress worked on Law Number 1420 regarding compulsory and free primary education there was great consternation because religion was to be excluded from school curricula, its teaching to be allowed only outside of the school schedule, by priests or ministers of the diverse creeds, not only by Catholics. This law was called 'the law of secular education' (*laica* in Spanish being reminiscent of the French *laïque*), the influential educational model of the ruling group. Catholics resisted, but they were overcome.[7] Something similar happened when, according also to the French pattern, marriage was secularized so that only civil marriage would have legal effect, and was compulsory prior to a religious ceremony.[8]

At certain moments even during the twentieth century, military, intellectuals, and men of the Church identified the Argentine people exclusively as members of the majority creed, ignoring minorities. The mentality was of a 'Catholic Argentina' as a reality without any possible nuance, and, due to the historical links, some proclaimed an alliance between the Cross and the sword. Authoritarian or totalitarian projects emerged, influenced by European ideologies (Fascism, Falangism, French Action, and, rarely, Nazism).[9] It would be a mistake, however, to characterize Argentine Catholicism as a whole in this way, for during these same decades there were those concerned with the great issues of the Church's Social Doctrine and its principles, and furthermore (and strongly) of its concerns with education and culture.

In 1943, after the coup that marked the beginning of Juan Perón's access to power, the military regime abolished Law 1420 and established compulsory Catholic religious education in schools, with the alternative of Moral Doctrine for those who rejected attending for

6 When we say 'liberal' in this context we mean the ideas of the US Constitution (followed closely by the framers of the Argentine Constitution) and not the current sense of 'liberal' in the US today, as left-leaning or 'progressive'.

7 Eduardo María Taussig, *Ley 1420 y Libertad de Conciencia* (Agape Libros 2006). On the topic of religion and education in Argentina, see also Norberto Padilla, 'Religious Education in Argentina', in Derek H. Davis and Elena Miroshnikova, eds., *The Routledge International Handbook of Religious Education* (Routledge 2013), 13.7, and Roberto Bosca, 'El Derecho Eclesiástico en la República Argentina en Materia Educativa'; Octavio Lo Prete, 'El Derecho a la Libertad Religiosa en Materia Educativa y Educación Pública y Religión en la Argentina'; and Jorge Gentile, 'La Libertad Religiosa en la Educación', all of which may be found at the website of Consejo Argentino para la Libertad Religiosa (CALIR) under the topic Libertad religiosa y educación, http://calir.org.ar/articulos.htm (accesssed 26 June 2018).

8 Arnoldo Canclini, *Historias y Anécdotas del Matrimonio en la Argentina* (Emecé 2005).

9 'The idea that Catholicism entailed a fundamental feature of a national identity conceived in essential terms was not something new. However, during the period between wars it almost became part of common sense, including beyond the Catholic Church boundaries. On that basis the concept of democracy started to gain a new sense: if the nation was Catholic, a constitution that did not adopt the Catholic creed as the religion of the State would not reflect genuinely the Argentine idiosyncrasy and therefore would be undemocratic. As to the "atheistic" law of education which had "banned God from schools", in order to put things in their place again, to reach true democracy, it was necessary to review completely the country's legal system. Time had arrived to obey God before men.' Roberto Di Stefano, 'El Catolicismo y la República', (2012) *Revista Criterio* No. 2388 (translation by the author). See also, among others, Jorge Emilio Gallardo, *Luchas Ideológicas Argentinas. Origen y Consecuencias de Nuestros Fanatismos* (Idea Viva 2006), 21, and Nestor Tomás Auza, 'La Iglesia Católica (1914–1960)', in *Nueva Historia de la Nación Argentina*, Vol. 8. La Argentina del Siglo XX (Academia Nacional de la Historia / Planeta, 1999), 303.

ideological or religious reasons. This of course was resented by those who did not want to participate in Catholic religion classes as they had to leave the classroom and join the other few in the Lectures on Moral Doctrine.[10] Ironically, Perón, at the end of his government, persecuted the Catholic Church by imprisoning priests and laymen, expelling prelates, and allowing the burning of churches. In that hostile mood, he banned the religious education instigated in 1943.[11] This conflict with the Church was one of the important reasons that Perón was overthrown in 1955, though this did not bring back Catholic education in public schools. Two decades later, Perón returned from exile, and he died in office in 1974, reconciled with the Catholic Church, to which most of his political and union leading figures were strongly connected.

Until the early 1920s, the non-Catholic communities composed of foreigners and their ministers and priests performed religious rites in their own languages. They understood that they had to acknowledge the Catholic identity of the majority, so they did not proselytize outside their communities, which at the same time were being reduced by interreligious marriages, generally with Catholics. This situation varied as Pentecostal, Baptist, Free Evangelicals, Congregationalists, and other Protestant groups began to merge, with Argentine ministers and communities integrated by Argentines and with the intention of missionary activity towards those christened in the Catholic faith but in many cases having little adherence to religious practice or education.

Immigrants of the Islamic faith were not part of this process until the mid twentieth century, when Islamic countries began to provide the necessary resources to build places for worship. The first two mosques in Argentina were built in Buenos Aires in the 1980s: one supported by the Islamic Republic of Iran, to serve the Shia community, and another, the Al Ahmad Mosque, to serve Sunni Argentinians. In 1996, the largest mosque in Latin America was completed as part of the King Fahd Islamic Cultural Center, built with the help of the Saudi King Fahd bin Abdulaziz Al Saud, Custodian of the Two Holy Mosques. The Center, which contains not only the mosque but also two schools, a library, and a park, was built on a 34,000-square-meter plot of state property in the district of Palermo, which was gifted by the government following a visit by President Menem to Saudi Arabia. Carlos Menem, who was president of the country for a decade, was the son of Syrian immigrants, and though he himself was a Catholic, he belonged to a Muslim family.

The Jewish community in Argentina is in many ways one of the most important in Latin America. Even though marked by prejudices, it nevertheless has played an important role in Argentine life.[12] To name only a few influential Jewish Argentinians: Russia-born Alberto Gerchunoff, journalist for *La Nación*, Argentina's leading newspaper, and author of the influential novel *Los Gauchos Judíos*, and internationally renowned musician and citizen-of-the-world Daniel Barenboim, born in Buenos Aires to Argentinian Jewish parents. A number of prominent Argentinian scientists are members of the Jewish community, including Hungarian-born Lazlo Biro, the inventor of the ballpoint pen, and most notably biochemist César Milstein, born in Argentina to Ukrainian immigrant parents, who received the Nobel Prize in Physiology or Medicine in 1984. Jewish political leaders in Argentina include

10 Mario Ringler, 'Historia y memoria de un judío argentino', in Robert Bosca, comp., *La libertad religiosa en la Argentina. Aportes para una legislación* (CALIR/Konrad Adenauer Stiftung 2003), 127.

11 Florencio José Arnaudo, *El Año en que Quemaron las Iglesias* (Librería Histórica 2005).

12 See Arnoldo Canclini, 'El Protestantismo', 363; Narciso Binayan Carmona, 'Iglesias y Religiones Orientales', 375; León Klenicki, 'El Judaismo', 389; in *Nueva Historia de la Nación Argentina*, supra note 9.

provincial and national congressmen, Ministers in the Cabinet, and a Provisional President of the Senate.

Rabbi Sergio Bergman is *Ministro de Ambiente y Desarrollo Sustentable* in President Mauricio Macris's Government, and Rabbi Abraham Skorka, rector of the Seminario Rabínico Latinoamericano in Buenos Aires, has been for many years a close friend and collaborator with another Argentine with a common background in chemistry: Jorge Mario Bergoglio, Archbishop of Buenos Aires, who in March 2013 became Francis, the 266th Pope of the Roman Catholic Church. Like his predecessor as Archbishop, Antonio Quarracino, as well as his successor, Cardinal Mario Aurelio Poli, Bergoglio is the son of Italian immigrants to Argentina.

Emblematic of this close association of Jews and Catholics in Argentina is the choice of Cardinal Quarracino to be buried in the Buenos Aires Cathedral next to the Shoah memorial built due to his initiative.[13]

Ecumenism and dialogue, irreversible commitment

With the Second Vatican Council, ecumenism and interreligious dialogue became a part of the life of the Catholic Church in Argentina.[14] It did not happen in a wink, nor was it something easy to accomplish. There was much to do, and on many occasions whether within the Church or outside, what must be done was not understood. We may mention, for example, those first meetings in the late sixties between professors and students from the Catholic, Protestant, and Jewish Divinity faculties; the work carried out by the review *Criterio*, which for many years had as editor Rev. Jorge Mejía, expert at the Vatican Council at the time and later a cardinal; the setting up of committees of ecumenism in the Archdiocese of Buenos Aires and in the Argentine Conference of Bishops. In short, considerable creative and constant work was undertaken by many, not only Catholics but also Protestants, Orthodox Christians, and Jews. Suddenly, people and institutions of different creeds discovered each other, and the integration of ecumenical commitment and dialogue between Catholicism and Judaism and other faiths began to take place in catechesis studies, parochial groups, convents, and seminars.

Something to emphasize is the creation of the Ecumenical Committee of Christian Church in Argentina (CEICA), made official in 1988 but which started to coalesce years earlier at the meetings of religious leaders for the Week of Prayer for the Unity of Christians. Among other expressions of the dialogue, we might mention the fruitful Declaration of Mutual Recognition of Baptism, sealed by the highest authorities of the Argentine Episcopal Conference of Bishops and the Evangelical Church of the Rio de la Plata and the Evangelical United Lutheran Church in 1989.[15]

13 Abraham Skorka, 'Judíos y católicos a cincuenta años del Concilio', and Norberto Padilla, 'Rostros, gestos y palabras de un reencuentro', in Ariel Stofenmacher and Abraham Skorka, eds, *El Concilio Vaticano II y los Judíos* (Seminario Rabínico Latinoamericano Marshall T. Meyer 2015), 51 and 62. The edition of this book planned to be published before 13 March 2013 has its first chapter by Cardinal Bergoglio on 'Nostra Aetate' and one of the Prefaces by His Holiness Pope Francis. Cardinal Jorge Mejia contributed, a short time before passing away, the chapter 'Cincuenta años de relaciones positivas con el Judaismo'.

14 Norberto Padilla, 'La Iglesia Católica (1961–1983)', 337, in *Nueva Historia*.

15 Declaración Conjunta sobre el Reconocimiento Mutuo del Sacramento del Bautismo, 1989. http://www.ceerjircea.org.ar/reconocimientomutuo.htm (accessed 26 June 2018).

During the 1970s, religious ministers, intellectuals, and youth involved in religion, many among them Catholic, trying to make use of Marxist categories to define the struggle for justice, chose violence, which is neither Christian nor according to the Gospel. At the same time, there were Catholics who used violent and evil methods to repress, to engage in torture and forced disappearance of people. In response, some Catholic Bishops, including the Bishop of Neuquén, Jaime de Nevares, who took part in the Second Vatican Council, acting on their own responsibility, joined with a number of Evangelical and other Protestant churches in 1976 to create the Ecumenical Movement for Human Rights (MEDH), whose purpose was to mobilize 'churches, institutions and people of good will to commit themselves to work for human rights'.[16]

The years of military dictatorship (1976–1983) also led to the creation of CONADEP (National Commission on Disappearance of People). In this endeavor Bishop Nevares joined with Rabbi Marshall Meyer, founder of the Latin-American Rabbinical Seminar,[17] a Methodist bishop, leaders belonging to the Churches of the Reformation, and other personalities bearing a clear pluralist character from politics, press, and intellectual life.

The institutional response of the Church and of some of its members during that tragic period is still a controversial matter.[18]

As the military regime declined, the Catholic Church made a valuable contribution to the debate on dialogue, reconciliation, and democracy with the document 'Iglesia y Comunidad Nacional' (Church and National Community) (1981). After the reestablishment of the democratic government (10 December 1983), the Church had to undergo the experience of a society in the process of change, now clearly pluralistic. Catholic interests had to confront, relate to, and coexist with stances that ranged from a respectful and positive secular view to certain kinds of secularism ('laicismo') that were particularly adverse to participation of religion on the public scene.[19]

At the same time the State (especially the State Office of Worship, *Secretaría de Culto*, in the Foreign Ministry[20]), in what can be considered to be an enduring public policy, made efforts to assign importance to and assess the religious factor, recognizing the contribution of interdenominational relations to national peace and brotherly coexistence. During the 1990s, sacred feast days of Jews and Muslims were declared holidays by national law, and Seventh-day Adventist students were exempted from attending exams, classes, and other

16 'Ecumenical Movement for Human Rights (MEDH): A Commitment to Life', http://www.derechos.net/medh/medh1.htm (accessed 26 June 2018).

17 Marina Volcovich, 'Marshall Meyer', in *Personalidades Religiosas de la Ciudad de Buenos Aires, Hombres y Mujeres que Dejaron Huella*, Marcos Gabriel Vanzini, comp., Alfredo Abriani, coord., (Gobierno de la Ciudad de Buenos Aires 2012), 147, available at http://cdn2.buenosaires.gob.ar/relaciones%20internacionales/cultos/personalidadesreligiosasdeba.pdf (accessed 26 June 2018).

18 Veit Strassner, 'Church and Civil Society in Latin America: Some Reflections on Limits and Possibilities', in Gerhard Kruip and Helmut Reifeld, eds., *Church and Civil Society* (Konrad Adenauer Stiftung 2007), http://www.calir.org.ar/docs/churchandcivilsociety.pdf (accessed 26 June 2018).

19 Norberto Padilla, 'Opción por la Democracia. A Treinta Años de "Iglesia y Comunidad Nacional"', expanded from the original in *Communio: Revista Católica Internacional*, Año 18, n° 3, Navidad de 2011, available at http://www.calir.org.ar/verPdf.php?doc=/docs/Opcionporlademocracia-PadillaA30anios2011.pdf (accessed 26 June 2018).

20 The term *Secretaría de Culto* is occasionally translated as Secretary of Cults, but this literal translation is misleading. *Culto* is better translated as worship. The Secretary or State Office in the Foreign Ministry can also be translated as Secretary for Religious Affairs. It must be noted that the Foreign Ministry has been named *Ministerio de Relaciones Exteriores y Culto* since 1898.

school activities during their Saturday Sabbath.[21] The non-Catholic churches were recognized beyond the bureaucratic relationship, and the *Secretaría de Culto* has been and continues to be a forum for dialogue and encounter between state and churches and of the churches between themselves. It was from the first multidenominational council constituted at the *Secretaría de Culto* between the years 2000 and 2001 that the Argentine Council for Religious Freedom (CALIR) gained a place as an essential reference in Argentina concerning all such matters.[22]

Still pending after more than thirty years since the first drafts were drawn is a regulation regarding protection and promotion of religious freedom and a code recognizing the legal status appropriate for denominations and non-Catholic religious communities.[23] This regulation is meant to replace Law 21.745, which created the *Registro Nacional de Cultos* (National Registry of Worship), in the State Secretary for Religious Affairs (*Secretaría de Culto*) during the last military regime. Even if its application has been benevolent, this law aims to control and forbids any kind of activity to those organizations that are not registered or that have their registration cancelled by any of the reasons specified in the law. The move towards legislation that includes specifically the principles of religious liberty as formulated in the UN Declaration of 1981,[24] and to turn the Registry from compulsory to voluntary for enhancing collaboration, was opposed by conservative Catholic groups in the 1990s. They feared the loss of the special status of the Catholic Church according to the Constitution and the advancing of foreign-financed sects. At the same time, on the Evangelical side, the criticism was that the law did not establish full equality between creeds. During the last twelve years of the Kirchner-Fernández government many promises were made, but no draft of law was ever sent to the Congress. In 2012, Representative Cynthia Hotton, a Baptist, after an informal consultation with Cardinal Bergoglio, introduced a draft in the Lower House, basically similar to CALIR's proposals. At a public hearing, a comprehensive representation of creeds in Argentina backed Hotton's draft, which other Representatives had also endorsed, as did the *Secretaría de Culto*. The future seemed assured: finally there would be a law. But some of the Protestant churches, who had been in favor of the draft bill, concluded that equality was not there, so they withdrew their support. The Government, which had in mind that Hotton had been a fierce opponent of the Same Sex Marriage Bill, also withdrew. The *Secretaría de Culto* of the present Argentine Government, following the earlier efforts, in a little more than one year has achieved a draft of law that seems to have gained wide consensus, and would be sent for discussion by the Congress in 2017.

21 Octavio Lo Prete, 'Los feriados de carácter "religioso" en la Argentina', available at http://www.calir.org.ar/pubrel04103.htm (accessed 26 June 2018).

22 In the field of relationships between state and religious communities, the *Secretaría de Culto* stands out as meeting point for encounter and interdenominational dialogue. In accordance with Resolution 1248/2000 of 16 May 2000, an advisory council was attached to this Office, made up of members of religious communities, all of them laypeople, acting without an official representation of the different creeds. This Council was created to advise on the drafting of a bill on freedom of worship.

23 See various law projects on the matter at http://www.calir.org.ar/proyecto.htm (accessed 26 June 2018). See also Juan G. Navarro Floria, 'The Relations between Church and State in the Argentine Republic', available at http://www.calir.org.ar/pubrel04102.htm (accessed 26 June 2018).

24 Declaration on the Elimination of All Forms of Intolerance and of Discrimination Based on Religion or Belief, adopted by the 36th session of the United Nations General Assembly on 25 November 1981.

One of the aspects to be considered when Congress has before it drafts of laws related to religion is that the elected members know very little about these issues and are afraid to get involved in a religious war. Only if churches and religious associations as a whole give their support will they be eager to go ahead. Another consideration is the confusion that many times arises between what the law is able to deal with and what can only be provided for or changed with an amendment to the Constitution. Though the Supreme Court has ruled[25] that neither the Constitution nor any federal laws declare the Catholic Church to be Argentina's official religion, yet the Constitution requires the government to 'support' the Church. At the same time, it must be said that in today's Argentina there is not a Catholic influence on governmental policies as in the past. Even the government's economic support is relatively unimportant in numbers, and tax exemptions and benefits apply to Catholic and non-Catholic educational and health institutions equally.[26] Even so, it may be hoped that a better way, inclusive of non-Catholic groups, as in Spain or Italy, can be reached in the future.

Good news came in 2015 with the (in many other aspects controversial) *Código Civil y Comercial.* [27] As in the former Civil Code, the Catholic Church is recognized as a 'public legal person' (Article 146) due to its place in the Constitution and the Agreement with the Holy See of 1966, among many other reasons. But what is a welcome change, in which CALIR played a decisive part, considering it would be 'a great step forward',[28] is that 'the churches, confessions, communities or religious entities' are recognized as 'private legal entities' (Article 149). Before this, such entities were categorized as merely civil associations, like sports clubs; there was no consideration of the characteristics of the organizational character of each entity. The work of adequation by state and creeds is yet to be done, with or without the long-delayed law.

The experience in pluralism

In the past twenty-five years awareness of the 'other' has become entrenched in the Argentine religious field. The first step is to accept the other, something which is not always easy. Many Catholics have considered other religious groups as 'sects', sent by 'Yankee imperialism' as a threat to the 'Catholic identity' of the country.[29] At the same time, for certain Evangelical groups, only they and certainly not the Catholics have the right to be called

25 Villacampa, Ignacio c/ Almos de Villacampa, María Angélica, Sentencia 9 de Febrero de 1989, SAIJ: FA89000012.

26 Norberto Padilla, 'Leyes en Material de Religión en el Siglo XXI. Desafíos y Dificultades en la Argentina', Consejo Argentino para la Libertad Religiosa, Congreso International: 'La Libertad Religiosa en el Siglo XXI. Religión, Estado y Sociedad', Facultad de Derecho y Ciencias Sociales, Universidad Nacional de Córdoba, Argentina, 3–5 Sedptember 2014, available at http://www.calir.org.ar/verPdf.php?doc=/congreso2014/Ponencias/PADILLA.Leyesenmateriadereligion.Argentina.pdf (accessed 26 June 2018).

27 *Código Civil y Comercial de la Nación*, entered into force 1 August 2015. On this subject see Juan G. Navarro Floria, 'Derecho Eclesiástico en el nuevo Código Civil y Comercial Argentino', (2016*) Anuario de Derecho Eclesiástico del Estado* (32), 501, and 'La personería jurídica de iglesias, confesiones y comunidades religiosas', in *Revista de Derecho Privado y Comunitario, Nueva Serie*, Vol. 2 (Editorial Rubinzal y Culzon 2015).

28 Consejo Argentino para la Libertad Religiosa, 'Declaración: Sobre el Nuevo Código Civil y Comercial', available at http://www.calir.org.ar/verPdf.php?doc=/docs/SobreCodigoCivil.5noviembre2014.pdf (accessed 26 June 2018).

29 Opposition of certain conservative Catholic groups to the projects of laws on freedom of worship claimed that the expansion of the so-called sects was favored.

Christians. However, for some time now dialogue and mutual collaboration have made possible remarkable advances.

In the educational area, denominations do an outstanding work: the oath of loyalty to the national flag for Jews, Christians, and Muslims all together in a common meeting; the planting in Plaza de Mayo in year 2000 of an olive tree as symbol of peace, in a ceremony performed by pupils of denominational schools together with Archbishop Bergoglio[30] and non-Catholic religious leaders; schools that invite their pupils to dialogue with ministers belonging to other creeds; initiatives such as *Construyendo Puentes* (Building Bridges, with the support of the US Embassy); Scouts with interdenominational camps.

We may also point to social work in shanty towns carried out by Caritas and Jewish philanthropic organizations; the Focolar movement and the Communitá di Sant Egidio; the YMCA; training courses for interreligious dialogue and transmission of religious values; the confluence of Catholic representatives and Evangelicals in statements in defense of unborn life, matrimony, and family;[31] the Archbishop of Buenos Aires taking part in a great meeting of Catholic and Pentecostals, and kneeling in the podium of the stadium receiving the blessing of pastors and congregation; Rabbi Abraham Skorka received as Doctor Honoris Causa by the Pontificia Universidad Católica Argentina, whose Grand Chancellor was that Archbishop, Cardinal Bergoglio.

The relationship between the cardinal and the rabbi would grow into a fruitful interfaith dialogue, and more than 30 conversations between the two men about matters of faith, ethics, and morality were recorded and shown on Catholic television, and later published as the bestselling 2010 book, *On Heaven and Earth.* [32]

The 1992 terrorist attacks against the Israeli Embassy in Buenos Aires and the AMIA (Asociación Mutual Israelita Argentina), in which Jews and Christians died or suffered injuries and destruction of their homes, opened minds to solidarity and to seeing the need of avoiding the isolation of the Jewish community, and as well to avoiding some subtle forms of Islamophobia. The same happened after the 9/11 attacks in the United States. In Buenos Aires, responding to a call from President de la Rúa, on short notice, the leaders of the most important religions, including Muslims, gathered with the national authorities and people to pray for peace at the Obelisk, in the center of the City.

Many Argentine religious leaders are now regular visitors in the Vatican. Two of them, Rabbi Skorka and Omar Abboud, a Muslim presently elected to the Buenos Aires City Legislature and director of the Institute for Inter-religious Dialogue in Buenos Aires, were embraced by Pope Francis at the Wall of Lamentation in Jerusalem, as part of a special pilgrimage to Jerusalem, Jordan, and the West Bank in 2014. And in New York, at Ground

30 On 7 September 2013 Pope Francis led in Saint Peter's Square at the Vatican a Vigil of Prayer for Peace, in the speech he delivered he recalled mentioned the planting of the olive tree: 'After the chaos of the flood when it stopped raining, a rainbow appeared and the dove returned with an olive branch. Today, I also think of that olive tree which representatives of various religions planted in the Plaza de Mayo, in Buenos Aires in year 2000, asking there be no more chaos, asking there be no more war, asking for peace.' The text of the address is available at http://www.vatican.va/holy_father/francesco/homilies/2013/documents/papa-francesco_20130907_veglia-pace_en.html (accessed 26 June 2018).

31 *Compromiso por la Vida*, 15.11.2011.http://www.ceercjircea.org.ar/COMPROMISOPORLAVIDA.pdf.

32 Rachael Kohn, 'The Embrace: Pope Francis and his Friends, Omar and Abraham', *The Spirit of Things*, ABC (Australia), 17 July 2015, http://www.abc.net.au/radionational/programs/spiritofthings/the-pope%E2%80%99s-and-his-friends,-omar-and-abraham/6624682 (accessed 26 June 2018).

Zero, the Pope held the hands of their American counterparts. Abboud, who draws inspiration from Pope Francis, has said of such events:

> For us who come from Argentina, where there has always been integration and good coexistence between the different faiths, this is not a novelty because the impulse to inter-religious dialogue was always a constant (element of our lives). ...
> Argentina does not have the same baggage that exists in the Middle East ... [T]hat does not mean that our model can be exported, but it can be an inspiration to others.[33]

As Jewish Australian radio journalist Rachael Kohn observed, 'Taking opportunities to foster co-existence is what matters most to Abboud, which is why he organised Argentina's first interfaith Middle East and Rome pilgrimage with 45 representatives from the Jewish, Muslim and Christian communities.'[34]

Pope Francis, an early supporter of Abboud's interfaith work, made 'the unprecedented step of praying at the wake of the Muslim community's beloved sheikh, Adel Made'.[35] Abboud calls Francis 'the spiritual authority of the modern world'.[36] 'It's a long time since the world has had such a strong spiritual leader', he says.[37]

A culture of encounter

For Argentine Catholics there has been an evolution towards comprehension and acceptance of the fact that we live in a pluralistic society. The price of acceptance is not to resign identity or to forget or deny the significance and importance of the legacy and presence of the Catholic Church in Argentina. But it is to admit the fact that religion does not mark and determine life in society as it did in the past, that many today have lost their religious roots, and that this not only should be a matter of regret but also should be a task of assuming the challenge of finding new ways of announcing and witnessing values that enhance the dignity of human beings. Churches and the other religious families have the possibility of finding common ground to serve individual men and women, from their own traditions and identities, and in dialogue and collaboration with so many that look for God with a sincere heart, perhaps without even being conscious of this search.

One of the consequences is the evolution in the State and Church relations: first, that non-Catholic creeds are part of that relation, for general benefit, and second, but not less important, the transition to independence from mutual influence and identification in favor of respectful cooperation. There is a model of relation that has rooted in the last decades, in which the Church has become over all the voice of the voiceless, as in the teachings of the Vatican Council, the popes, and the regional bishops' conferences of Medellín (1968), Puebla (1979), and Aparecida (2007).

In today's Argentina, the religious creeds express pluralism in society, based on respect, coexistence, and cooperation. This is very important, for at the same time, in politics in

33 Gerard O'Connell, 'It's a long time since the world has had such a strong spiritual leader', *Vatican Insider News*, 23 May 2015, http://www.lastampa.it/2014/05/23/vaticaninsider/eng/world-news/its-a-long-time-since-the-world-has-had-such-a-strong-spiritual-leader-HZFVmPGKPUES3MlylIQNFN/pagina.html (accessed 26 June 2018).

34 Kohn, supra note 32.

35 Kohn.

36 Kohn.

37 O'Connell, supra note 33.

recent years, dialogue and 'social friendship' has been replaced by the 'friend–foe logic'. We can also see some expressions of 'lay intolerance' towards religion from certain political and intellectual groups.[38]

This experience of being a country that learned to live religious pluralism has been strengthened, although it may seem paradoxical, by the fact that an Argentinian has been elected Pope, and that, as we have mentioned above, he has been so strongly involved, and has been so dynamic in the promotion of dialogue and encounter. Argentine Catholics' enthusiasm for Pope Francis's election was shared by the whole religious spectrum. We say that it may seem a paradox, because far from any temptation of triumphalism, Catholics had seen in the Pope's life teaching a model of respect and openness towards those belonging to other faith communities and also to nonbelievers. It can be said that the some of the most enthusiastic reactions to the new Pope came from ministers of other creeds, in particular of the Jewish community. It has been noticed, as well, that for the first time there is someone as head of the Catholic Church who has such a deep knowledge of Judaism, not only regarding the Hebrew language or due to Biblical studies, but about life itself. In some way, the Argentine experience gains a worldwide scope.

To summarize we may say that although Argentina's society can be at times egotistic and intolerant, and confrontation appears in many ways, it is a society capable of great solidarity, in which religions play an important role very much in tandem with others not having any religious affiliation. In times of crisis, a 'revolution of solidarity' has emerged towards the less favored. This is very good example of what Pope Francis refers to as 'the culture of encounter'.[39] To promote it is a task for the Church that can be fully shared by other creeds and by all men and women of good will.

38 In September 2013 a group of students of the historical *Colegio Nacional de Buenos Aires* got into, through a tunnel and during the night, the Church of San Ignacio, the oldest church in Buenos Aires. The students' acts of vandalism included writing graffiti stating 'The church that gives light is the church in flames.' The most rapid condemnation of this barbaric felony came from the DAIA, the Jewish community organization, followed by all other creeds. At the mass, conducted by Archbishop Mario Poli, national and town authorities, the Rector of the *Colegio Nacional Buenos Aires*, representatives of the Protestant, Evangelical, Jewish, Christian Orthodox, and Muslim faiths attended. There were also, at the same time, the burning of a Methodist church in Rosario, where files of the MEDH where kept, and hostile phrases put on the walls of some Mormon centers in the provinces. All of these grievances were strongly repudiated by CALIR as well other groups and all the media. The Archbishop, together with strong concepts on the duty to respect sacred places, showed himself as open to dialogue with the offenders. The full text of the homily can be found here: http://www.arzbaires.org.ar/inicio/homiliaspoli.html (accessed 26 June 2018).

39 Pope Francis, Meeting with the Brazilian Leaders of Society, Rio do Janeiro, 27 July 2013: 'To complete this reflection, in addition to an integral humanism which respects cultural distinctiveness and fraternal responsibility, an element that I consider essential for facing the present moment is constructive dialogue. Between selfish indifference and violent protest there is always another possible option: that of dialogue. Dialogue between generations, dialogue within the people, because we are all that people, the capacity to give and receive, while remaining open to the truth. A country grows when constructive dialogue occurs between its many rich cultural components: popular culture, university culture, youth culture, artistic culture, technological culture, economic culture, family culture and media culture: when they enter into dialogue. It is impossible to imagine a future for society without a significant injection of moral energy into a democratic order that tends to remain imprisoned in pure logic or in a mere balancing of vested interests. I consider fundamental for this dialogue the contribution made by the great religious traditions, which play a fruitful role as a leaven of society and a life-giving force for democracy. Peaceful coexistence between different religions is favoured by the laicity of the state, which, without appropriating any

As in the past, when governments put education at the top of their scale of values, schools have a fundamental role to help open a respectful interreligious dialogue in order to avoid differences, even with those who have forgotten or simply are unaware of the transcendental dimension, essential to all human beings. Religious creeds have the important responsibility of teaching and transmitting peace, a characteristic that belongs to their own religious patrimony, in order that society will find in religious men and women the first and most determined builders of a more peaceful and fraternal society. In Argentina it is a tireless task; it is a 'work in progress' in which we are all engaged.

one confessional stance, respects and esteems the presence of the religious dimension in society, while fostering its more concrete expressions. When leaders in various fields ask me for advice, my response is always the same: dialogue, dialogue, dialogue. *The only way for individuals, families and societies to grow, the only way for the life of peoples to progress, is via the culture of encounter, a culture in which all have something good to give and all can receive something good in return.* Others always have something to give me, if we know how to approach them in a spirit of openness and without prejudice. This open spirit, without prejudice, I would describe as "social humility", which is what favours dialogue. Only in this way can understanding grow between cultures and religions, mutual esteem without needless preconceptions, in a climate that is respectful of the rights of everyone. Today, either we take the risk of dialogue, we risk the culture of encounter, or we all fall; this is the path that will bear fruit.' (emphasis added), available at http://www.vatican.va/holy_father/francesco/speeches/2013/july/documents/papa-francesco_20130727_gmg-classe-dirigente-rio_en.html (accessed 28 June 2018).

9 The quest for religious pluralism in post-apartheid South Africa

Mary-Anne Plaatjies-van Huffel

The place of religion in South African society

One of most important challenges facing post-apartheid South Africa is how to manage moral and religious diversity. Religion is one of the most powerful and influential forces in human society. It shapes peoples' relationships with one another, influencing families, communities, and economic and political life. People use their belief system or worldview to make choices, interpret events, and plan their actions. Religious beliefs provide a particularly strong guidance system, helping individuals identify good and bad, right and wrong.

The word 'religion' itself is a Western word, from the Latin *religare*, meaning to bind fast. It is commonly, though not always, associated with traditional majority, minority, or new religious beliefs in a transcendent deity or deities. In human rights discourse protections accorded to religion are usually extended to non-religious beliefs as well. For example, the 1993 United Nations Human Rights Committee, in General Comment 22 on Article 18 of the International Convenant on Civil and Political Rights (ICCPR), mentioned 'theistic, non-theistic and atheistic beliefs, as well as the right not to profess any religion or belief'.[1] In the language of the UN's '1981 Declaration', the right to freedom of thought, conscience and religion includes freedom for everyone 'to have a religion or whatever belief of his choice'.[2]

Freedom of belief, then, is absolute in human rights law. Expression of belief, however, is subject to limitation. It is generally agreed that such limits must be prescribed by law and be necessary to achieve a legitimate aim, such as to protect the rights of minorities.[3] This is a point of considerable importance in South Africa, and freedom of religion or belief is protected by national legal instruments as well as by the international legal instruments to which the country subscribes.

1 UN Human Rights Committee (HRC), *CCPR General Comment No. 22: Article 18 (Freedom of Thought, Conscience or Religion)*, 30 July 1993, CCPR/C/21/Rev.1/Add.4, available at http://www.refworld.org/docid/453883fb22.html.

2 UN General Assembly Resolution 36/55, Declaration on the Elimination of All Forms of Intolerance and of Discrimination Based on Religion or Belief, A/RES/36/55 (25 November 1981), available at http://www.un.org/documents/ga/res/36/a36r055.htm.

3 See Karima Bennoune, 'Secularism and Human Rights: A Contextual Analysis of Headscarves, Religious Expression, and Women's Equality Under International Law', (2007) 45 *Columbia Journal of Transnational Law*, 368, available at http://ssrn.com/abstract=989066.

South Africa is often characterized as a highly religious country. Approximately 85 percent of South Africans declare a religious affiliation, and many consider their religious beliefs to be central to their lives. According to the census of 2001, the last census in which religious affiliation was tracked, almost 80 percent of South Africa's population follows the Christian faith. The Christian majority can be further subdivided, giving rise to many religious minorities. The African Independent Churches – comprising Zion Christian Church (approximately 11 percent of the population), the Apostolic Church (approximately 10 percent), and a number of Pentecostal and charismatic groups – are the largest group, but there are also Methodists, Anglicans, Baptists, Lutherans, Presbyterians, Roman Catholics, Seventh-day Adventists, and members of the Greek Orthodox, Dutch Reformed, and Congregational Churches. Other major religious groups (present in relatively small numbers) are Hindus, Muslims, Jews, and Buddhists. A minority of South Africa's population do not belong to any of the major religions, but regard themselves as traditionalists of no specific religious affiliation.[4]

A 2008 South Africa Social Attitudes Survey (SASAS)[5] survey revealed that the vast majority of South Africans (83 percent) expressed high levels of confidence or trust in religious institutions, especially relative to politicians and political parties, the latter receiving a mere 29 percent approval.[6] It seems clear, then, that people would probably expect these institutions and affiliated leaders, as part of their role in the spiritual and moral welfare of the people, to make statements about important social and political concerns and raise their voices in related debates.

The Constitution of the Republic of South Africa no. 108 of 1996 [7] ('the Constitution') provides for freedom of religion as a fundamental right.[8] Freedom of religion includes the freedom to practice one's religion. This implies also an obligation to accommodate religions. South Africa thus upholds the right to freedom of religion and belief and the right to freedom from discrimination on the grounds of religious or other belief. There is therefore in South Africa a legal obligation to accommodate religious minorities and their religious beliefs and practices.

4 South African Government, http://www.info.gov.za/aboutsa/people.htm. See also United States Deparment of State, *International Religious Freedom Report for 2015 – South Africa*, https://www.state.gov/j/drl/rls/irf/religiousfreedom/index.htm?year=2015&dlid=256071.

5 Human Sciences Research Council, South African Social Attitudes Survey, http://www.hsrc.ac.za/en/departments/sasas.

6 Human Sciences Research Council, *Attitudes towards the Role of Religion in Politics: South African Social Attitudes Survey* 2009.

7 Available at http://www.gov.za/sites/www.gov.za/files/images/a108-96.pdf.

8 The right to freedom of religion is enshrined in the Constitution of South Africa. Chapter 2, containing the Bill of Rights, states that everyone has the right to freedom of religion, belief and opinion. Section 9, the equality clause, prohibits unfair discrimination on various grounds including religion. Section 31 protects the right of persons belonging to a religious community to practise their religion together with other members of that community and form voluntary religious associations. Sections 185 and 186 provide for a commission for the promotion and protection of the rights of cultural, religious and linguistic communities. See specific details in the notes following.

The Constitution makes accommodation for religious diversity in the Freedom of Religion provision,[9] the Equality provision,[10] and the General Limitations provision.[11]

Recognition of rights of religions in post-apartheid South Africa

A basic question in this discussion is whether religion per se has a place in the public space, and if so, how might a diversity of belief systems be accommodated? Is there in post-

9 Chapter 2, Bill of Rights. Section 15. Freedom of religion, belief and opinion. –
(1) Everyone has the right to freedom of conscience, religion, thought, belief and opinion. –
(2) Religious observances may be conducted at state or state-aided institutions, provided that –
(a) those observances follow rules made by the appropriate public authorities;
(b) they are conducted on an equitable basis; and
(c) attendance at them is free and voluntary.

(a) This section does not prevent legislation recognising–
(i) marriages concluded under any tradition, or a system of religious, personal or family law; or
(ii) systems of personal and family law under any tradition, or adhered to by persons professing a particular religion
(b) Recognition in terms of paragraph *(a)* must be consistent with this section and the other provisions of the Constitution.

10 Equality –
(l) Everyone is equal before the law and has the right to equal protection and benefit of the law.
(2) Equality includes the full and equal enjoyment of all rights and freedoms. To promote the achievement of equality, legislative and other measures designed to protect or advance persons, or categories of persons, disadvantaged by unfair discrimination may be taken.
(3) The state may not unfairly discriminate directly or indirectly against anyone on one or more grounds, including race, gender, sex, pregnancy, marital status, ethnic or social origin, colour, sexual orientation, age, disability, religion, conscience, belief, culture, language and birth.
(4) No person may unfairly discriminate directly or indirectly against anyone on one or more grounds in terms of subsection (3). National legislation must be enacted to prevent or prohibit unfair discrimination.
(5) Discrimination on one or more of the grounds listed in subsection (3) is unfair unless it is established that the discrimination is fair.
Section 31. Cultural, religious and linguistic communities.–
(l) Persons belonging to a cultural, religious or linguistic community may not be denied the right, with other members of that community –
(a) to enjoy their culture, practise their religion and use their language; and (b) to form, join and maintain cultural, religious and linguistic associations and other organs of civil society.
(2) The rights in subsection (1) may not be exercised in a manner inconsistent with any provision of the Bill of Rights.

11 Section 36. Limitation of rights. –
(1) The rights in the Bill of Rights may be limited only in terms of law of general application to the extent that the limitation is reasonable and justifiable in an open and democratic society based on human dignity, equality and freedom, taking into account all relevant factors, including–
(a) the nature of the right; (b) the importance of the purpose of the limitation; (c) the nature and extent of the limitation; (d) the relation between the limitation and its purpose; and (e) less restrictive means to achieve the purpose.
(2) Except as provided in subsection (1) or in any other provision of the Constitution, no law may limit any right entrenched in the Bill of Rights.

apartheid South Africa, as the European Commission has identified as being crucial in Europe, a 'shared ethos' that 'can produce a better understanding of the impact of plural values and religions ... and their role in relation to changes in society'?[12] Is such a shared ethos possible in a 'rainbow nation' with 11 official languages?[13]

Religion in pre-colonial southern Africa to was seen to conceptualize the divide between good and evil in society. This important notion should be taken into account in discourse on religious diversity in post-apartheid South Africa. One of most important challenges in this regard, indeed 'one of the important challenges facing contemporary society is how to manage moral and religious diversity'.[14] Should members of certain groups be treated differently from others? Should some be exempt from certain laws on the basis of their particular religious or ethical beliefs?

In apartheid South Africa (pre-1994) there was a state religion that was historically associated with the nation and occupied a prominent position in public and political life. Bible study was taught in public schools, and even the state constitution (1983) referred to a specific religion.[15] The state, then, gave official recognition to the majority religion. Such recognition often entails a series of privileges such as exemption from taxation, state subsidies, and official recognition of some religious celebrations (for example Easter and Christmas).[16] There had been a strong link between certain churches during apartheid and in the apartheid government. Members of other religions and even those who were not adherents to any religion were marginalized. African Traditional Religions (ART), for example, have been subjected to misrepresentation, underestimation, and basic stigmatization.

Minority group relations refer to the phenomena that arise when groups of people who differ racially or culturally come into contact. The term 'minority group' refers to any subgroup within a culture which is singled out for differential and unequal treatment. Members of such groups can regard themselves as objects of collective discrimination, as their status can carry with it the exclusion from full participation in the life of society.[17]

The 1996 Constitution provides for freedom of religion as a fundamental right, so that everyone has the right to his/her religion or belief, either individually or in community with

12 See Directorate-General for Research and Innovation Socio-economic Sciences and Humanities, *Pluralism and Religious Diversity, Social Cohesion and Integration in Europe: Insights from European Research* (European Commission 2011), 13, available at http://www.net4society.eu/_media/pluralism-and-religious-diversity_en.pdf.

13 South African Government / About / South Africa's People, http://www.gov.za/node/66. 'According to the 2011 Census, English is most widely used for official and commercial communication. IsiZulu is the most common home language spoken by 22,7% of the population, followed by isiXhosa at 16%, Afrikaans at 13,5%, and English at 9,6%, Sepedi at 9,1%, Setswana at 8%, Sesotho at 7,6%, and Xitsonga at 4,5%. Siswati is spoken by 2,5% of the population, Tshivenda by 2,4% and isiNdebele by 2,1%.'

14 Jocelyn Maclure and Charles Taylor, *Secularism and Freedom of Conscience* (Harvard University Press 2011), 1.

15 The drafters of the 1983 Republic of South Africa Constitution Act declared themselves to be conscious of their 'responsibility towards God and man; ... convinced of the necessity of standing united and of pursuing the following national goals: To uphold Christian values and civilized norms, with recognition and protection of freedom of faith and worship....'

16 Anna Triandafyllidou, *Addressing Cultural, Ethnic and Religious Diversity Challenges in Europe A Comparative Overview of 15 European Countries*. The Accept Pluralism Project, European University Institute Robert Schuman Centre for Advanced Studies, RSCAS Research Project Reports (Cadmus 2012), 29–30. http://cadmus.eui.eu/handle/1814/19254.

17 Hendrik W. van der Merwe, 'What is a Minority Group?' in Peter Randall, *South Africa's Minorities: The Study Project on Christianity* (Golden Era Printers & Stationers 1971), 11.

others. The religious freedom of citizens in South Africa is thus respected and safeguarded by law. This freedom includes the right to profess freely, without prejudice to his/her responsibility under the law. In the exercise of this right all people should be free from coercion, whether by individuals, by social groups, or by any human power. No one is forced to act against his conscience; no one is to be impeded, within appropriate limits, in private or in public, alone or together with others, from acting according to his/her conscience. In addition to the constitutional provisions, some legislation explicitly protects this freedom, including the anti-discrimination provisions in employment and education legislation.

The role of religion in politics up to 1994 was essentially undisputed. The Dutch Reformed Church (DRC) theologically justified apartheid, helping to present the apartheid state as Christian. Consequently, in the post-apartheid state the religious diversity of South Africa was appropriately accommodated so as to prevent religion-based conflict. One of most important challenges facing post-apartheid South Africa is how to manage this moral and religious diversity consistently, in such a complex society. Maclure and Taylor have observed that moral and religious diversity 'is a structuring and, as far as we can see permanent characteristic of democratic societies.'[18] How does the structuring work in South Africa?

The post-apartheid South African state seeks to treat all faith communities and even those who profess no religion at all equally before the law. This means in effect that all such communities should be free from discrimination on the grounds of religious or other belief, which must include '[r]uling out once and for all the view of an assumed spiritual inferiority of African peoples....'[19] Recall that Section 15(3) seeks to define how the right to freedom of religion, belief, and opinion is balanced against tradition and custom, as it 'does not prevent legislation recognizing marriages concluded under any tradition, or a system of religious, personal or family law; or systems of personal and family law under any tradition, or adhered to by persons professing a particular religion.'

Perhaps not surprisingly, even with such protections in place, religion-related and ethnic conflicts regularly occur. Incidents involving preventing learners from attending school because of their Islamic headgear are examples. The Department of Basic Education's National Guidelines on School Uniforms provides: 'If wearing a particular attire ... is part of the religious practice of pupils or an obligation, schools should not, in terms of the constitution, prohibit the wearing of such items.'[20] Schools, therefore, cannot prohibit the wearing of items such as yarmulkes or headscarves if these items are part of pupils' religious practice. All the same, some public schools have prohibited Muslims from wearing the hijab (a headscarf) or the jilbab (a dark cloak) or the fez (for boys).[21] Children are usually told to remove the headcovering, as it is not part of the school uniform. Such prohibitions are not in line with the Constitution, and are seen as a violation of human rights.

A similar conflict, though concerning racial rather than religious differences, erupted recently at Pretoria High School for Girls, a school once restricted to whites only, but now

18 Maclure and Taylor, supra note 14 at 106.

19 Daniele Mezzana, 'The End of a Stigma: African Traditional Religions and Modernity', *African Culture and Women*, 21 Feburary 2011, http://cultureafrico.blogspot.com/2011/02/end-of-stigma-african-traditional.html.

20 National Guidelines on School Uniform, 'Religious and Cultural Diversity', Section 29 (2), http://www.ecdoe.gov.za/documents/parents/docs/school-uniforms.pdf

21 See, for example, 'Fez, scarf get siblings expelled', *IOL News South Africa*, 24 January 2013, http://www.iol.co.za/news/south-africa/western-cape/fez-scarf-get-siblings-expelled-1457634.

open to all. In this instance protests began in response to 'black students, even teachers, [being] teased and humiliated, broken as they were forced to sacrifice their cultures and identities' by school policies and the behavior of other students and staff. As one example, the protesters pointed to a policy forbidding natural hair styles that were deemed 'unladylike' and to prohibition of the speaking of local African languages in school. Students had been pulled out of class and given Vaseline to flatten their hair and had been told to 'stop making noises' when they had been speaking their languages in classes where Afrikaans conversations were ongoing. In response to the protests, graduates of the school explained how criticism by staff and students of 'the way black girls speak, walk, talk, and look' were a sort of indoctrination into self-hate that produced lasting damage to their confidence in their own abilities and a hypervigilant 'mistrusting of almost any white space'.[22]

The damage done by such 'add blacks and stir'[23] models in former white schools is incalculable. Such situations shock the conscience and are unquestionable violations of the Constitution.[24]

A South African Charter of Religious Rights

Albie Sachs, who would serve as a Justice of the South African Constitutional Court from 1994 to 2009, suggested in 1990:

> Ideally in South Africa, all religious organisations and persons concerned with the study of religion would get together and draft a charter of religious rights and responsibilities ... it would be up to the participants themselves to define what they consider to be their fundamental rights.[25]

The South African Constitution is unique in its provision in Section 234 that charters of rights consistent with constitutional provisions can be adopted.[26] Accordingly, a group of legal and theological academics, along with religious leaders, statutory commissioners, and

22 Reported by Greg Nicolson, 'Pretoria Girls High: A protest against sacrificed cultures and identities', *Daily Maverick*, 30 August 2016, https://www.dailymaverick.co.za/article/2016-08-30-pretoria-girls-high-a-protest-against-sacrificed-cultures-and-identities#.WRGLJNorJaQ.

23 See Panashe Chigumadzi, 'Why I call myself a "coconut" to claim my place in post-apartheid South Africa', *The Guardian*, 24 August 2015, at https://www.theguardian.com/world/2015/aug/24/south-africa-race-panashe-chigumadzi-ruth-first-lecture.

24 Section 28. Children. – (1) Every child has the right— ...

> (f) not to be required or permitted to perform work or provide services that –
> (ii) place at risk the child's well-being, education, physical or mental health or spiritual, moral or social development; ...
> [This provision, though no doubt not intended for this particular application, arguably could be raised in this context.]

Section 30. Language and culture. – Everyone has the right to use the language and participate in the cultural life of their choice.... Section 31. Cultural, religious and linguistic communities. –

> (1) Persons belonging to a culture, religious or linguistic community may not be denied the right, with other members of that community —
> (a) to enjoy their culture, practise their religion and use their language; ...

25 Albie Sachs, *Protecting Human Rights in a New South Africa*, Contemporary South African Debates Series (Oxford University Press Cape Town 1990), 46–47.

26 Section 234: 'In order to deepen the culture of democracy established by the Constitution, Parliament may adopt Charters of Rights consistent with the provisions of the Constitution.'

international legal experts, consulting with all major religious, human rights, and media groups in South Africa, joined in drafting, over a number of years, a document intended to define the religious freedoms, rights, and responsibilities of South African citizens.[27] A first draft of the South African Charter of Religious Rights and Freedoms (SACRRF) was unveiled in February 2008. Further revisions by the Continuation Committee resulted in the draft of October 2010, which was signed by representatives from all major religions in South Africa as well as by the Commission for the Promotion and Protection of the Rights of Cultural, Religious and Linguistic Communities.[28]

SACRRF was designed to protect individuals' rights to believe and make choices according to their convictions, to change their faith, and to refuse to perform certain duties or assist in certain activities that violate those beliefs.

Not all minority groups favored these objectives. According to the Freedom from Religion South Africa action group – an association of freethinkers, atheists, sceptics, and agnostics committed to a secular state – SACRRF would undermine secularity, democracy, and freedom in South Africa. The group was concerned that instead of advancing freedom of religion SACRRF would advance majority religion and inhibit the religious freedom of those in minority religions as well as of those who are not religious. The group further asserted that SACRRF aimed to entrench religion in educational and state institutions using state powers and state funds. According to this group the SACRRF would grant rights to conduct religious observances, expression, and activities in state or state-aided institutions. This, they asserted, will be used by persons of religion to conduct public prayer or activities/ sermons in state institutions. Although such activities would be voluntary and not coerced, those of a minority religion, atheists, or freethinkers would be identified and classified by others as being of a different religion or as being unbelievers, resulting in prejudice and discrimination against these persons.

The Charter was made available in six of South Africa's official languages: English, Afrikaans, isiXhosa, isiZulu, Sepedi, and Tswana. Signatories included representatives of religious groups and organizations, human rights organizations, legal and academic entities and media bodies. After the public endorsement of the Charter, the South African Council for the Protection and Promotion of Religious Rights and Freedoms was established to oversee the process of the Charter being formally enacted into South African law by Parliament.[29] By the time of the First Annual General Meeting of the South African Council for the Protection and Promotion of Religious Rights and Freedoms in 2011, 67 religious organizations including numerous Christian denominations representing approximately 8–10 million South Africans, had signed the Charter.

Though the South African Charter of Religious Rights and Freedoms has yet to become a formal part of South African law, its text, and the process of drafting it, are of great importance. Erasmus (Rassie) Malherbe, one of the participants in the process, has noted:

27 See Rassie Malherbe, *The Background and Contents of the Proposed South African Charter of Religious Rights and Freedoms*, (2011) *BYU Law Review* (3) 613–635, available at http://digitalcommons.law.byu.edu/cgi/viewcontent.cgi?article=2600&context=lawreview.

28 See Iain T. Benson, 'South African Charter of Religious Rights and Freedoms', (2011) 4 *International Journal of Religious Freedom* (1), 125–134, available at http://researchonline.nd.edu.au/cgi/viewcontent.cgi?article=1057&context=law_article.

29 See CRRF, 16 May 2016, at http://www.crlcommission.org.za/docs/sacrrf.pdf.

> First, I believe the Charter represents a major step in the effective protection of the right to freedom of religion, and will provide a firm foundation for ensuring a healthy relationship between religion and the state. ...
> Second, the Charter can secure the tolerant spirit prevailing among religious communities in South Africa. ... The Charter will also deepen our understanding of basic values of justice, love, compassion, human dignity, democracy, rights and responsibilities, and basic good relations with others. As such, the Charter can make an invaluable contribution in determining the rightful place of religion in society, an issue with which many countries struggle from time to time.[30]

Religious pluralism and the building of a better society

South Africa – its people, its institutions, its society, its government – must repond to the societal challenges they face. It is particularly clear in South Africa that religion influences society and society influences religion. The question is whether religion can build a better society. In coming to an answer, other questions might be asked along the way: What kinds of conflicts arise in South Africa with regard to ethnic, cultural, and religious diversity? What do we understand by the concept of 'pluralism'? In what ways is 'pluralism' more than the mere existence, or even tolerance of 'diversity'?

The notion of cultural diversity may be applied to individuals or groups that have different ethnic descent from the majority group in a country (ethnic diversity), different physical traits (racial diversity), different cultural traditions, customs, and language (cultural diversity), and/or different religions (religious diversity). In sociological studies the terms 'ethnic' and 'cultural' are often used synonymously to refer to different language, customs, and traditions including codes of behavior, codes of dress, and value orientations. Similarly, it is often difficult to tell whether a given group is facing ethnic or racial prejudice. Religious diversity, by contrast, is more often clearly distinguished. Indeed, people of different ethnic backgrounds may share the same religion.[31]

Handling the politics of cultural diversity in all its aspects is therefore of utmost importance. Cultural diversity should be seen as a matter of enrichment rather than division. The questions to ask here concern what views and practices are – and are not – tolerated, accepted, and respected in South Africa. What kind of policies and practices need to be developed for South Africa to become more respectful of cultural diversity?[32]

Pluralism and tolerance are the hallmarks of a democratic society,[33] and the South African Constitution provides a firm foundation for the flourishing of such a society. In making provision for persons belonging to national minorities to maintain and develop their culture, and to preserve the essential elements of their identity, namely their religion, language, traditions and cultural heritage, the Constitution provides a strong support for communities seeking to promote a plurality of values, seeking to eliminate racism, xenophobia, anti-Semitism, and intolerance by combating discrimination and prejudice on grounds of race, color, language, religion, nationality, and national or ethnic origin.

30 Rassie Malherbe, 'The Background and Contents of the Proposed South African Charter of Religious Rights and Freedoms', (2011) *Brigham Young University Law Review* (3) 613.

31 Triandafyllidou, *Addressing Cultural, Ethnic and Religious Diversity Challenges*, supra note 16.

32 *Pluralism and Religious Diversity*, supra note 12 at 6.

33 See Willi Fuhrmann, 'Perspectives on Religious Freedom from the Vantage Point of the European Court of Human Rights', (2000) *Brigham Young University Law Review* (3), 838.

At the same time, faith communities and their members should have a right to safety and security. It is important to clarify that the relationship between tolerance and respect or recognition of difference is not necessarily a hierarchical one. Respect is not necessarily or always a better institutional or practical solution for accommodating difference. While tolerance may be appropriate for some diversity claims and may satisfy some requests of minority groups or individuals, respect and public recognition may be a better 'fit' for other types of diversity claims. This means that no religious group, or its practical conduct or customs, will be regarded to be less important or inferior to, for example, Christianity as majority religion. Because those who draft relevant codes may be unaware that they are merely codifying assumptions, prejudices, or beliefs that they themselves are steeped in, they often seem incapable of accepting this fact.

A 2013 Supreme Court of Appeal judgment confirmed that the dismissal of several Correctional Services officers for failing to adhere to the Department of Correctional Services Dress Code, namely to cut their dreadlocks, was unlawful. This judgement illustrates that seemingly neutral codes of conduct often discriminate against individuals or groups who do not belong to the dominant economic, religious, or cultural group in a society or in an organization.[34]

Successful bridging of diversity has a great deal to do with clear, shared definitions. How one defines 'religion' shapes one's explanation of the role of belief systems in society, and influences how one thinks about religious diversity. One way to understand one's own definition of religion is to determine whether it excludes either 'Supreme Being' religion or other kinds of belief systems. A Pagan critique of the South African Charter of Religious Rights and Freedoms is that it will only enhance dominant religions in post-apartheid South Africa. How can this critique be answered?

Another essential consideration is an understanding of the meaning and value of 'secularism'. Even defining this term is not a clear-cut matter. Members of the South African Pagan Council[35] expressed concern that SACRRF would be used to enforce religious discrimination in society by, for example, providing the unlimited right to refuse service to South African citizens on the grounds of religious conscience, and would result in state-subsidized religious education in an avowedly secular state. At the same time, the concept of 'secular' was misunderstood by many others as referring to a godless or even immoral state. Traditional definitions and prescriptions of the 'secular' are increasingly being questioned as religion re-emerges as an important element of the public sphere in various nation-states. Secular nation-states with official policies of freedom of religion are increasingly challenged to redefine assumptions about the public role of religion.[36]

South Africa is not an exception as regards the definition and redefinition of the role of religion in the public sphere. In the pre-1994 dispensation there was nominal freedom of

34 See *Department of Correctional Services & another v. POPCRU & others* (107/12) [2013] ZASCA 40 (28 March 2013).

35 See South African Pagan Council: Unity through Diversity, at http://www.sapagancouncil.org.za/.

36 For a useful distinction between 'secularism' ['an ideological position that is committed to promoting a secular order' (e.g. France)] and 'secularity' ['an approach to religion-state relations that avoids identification of the state with any particular religion or ideology (including secularism itself)' (e.g. United States)], see discussion in Chapter 1; see also W. Cole Durham, Jr. and Brett G. Scharffs, *Law and Religion: National, International, and Comparative Perspectives* (Wolters Kluwer, 2nd edn, forthcoming 2019), chapter 4; and Brett G. Scharffs, 'Four Views of the Citadel: The Consequential Distinction between Secularity and Secularism', (2011) 16 *Religion and Human Rights* 109–126.

religion in South Africa, but South Africa claimed to be a specifically *Christian* state, in which a specific version of Protestant Christianity informed apartheid policies and legislation. Christian National Education (CNE) furthermore deliberately endorsed and promoted this version of Protestant Christianity and excluded other Christian denominations, other religions, and African traditional religion from curricula. The new South African Constitution guarantees not only religious freedom, practice, and expression but also freedom from coercion. The question of how religion can bridge diversity will therefore also have to attend to the question of how to address religion in the context of school curricula.

The National Policy on Religion and Education (2003) actively promotes the role of religion in education and teaching about religion, but also embraces teaching about secular worldviews. Different groups in post-apartheid South Africa have contested and are still contesting the Policy. These groups have used concepts like 'secular' and 'secularization' interchangeably to mean 'anti-religion' and even atheism.[37] However, after constitutional experts had emphasized that a secular state by necessity implies religious freedom and religious tolerance, the popular dissatisfaction lessened, because no one wants to be known in the public domain as being intolerant to other religions or worldviews. Still, it is significant that the term 'secular state' was eventually not included in the 1996 Constitution, which may be explained by the highly religious nature of South African society and the perceived need to respect that.

A closely related issue raised in drafting the Constitution was whether the preamble should refer to God and if so in what way. Since a preamble gives an important indication about a constitution's fundamental values, this did cause some debate, but eventually a compromise was reached by taking the views of all the negotiating parties into account to some extent, and by ending the preamble with: 'May God protect our people.' It was thus considered acceptable for the Constitution not to be a religiously neutral document.[38]

The best way to describe the government of South Africa is to say that it is a constitutional democracy. Secularism in South Africa's context should therefore be understood under a broad framework of diversity of beliefs and values that the citizens of South Africa embrace. A secular state is at a basic level a state with no state religion and in which the state is officially neutral in matters of religion, neither supporting nor opposing any particular religious beliefs or practices. Strictly speaking, South Africa cannot be seen as this sort of a 'secular' state. It is important to be clear that a secular state is properly distinct from an atheistic state (North Korea, China, the former Soviet Union), in which the state officially opposes all religious beliefs and practices. In some nominally 'secular' states there is a majority religion among the population (for example Turkey); in others there may be great religious diversity (India). States that may be called 'semi-secular' are those with no particular or official state religion but with a dominant religion that to a great extent influenced the development of or underpins society and law.[39] Pakistan is sometimes identified as a semi-secular state, though this is a matter of considerable debate.[40]

37 Paul Prinsloo, 'The South African Policy on Religion and Education (2003): A Contradiction in a Secular State and Age?', (2009) Alter*nation Journal*, Special Edition 3, 31–54, http://alternation.ukzn.ac.za/pages/volume-16-2009/special-edition-no-3-2009.aspx.

38 See Kristin Henrard, 'The Accommodation of Religious Diversity in South Africa', (2011) 45 *Journal of African Law* 1, 51–72.

39 Anél du Plessis, 'The Fulfillment of Human Rights Related to Religion: Some Current Challenges in South Africa.' This paper is an elaborated version of an essay written for a workshop of the Irmgard-Coninx-Stiftung (ICS) on 'Secular and Religious Sources of Human Rights' in Berlin, May 2006.

40 See, for example, Shamil Shams, 'An Islamic or Secular Pakistan?', *Deustche Welle*, 26 December 2013, http://www.dw.com/en/an-islamic-or-secular-pakistan/a-17325395.

'Secularism' is typically used to describe the philosophy underlying a political and legal system whose function is to establish a certain distance between the state and religion and to guarantee the religious neutrality of the state. It also has to do with the appropriate distinction between the public sphere and the private sphere, and between public and religious institutions. Two aims of such secularism today are 'respect for the moral equality of individuals and the protection of freedom of conscience and of religion'.[41]

How can religion bridge diversity?

Perhaps in our journey to bridge religious diversity to create the conditions of true religious pluralism we should revisit, once again, basic concepts such as tolerance, recognition, acceptance, respect, equality, accommodation, integration, assimilation, and multiculturalism, terms which may be used interchangeably but which have important differing meanings and implications. We will look at the interplay of these terms in the following discussion.

On the most basic level, the acceptance of ethnic, cultural, and religious diversity in society is of utmost importance. For a long time in South Africa tolerance meant recognition, but not acceptance, and in fact meant either an exclusion or marginalization of certain religions or worldviews. An absolute secularism confines religion to the private realm, separate from public institutions and politics (for instance there can be no religious political parties, no state support for religious organizations, and religion is kept out of public schools). As we have noted, among European Union states only France comes near to an absolute secularism model. The secularism model of South Africa moderates the concept, including measures such as the funding of religious schools, adopting the official holidays of the majority religion (Christianity), and generally accommodating the majority religious calendar within the school programme. Such a moderate secularism upholds the division between political and religious institutions but recognizes religion as an aspect of public and political life. It sees organized religion as a potential public good or national resource, not just a private matter, and provides a degree of recognition and support for minority religions.

The 1996 South African Constitution echos the provisions of Article 18 of the *Universal Declaration on Human Rights of 1948*:

> Everyone has the right to freedom of thought, conscience and religion; this right includes freedom to change his religion or belief, and freedom, either alone or in community with others and in public or private, to manifest his religion or belief in teaching, practice, worship and observance.[42]

We can speak of the Constitution as protecting a multicultural citizenship, in the sense that there is 'a set of rights and duties that takes into account the cultural, ethnic, and religious diversity of the groups that make part of a state and integrates their needs appropriately into an existing set of rights and duties that follow their citizenship'.[43] While both pluralists and multiculturalists appreciate the connection between religion and identity, multiculturalists

41 See Maclure and Taylor, supra note 14 at 4.

42 United Nations, *Universal Declaration of Human Rights*, GA Resolution 217A, 10 December 1948. See discussion in Jim Murdoch, *Freedom of Thought, Conscience, and Religion: A Guide to the Implementation of Article 9 of the European Convention on Human Rights*, Human Rights Handbooks, No. 9 (Directorate General of Human Rights and Legal Affairs Council of Europe 2007).

43 Triandafyllidou, *Addressing Cultural, Ethnic and Religious Diversity Challenges*, supra note 16 at 26.

would tend to view majority manifestations of religion with distrust, perhaps viewing them as symbols of dominance rather than as group expressions of identity.

This particular strand of argument presses the question of whether accommodationism can indeed promote pluralism. 'Accommodation' refers to an approach to the Religion Clauses that values individual religious practice, the autonomy of religious groups, and the presence of religion in public life. A democratic state like South Africa should be neutral or impartial in its relations with different faiths. It should treat all citizen equally notwithstanding their world-views or religious beliefs. Religious communities, groups, and associations play important roles in South Africa.[44] The state and religions act independently and autonomously.

The core principles of a liberal democratic state – 'human dignity, basic human rights, and popular sovereignty'[45] – are the constitutive values of South African democracy. These values help people from diverse religions defend the diverse principles that comprise fundamental rights and freedoms. The state should therefore not only adopt a position of neutrality towards religions but should also be sovereign in its jurisdiction. Public institutions should also be neutral: meaning the state and the institutions that embody it should not be identified with a particular religion or with religion in general.[46] In principle the public institutions serve the common good. Public schools and universities, for example, are institutions belonging to the state and as such ought not to be identified with a particular religion. Such identification would hamper bridging diversity.[47] Likewise, the wearing of religious symbols by state officials executing their tasks in the public sphere can have a negative impact on religious diversity, even lead to religious conflict. As individuals, as citizens, all have the right display religious affiliations both in the private sphere and in the public sphere.[48] State officials, however, agree to embody or personify the state's neutrality toward religions. State officials should therefore demonstrate impartiality in the exercise of their duty.

The limitations of religious-based rights came to the fore in *Prince v. President of the Law Society, Cape of Good Hope*. In this case the court confirmed that the right to religious freedom has two legs, namely the right to have religious beliefs and the right to practice those beliefs.[49] *Prince* was a Rastafarian who possessed and used cannabis as part of his religion. Section 4 (b) of the *Drugs and Drug Trafficking Act* 140 of 1992 prohibited the use and possession of cannabis. The applicant argued that his possession and use of cannabis was constitutionally protected in terms of the freedom of religion clause and that the particular case was therefore unconstitutional (paras 979–980). The court referred to foreign case law and came to the conclusion that section 4(b) limited the applicant's freedom to practice his religion. The purpose of section 4 is to protect public safety, order, health, morals, and the fundamental rights and freedoms of others, which outweighs the right of Rastafarians to practice their religion; as a result the limitation is justifiable in terms of the limitations clause.[50]

44 See extensive discussion of religious communities, groups, and associations in Richard W. Garnett, 'Religious Freedom and (and in) Institutions', in Gerard V. Bradley, ed., *Challenges to Religious Liberty in the Twenty-First Century* (Cambridge University Press 2012), 71–89.

45 Maclure and Taylor, supra note 14 at 11.

46 Maclure and Taylor at 43.

47 Maclure and Taylor at 38.

48 Maclure and Taylor at 40.

49 *Prince v. President of the Law Society of the Cape of Good Hope and Others* (CCT36/00) [2000] ZACC 28; 2001 (2) SA 388; 2001 (2) BCLR 133 (12 December 2000).

50 *President of the Law Society, Cape of Good Hope* 1998 8 BCLR 976 (C). See the discussion of Christa Rautenbach in *The Constitution of the Republic of South Africa, 1996: An Introduction for Members of the Executive 2nd; Prince v President of the Law Society of the Cape of Good Hope and*

Freedom of religion implies efforts to heal the divisions of the past; to establish a non-racial and non-sexist society based on democratic values, to promote equality between the religions; to promote respect for, and the protection of, the rights of cultural, religious, and linguistic communities; and to promote unity in diversity.[51] Mutual respect among cultural, religious, and linguistic communities must be fostered. Education is a most important area where action can be taken to foster tolerant and respectful behaviors towards diversity.

The concept of tolerance is not new in the political theory literature. In its basic form, tolerance means to refrain from objecting to something with which one does not agree. It involves rejecting a belief or a behavior, believing this objection to this behavior or idea is legitimate, and disposing of the means to combat or suppress it and still deciding to tolerate this negative behavior and even its possible consequences.

We should note, however, that tolerance is meaningful when the 'tolerator' has the power to suspend an act but does not exert this power or voluntarily suspends it. Tolerance or toleration describe contexts and practices where practices or attitudes, though disapproved of, are allowed to exist.

The term 'tolerance' is often used interchangeably with 'assimilation'. Beyond meaning to tolerate someone or some practice, tolerance may also be thought of as a prohibition of discrimination.[52] Assimilation on the other hand is a social process by which the someone from outside a group completely adapts to the traditions, culture, religion, and mores of that group, perhaps a host nation or a dominant religion, and eventually becomes part of it, gradually abandoning their own ethnicity, culture, religion, and traditions. Assimilation is indeed a one-way process that may involve people's efforts to adapt and fuse themselves into a country and its dominant culture. Assimilation in this sense must be distinguished from integration,[53] and we should be careful not to confuse assimilation with religious diversity.

In the exercise of their rights, individuals as well as communities are obliged by moral law to take into account the rights of others, with their own duties toward others and the common good of all. The South African Constitution protects an individual's core belief system and the right to manifest such beliefs either individually or with others, and both in private as well as in the public sphere.[54] Multiculturalism by contrast dictates that different communities should not be forced to integrate but should rather be allowed to maintain their own cultures and identities and live in 'parallel societies' within a single state. The question is how to deal with individual and collective ethnic, cultural, and religious diversity.[55] As religion is in general an important part of people's identity in South Africa, it entails a need for an appropriate governmental attitude towards religious diversity.

Civil society in addition has the right to protect itself from abuse under pretense of religious freedom. However, this protection should not be undertaken arbitrarily or in a manner that unduly

Others (CCT36/00) [2000] ZACC 28; 2001 (2) SA 388; 2001 (2) BCLR 133 (12 December 2000).

51 Act No. 19, 2002, Commission for the Promotion and Protection of the Rights of Cultural, Religious and Linguistic Communities Act, available at http://www.crlcommission.org.za/docs/crl-act.pdf.

52 Triandafyllidou, *Addressing Cultural, Ethnic and Religious Diversity Challenges*, supra note 16 at 28.

53 Triandafyllidou at 28.

54 Murdoch, supra note 42.

55 Triandafyllidou, *Addressing Cultural, Ethnic and Religious Diversity Challenges*, supra note 16 at 28. See also Anna Triandafyllidou, *Tolerance, Pluralism and Social Cohesion: The Accept Pluralism Tolerance Indicators Toolkit* (The European University Institute Robert Schuman Centre for Advanced Studies 2013).

favors a certain group, and it must be done according to legal standards that are consistent with the objective moral order. In our bridging religious diversity we should take note of the potential power of identity and influence of religious groups. At this point in time the only rival to the state as an institution able to coordinate the actions of large numbers of people is organized religion.[56]

Within South Africa these 'organized religions' are increasingly challenged by religious diversity. But a commitment to religious pluralism, an active bridging of diversity, implies that we ought to seek out people who are different from us and work to understand them, learn from them, and respect them in their differences. Religious pluralism is thus a challenge that can potentially enrich both religion and society. According to John Rex, just as religion plays a part in the creation of ethnicity, so it may play a part in the development of the mediation process. The real problem today is conflict resolution between people of diverse religion backgrounds, of achieving peace with justice between adherents from different faith communities.[57] Dialogue between adherents of diverse religions is essential to transform mistrust and reconcile the complex divisions within our society.[58]

Freedom of thought, conscience, and belief is indeed a vital human right, viewed primarily as an individual right often exercised in association with others. A proper appreciation of the underlying principles and ideals in different religions and worldviews is critical if we want to embark upon a true religious pluralism: in particular, freedom of thought, conscience and religion must be seen as helping to maintain religious diversity. Furthermore, 'the autonomous existence of religious communities is indispensable for pluralism in a democratic society. In other words, the protection of individual belief must promote rather than discourage mutual respect for and tolerance of others' beliefs.'[59]

Thus the duties that fall upon the South African State are to ensure that all adhere to our constitution. Government and faith communities have a responsibility to build and maintain positive relationships with each other, and to promote mutual respect and understanding.[60] Reasonable steps should be taken in educational and work environments and in the delivery of public services to recognize and accommodate diverse religious beliefs and practices. Schools should teach an understanding of different religious and spiritual traditions in a manner that reflects the diversity of their national and local community.

In short, religious communities should develop the ethical and political knowledge that will allow them to engage in a fair and consistent manner with the moral and spiritual diversity in the country. The state should treat with equal respect the core beliefs of all religious people in South Africa. We should take it for a given that moral and religious diversity is a structuring of democratic societies. Even though we have sometimes irreconcilable representations of the world and value systems, we must learn to cooperate and to resolve our divergences. We should develop an ethic of concern to each other. We must learn to co-exist and to establish bonds of solidarity with each other. We should opt for an ethics of dialogue, which will be helpful in bridging religious diversity.

56 Michael Banton, *Ethnic and Racial Consciousness* (Longman, 2nd edn, 1997), 159.
57 John Rex, *Ethnic Minorities in the Modern Nation State: Working Papers in the Theory of Multiculturalism and Political Integration* (Palgrave Macmillan UK 1996), 214.
58 Richard Norris Armitage, *Issues of Religious Diversity Affecting Visible Minority Ethnic Police Personnel in the Workplace,* a thesis submitted to The University of Birmingham for the degree of PhD (2006), 8.
59 Murdoch, supra note 42.
60 Paul Morris, *Religious Diversity in the New Zealand Workplace Questions & Concerns* (Human Rights Commission of New Zealand 2011), https://www.hrc.co.nz/files/6014/2388/1002/HRC_Religious-DiversityV6.pdf.

10 National Human Rights Institutions and the accommodation of religious diversity in Africa

Enyinna S. Nwauche

National Human Rights Institutions in Africa

Africa is made up of 53 states that reflect three colonial legal heritages – English, French, and Portuguese. Given this history, discussions about accommodation of religious diversity across the continent are complex. Recommendations can only be suggestions, and tentative, but we may make a beginning by considering National Human Rights Institutions (NHRI).

National Human Rights Institutions (NHRI) are constitutional and statutory bodies established by African States for the protection and promotion of human rights generally through non-judicial strategies such as the receipt and handling of complaints, advocacy, public awareness, and research.[1] The common goal of NHRI is adherence and commitment to the Principles Relating to the Status of National Institutions (Paris Principles).[2] Two types of institutions are contemplated by this definition. The first are broad-based human rights institutions established by African States. Examples include the South African Human Rights Commission, the Nigerian Human Rights Commission, the Ugandan Human Rights Commission, and the Commission on Human Rights and Administrative Justice. Another type of NHRI are national institutions whose mandate is specific to religious issues such as Nigeria's Advisory Committee on Religious Affairs and South Africa's Commission for the Protection of Cultural Linguistic and Religious Communities.

1 These institutions exist in Algeria (The National Human Rights Commission of Algeria); Angola (Provedor di Justicia de Direitos); Benin (The Benin Human Rights Commission); Burkina Faso (The National Human Rights Commission of Burkina Faso); Cameroon (The National Commission on Human Rights and Freedoms); Chad (The Chad National Human Rights Commission); Democratic Republic of Congo (The National Human Rights Observatory); Egypt (The National Council on Human Rights); Ethiopia (The Ethiopia Human Rights Commission); Gabon (The National Human Rights Commission); Ghana (The Commission on Human Rights and Administrative Justice); Kenya (The Kenya National Human Rights Commission); Madagascar (The National Human Rights Commission); Malawi (The Malawi Human Rights Commission); Mali (Commission nationale consultative des droits de l'homme); Mauritania (Commissariat aux droits de l'homme, a la Lutte contre la Pauvrete et l'insertion); Mauritius (The National Human Rights Commission); Morocco (The Human Rights Advisory Council); Namibia (The Office of the Ombudsman); Niger (The National Commission on Human Rights and Fundamental Freedoms); Nigeria (The National Human Rights Commission); Rwanda (The National Commission of Human Rights); Senegal (The Senegalese Committee for Human Rights); South Africa (South African Human Rights Commission); Tanzania (The Commission for Rights and Good Governance); Togo (The National Human Rights Commission); Tunisia (The Higher Committee on Human Rights and Fundamental Freedoms); Uganda (The Ugandan Human Rights Committee); and Zambia (The Permanent Human Rights Commission).

2 UNGA Res 134 (1993) GAOR 48th Session UN Doc A/RES/48/134 (Paris Principles).

Human Rights Commissions: South Africa, Ghana, and Nigeria

Three human rights commissions – the South African Human Rights Commission (SAHRC), the National Human Rights Commission (NHRC) of Nigeria, and Ghana's Commission on Human Rights and Administrative Justice (CHRAJ) – illustrate the protection of religious rights by human rights commissions established by African States. It should be added that human rights institutions include the Office of Ombudsman, whose mandate is directed towards administrative justice.[3] It is often imagined, albeit wrongly, that administrative justice and anti-corruption are outside the purview of human rights. Recent constitutional design has seen the inclusion of the right to administrative justice in Bills of Rights, a notable example of which is South Africa, which protects the right to administrative justice in Section 33 of its 1996 Constitution.

The South African Human Rights Commission (SAHRC)

The SAHRC is a Chapter 9 institution[4] supporting democracy.[5] The SAHRC is endowed with the functions prescribed by Section 184(1) of the Constitution: '(a) promote respect for human rights and a culture of human rights, (b) promote the protection, development and attainment of human rights; and (c) monitor and assess the observance of human rights in the Republic.' An interesting manifestation of the monitoring power of the SAHRC was recognized in *Government of South Africa v. Grootboom* [6] where the Constitutional Court mandated the SAHRC to oversee the implementation of aspects of its judgment.

The broad powers of the Commission are set out in Section 184(2) of the Constitution and include the power to '(a) investigate and to report on the observance of human rights; (b) to take steps to secure appropriate redress where human rights have been violated; (c) to carry out research and (d) to educate.' The SAHRC Act has further elaborated the powers of the Commission. These powers include the power to maintain close liaison with institutions bodies or authorities similar to the Commission in order to foster common policies and practices;[7] the power to carry out and publish studies on fundamental human rights as may be referred to it by the President;[8] and the power to bring proceedings in a competent court or tribunal in its own name, or on behalf of a person or a group of class of persons.[9] A related power in the protection of human rights is in respect of constitutional interpretation. Professor Klarren believes that the recognition by the South African Constitutional Court in *S v. Jordan* [10] of the persuasive role of the Commission for Gender Equality in constitutional

3 See John Hatchard 'The Institution of the Ombudsman in Africa with a Special Reference to Zimbabwe', (1986) 35 *International and Comparative Law Quarterly*, 360; 'The Ombudsman in Africa Revisited', (1991) 40 *International and Comparative Law Quarterly*, 938.

4 Chapter 9 of the Constitution of the Republic of South Africa 1996 lists seven institutions that support constitutional democracy to include the SAHRC. Other institutions are the Public Protector; the Commission for the Promotion and Protection of Cultural Religious and Linguistic Communities; the Commission for Gender Equality; the Auditor General; the Electoral Commission; and the Independent Authority to Regulate Broadcasting.

5 Established in 1995 pursuant to the South African Human Rights Act (Act No. 54 of 1994). Hereafter the SAHRC Act, available http://www.justice.gov.za/legislation/acts/2013-040.pdf (accessed 28 March 2017).

6 2001 (1) SA 46 (CC).

7 Sec. 7(1)b of the SAHRC Act.

8 Sec. 7(1)d of the SAHRC Act.

9 Sec. 7(1)e of the SAHRC Act.

10 *S v. Jordan*, 2002 (6) SA 642 (CC).

interpretation should ordinarily extend to the SAHRC, since both institutions are Chapter 9 institutions.[11] The Commission can engage in mediation conciliation or negotiation to discharge its functions.[12] Section 9(1) of the SAHRC empowers it to conduct investigations in order to enable it to exercise its powers and perform its duties and functions.[13]

There is little evidence that in the work of the SAHRC the protection of religious rights has occupied pride of place. An observer[14] of the SAHRC notes that in the first ten years the Commission has been involved in combating racism and promoting economic and social rights.[15] Available evidence of its second decade indicates the same. In its first decade, however, a report of the SAHRC documents some involvement in the protection of religious rights.[16] What follows hereafter is a review of the reported cases of such intervention. In the *Matter Involving Rastafarian Learners* (2000), Grayden Peterson, a seven-year-old Rastafarian boy, was refused admittance to four schools because of his parents' religion. After much endeavour by the SAHRC, including writing a letter to the National Minister of Education asking for his intervention, Grayden attended the school of his parents' choice, Arcadia Primary School.

The Commission has also reported that in another case, a Rastafarian mother lodged a complaint with the SAHRC that she was unable to enroll her son in a school because he had dreadlocks. The SAHRC made recommendations that he cover his head while attending school, but the school was not willing to accept this. The SAHRC wrote to the school concerned, the MEC for Education and the Honourable Minister of Education. In a prompt response, the Minister advised that he has directed the MEC to attend to the matter urgently and to ensure that the learner was admitted to the school immediately.

In the *Goudini Spa Investigation* (2000) the Commission found that persons who were refused entry to a spa on the grounds that they were not Christians was not unfair discrimination because the position of the operators that they admitted only Christians was fair discrimination since they acted in accordance with Section 31 of the Constitution in furtherance of their right to promote their religious community.

In another matter, *In re: Constitutionality of the Practice of Mogaga* (1999), Mrs Tumane, a widow living in a rural area administered by tribal authority, was required to perform

11 See Jonathan Klarren 'South African Human Rights Commission', in Stu Woolman and Michael Bishop, eds, *Constitutional Law of South Africa* (RS 5 2013), Chapter 24C-9.

12 Sec. 8 of the SAHRC Act. The SAHRC has been involved in a number of litigations. A representative sample includes *S v. Twala (South African Human Rights Commission Intervening)* 2000 (1) SA 879 (CC); *National Coalition for Gay and Lesbian Equality & Another v. Minister of Justice* 1999 (1) SA 6; *Bhe v. Magistrate Khayelitsha; Shibi v. Sithole & Others; South African Human Rights Commission v. President of the Republic of South Africa* 2005 (1) SA 580 (CC).

13 A number of reports have been issued after investigations, including a report on its investigation into racism in the media. See Daryl Glaser 'The Media Inquiry Reports of the South African Human Rights Commission: A Critique' 99 (2000) *African Affairs* 373.

14 See Jonathan Klarren, supra note 11, 24C-8.

15 Indeed Section 184(3) of the 1996 Constitution mandates the SAHRC to request organs of state to provide the Commission with information on the measures they have taken towards the realization of the rights in the Bill of Rights concerning housing, health care, food, water, social security, education, and the environment.

16 Some of these cases are examined in Chris Peter Maina 'Human Rights Commissions in Africa: Lessons and Challenges', in Anton Bosl and Joseph Diescho, eds, *Human Rights in Africa: Legal Perspectives on their Protection and Promotion* (KAS Windhoek 2009), 351. Information on the work of the Commission with respect to the right to freedom of belief, conscience, and religion is available at http://www.sahrc.org.za/index.php/component/search/?searchword=Religion&searchphrase=all&Itemid=780 (accessed 28 March 2017).

certain traditional practices as a result of the death of her husband. These practices were against her religion. When she refused to follow the custom, she was placed under house arrest. Two commissioners travelled to Moruleng village in June 1998 to investigate Mrs Tumane's complaint and to attempt to mediate a solution to this impasse. The Commission determined that the conduct of the traditional leader violated the widow's right to freedom of movement, of religion, belief, conscience, and of association. However, negotiations failed. Recognizing the need to balance the tribe's right to enjoy their culture with Mrs Tumane's rights, and its mandate to protect human rights as defined in the Constitution, the Human Rights Commission, was obliged to take further action. When Kgosi Pulane reneged on his agreement to allow Mrs Tumane to leave her house without any negative repercussions, the Commission decided to take the matter to court.

Commission on Human Rights and Administrative Justice (CHRAJ) of Ghana

The CHRAJ[17] is a constitutional body created by Article 218 of the 1992 Ghanaian Constitution as an independent institution which is mandated to protect human rights. Under the Act the human rights mandate[18] of the CHRAJ includes investigation of complaints of violations of fundamental human rights and freedoms, injustice, corruption, abuse of power, and unfair treatment of any person by a public officer in the exercise of his official powers; and the investigation of complaints concerning practices and actions by persons, private enterprises, and other institutions where those complaints allege violations of fundamental rights and freedoms. To be able to discharge its functions the Act confers far-reaching powers of investigation on the CHRAJ. These powers include the power to issue subpoenas requiring any person to appear before the Commission to produce any document or record relevant to any matter under investigation by the Commission; to cause any person contemptuous of such subpoena to be prosecuted before any court of law; to question any person in respect of any subject matter under investigation before the Commission.[19] To resolve complaints brought before it the CHRAJ has the powers to apply before a court of law to enforce its judgment. It can seek any remedy it deems sufficient to resolve any human rights violation.[20]

Available statistics reveal that even though the CHRAJ is involved in the protection of the right to freedom of religion, such activity represents a relatively small percentage of its overall work, especially in terms of the complaints by Ghanaians of breach of human rights. For example of the more than 65,000 human rights complaints received by the CHRAJ between 2006 and 2010 only seven were listed as violations of the rights to freedom of worship.[21] If the complaints listed as witchcraft accusations are considered as part of Traditional African Religion, the number of complaints about breach of religious rights still

17 Established by the Commission on Human Rights and Administrative Justice Act 1993 (hereinafter CHRAJ). See Emmanuel Kofi Quashigah 'The Ghana Commission on Human Rights and Administrative Justice', in Birgit Lindsnaes, Lone Lindholt, and Kristine Yigen, eds, *National Human Rights Institutions: Articles and Working Papers* (Danish Centre for Human Rights 2000). 201.

18 The CHRAJ is also mandated to be an Anti-Corruption Agency and an Ombudsman.

19 See Section 219 of the 1992 Ghana Constitution.

20 See Section 229 ibid.

21 See The Commission on Human Rights & Administrative Justice (CHRAJ), Seventeenth Annual Report, 2010, available at www.chrajghana.com/wp-content/uploads/2012/08/Annual_Report_2010.pdf, 61 (accessed 28 March 2017).

remains low. The evidence of the nature of complaints of restrictions on the freedom of worship is predominantly about CHRAJ intervention in respect of certain practices of traditional African religions.[22] The CHRAJ has extensively sought to contain the practice of *trokosi*, [23] whereby women and children are sent to shrines of traditional African religions as a punishment for alleged transgressions by their family. In this regard the CHRAJ 'has succeeded in securing the release of some women and children from fetish shrines. In 1996, for example Commissioner Short took part in several liberation ceremonies in which some 400 *trokosis* were freed.'[24] A related human rights protection activity of the CHRAJ reported in the 2010 Annual Report is the monitoring of refugee camps of persons accused of witchcraft.[25]

National Human Rights Commission (NHRC) of Nigeria

The NHRC of Nigeria[26] is statutorily empowered[27] to:

a deal with all matters relating to the protection of human rights as guaranteed by the Constitution of the Federal Republic of Nigeria 1999, the African Charter on Human and Peoples' Rights, the United Nations Charter, and the Universal Declaration on Human Rights and other International Treaties on human rights to which Nigeria is a signatory;

b monitor and investigate all alleged cases of human rights violation in Nigeria and make appropriate recommendation to the President for the prosecution and such other actions as it may deem expedient in each circumstance;

c assist victims of human rights violation and seek appropriate redress and remedies on their behalf;

d undertake studies on all matters pertaining to human rights and assist the Federal Government in the formulation of appropriate policies on the guarantee of human rights;

e publish, from time to time, reports on the state of human rights protection in Nigeria;

f organise local and international seminars, workshops, and conferences on human rights issues for public enlightenment;

g liaise and co-operate with local and international organizations on human rights with the purpose of advancing the promotion and protection of human rights;

h participate in all international activities relating to the promotion and protection of human rights;

i maintain a library, collect data and disseminate information and materials on human rights generally; and

22 The CHRAJ has *suo motu* intervened in protecting the rights of sick children whose parents refuse medical intervention on religious grounds. See International Council on Human Rights Policy, *Performance and Legitimacy: National Human Rights Institutions* (2004), 15, available at http://www.ichrp.org/files/reports/17/102_report_en.pdf (accessed 28 March 2017).

23 Iheanyi Enwerem, *A Dangerous Awakening: The Politicisation of Religion in Modern Nigeria* (Institut français de recherche en Afrique 1995).

24 Enwerem at 16.

25 CHRAJ Report, supra note 21 at 124.

26 Established by the National Human Rights Commission Act Cap N46 Laws of the Federation 2004.

27 NHRC Act Section 5.

j carry out all such other functions as are necessary or expedient for the performance of its functions under this Act.[28]

There is not much evidence of the work of the NHRC in the protection of religious rights. The statutory reports available at its website[29] do not document any involvement in the protection of religious rights, even though this seems unlikely in a country of religious intensity.

Religious human rights organizations in Africa

Two of what can be described as 'religious human rights organizations' established by African States to specifically protect religious rights are the South African Commission for the Protection of Cultural Religious and Linguistic Communities (CRL Commission) and the Nigerian Advisory Committee on Religious Affairs.

South African Commission for the Protection of Cultural Religious and Linguistic Communities

The South African Commission for the Protection of Cultural Religious and Linguistic Communities (CRL Commission) is a Chapter 9 institution established like the SAHRC to support democracy. Section 185 of the FC provides that the objects of Commission are

> (a) to promote respect for the rights of cultural, religious and linguistic communities;
> (b) to promote and develop peace, friendship, humanity, tolerance and national unity among cultural, religious and linguistic communities, on the basis of equality, non-discrimination and free association; and
> (c) to recommend the establishment or recognition, in accordance with national legislation, of a cultural or other council or councils for a community or communities in South Africa.

The CRL Commission was established by the Commission for the Promotion and Protection of the Rights of Cultural Religious Communities Act 2002. The functions of the Commission are as follows:

1. Conduct information and education programmes to promote public understanding of the objects, role and activities of the Commission;
2. Conduct programmes to promote respect for and further the protection of the rights of cultural, religious and linguistic communities;
3. Assist in the development of strategies that facilitate the full and active participation of cultural, religious and linguistic communities in nation-building in South Africa;
4. Promote awareness among the youth of South Africa of the diversity of cultural, religious and linguistic communities and their rights;
5. Monitor, investigate and research any issue concerning the rights of cultural, religious and linguistic communities;

28 NHRC Act Section 5.
29 National Human Rights Commission, www.nigeriarights.gov.ng/resources (accessed 28 March 2017).

6 Educate, lobby, advise and report on any issue concerning the rights of cultural, religious and linguistic communities;
7 Facilitate the resolution of friction between and within cultural, religious and linguistic communities or between any such community and an organ of state where the cultural, religious or linguistic rights of a community are affected;
8 Receive and deal with requests related to the rights of cultural, religious and linguistic communities;
9 Make recommendations to the appropriate organ of state regarding legislation that impacts, or may impact, on the rights of cultural, religious and linguistic communities;
10 Establish and maintain databases of cultural, religious and linguistic community organizations and institutions and experts on these communities; and
11 Bring any relevant matter to the attention of the appropriate authority or organ of state, and, where appropriate, make recommendations to such authority or organ of state in dealing with such a matter.

In addition, the Commission may report any matter which falls within its powers and function to the South African Human Rights Commission for investigation. This possibility means that the SAHRC can initiate litigation on behalf of the CRL Commission. Learned commentators suggest that the Commission can act as *amicus curiae* in matters within its competence[30] giving it a credible opportunity to enforce its mandate. However, the absence of the power to litigate in furtherance of its mandate has been described as putting the CRL Commission in the place of 'a consciousness raiser rather than as an agent of change'.[31]

The CRL Commission has adopted a comprehensive procedure for complaints and resolution.[32] The preamble to the CRL Manual recounts that the Commission 'has to ensure equality of cultural, religious and linguistic rights between and among diverse communities, as well as to resolve conflict between and among communities and organs of state or private institutions'. This objective is to be facilitated by individuals as well as religious communities complaining to the Commission that their rights have been threatened or that they are denied the right to practice their religion as well denied the right to freely form, join, and maintain religious associations. On the receipt of the complaint the Commission screens the complaint to determine whether it falls within its mandate. The complaint is forwarded to the alleged perpetrator, who has seven days to respond, and the response is then forwarded to the complainant. If the alleged perpetrator fails to respond after repeated reminders, the Commission will invoke its powers under Section 7(2) of the CRL Commission Act to give evidence and/or produce appropriate documents. The ICR manual points out that failure to honor a summons is a ground for prosecution and conviction under Section 41 of the CRL Commission Act. If the Commission decides that the rights of the individual are violated, it may decide to investigate and mediate between the parties with a view to resolution of the conflict and reconciliation of the parties. If no settlement is reached between the parties, the Commission may refer the matter to other institutions or institute a complaint at the Equality Courts.

30 See Stuart Woolman and Julie Soweto-Aullo 'Commission for the Promotion and Protection of the Rights of Cultural Religious and Linguistic Communities', in Stuart Woolman, Michael Bishop, and Jason Brickhill, eds, *Constitutional Law of South Africa* (Juta, 2nd edn, OS 02–05), 24F-15.
31 Woolman and Soweto-Aullo at 24F-15.
32 *ICR: Complaints Handling Manual* (hereinafter CRL Manual). The CRL Manual is available at http://www.crlcommission.org.za/complaints.html (accessed 28 March 2017).

Available evidence of the work of the CRL Commission is contained in two reports of its work launched in April 2013. In *Public Holidays vs Religious/Cultural Holydays: In Pursuit of Equality Among Religious and Cultural Groups* [33] the CRL Commission dealt with a number of complaints of discrimination by members of the public on account of the Public Holidays Act 36 of 1994, which prescribes and entrenches Christmas and Good Friday, based on their Christian character as religious holy days, to the exclusion of significant religious days of other religious groups such as Jews, Muslims, members of African Traditional Religion, and Hindus. The complainants argued further that followers of other faiths have to sacrifice their annual leave days from work whenever they have to observe their significant religious days. Furthermore, examinations are scheduled on their religious holy days by schools and institutions of higher learning. The CRL Commission decided to investigate the matter by engaging in public consultative hearings. After extensive public consultations the Commission handed out a reasoned opinion[34] that tracks the existing jurisprudence on the equality of religions and the protection of the right to freedom of religion in South Africa by an extensive discussion of the Constitutional Court decisions in *S v. Lawrence, S v. Nagel,* and *S v. Solberg*. The Commission concentrated on *S v. Solberg,* [35] which involved a woman, Mrs Solberg who was accused of selling wine on a Sunday. Mrs Solberg argued that the prohibition of liquor sales on such closed days was to compel observance of the Christian Sabbath and Christian holidays, which is inconsistent with the freedom of religion of those who do not share such a belief. The Report drew attention to the judgment of O'Regan in *S v. Solberg* to the effect that the requirement of equity demands that the State act even handedly in relation to different religions.

The Commission also examined another Constitutional Court case, *National Union of Metal Workers of South Africa v. Bader Bop (Pty) Ltd,* [36] to reach the conclusion that the rights of minority religions to equality with respect to unfair discrimination solely on grounds of religion are 'classified as non-derogable rights under Chapter 2 of the Bill of Rights in the Constitution'.[37] The Commission found that there is mischief in the Public Holidays Act because it endorses Christianity and excludes other religions. It also found that the Basic Conditions of Employment Act (BCEA) does not regulate leave for religious holidays.[38] Accordingly, the Commission recommended *inter alia* amending the Public Holidays Act to add religious holidays of African Traditional Religion, Hinduism, Judaism, Islam, Bahá'í, Rastafarianism, and Buddhism and that each of these religions should be allotted only one day. To create space for these new religious holidays the Commission recommended that a number of 'secular' holidays should be dropped. Other important holidays of religious groups should be brought to the attention of the public. Furthermore, the Commission directed that the Department of Labour must consider amending the BCEA to accommodate workers by allowing workers to take annual paid leave for religious holydays that are not a public holiday. To the Department of Basic Education, the Commission recommended the development of plans and policies that will ensure that examination timetables do not clash with religious holidays in accordance with the recommendation of the Commission.

33 Hereinafter *Public Holidays Report*, available at http://www.crlcommission.org.za/docs/public-holidays-report.pdf (accessed 28 March 2017).
34 *Public Holidays Report* at 23.
35 *S v. Solberg*, 1997 (4) SA 1176.
36 *National Union of Metal Workers of South Africa v. Bader Bop (Pty) Ltd*, 2003 (3) SA 513 (CC).
37 *S v. Solberg* at 28.
38 *S v. Solberg* at 33.

Another report of the CRL Commission was *The Laws and Practices in the Workplace and Institutions of Learning vs Cultural and Religious Rights of Communities (Dress Code, and Challenges of Traditional Healers)*, [39] in which the Commission made recommendations after seminars it convened to deal with complaints concerning employees at certain workplaces who were not granted leave to train as traditional healers, and learners/pupils at certain schools who were ordered to remove their cultural or religious symbols, such as wrist strings, Isiphandla (animal wrist bands), nose studs, beads, forehead dots, and dreadlocks.[40] The seminars were organized to 'propose amendments to legislation, national policy internal policies, rules and circulars in order to address the discriminatory conduct which undermines peoples' rights to equality human dignity freedom of religion belief and opinion, freedom of expression and freedom to practice their cultures and religions'.[41]

The recommendations of the Commission with respect to dress codes at workplaces and schools are based on *MEC for Education: Kwazulu Natal v. Pillay*, [42] which the Report correctly identifies as requiring institutions like schools to reasonably accommodate the religious beliefs and practices of learners, employees, and members. On the question of leave application and medical certificates of traditional healers, the Report discusses *Kievits Kroon Country Estate Ltd v. Johanna Mmoledi*, [43] where the Court upheld the right of a worker to go on unpaid leave to become a traditional healer. Based on these two decisions and other comparative jurisprudence the Report adopts the principle of reasonable accommodation to recommend that any policy on dress code by organs of state in South Africa must incorporate reasonable accommodation for religious and cultural purposes. Furthermore, the Report recommends that the BCEA must be amended to provide leave to those who have to undergo training for religious or cultural purposes.

The Nigerian Advisory Council of Religious Affairs (ACRA)

The Nigerian ACRA was established in the aftermath of the considerable opposition to Nigeria's joining of the Organisation of Islamic States (OIC) [since 2011 known as the Organisation of Islamic Cooperation].[44] The ACRA is enabled by the Advisory Council of Religious Affairs Act,[45] and its functions are:

a promoting and inculcating moral values in the Nigerian society;
b serving as an avenue for articulating cordial relationship amongst the various religious groups and between them and the Federal Government;

39 *The Laws and Practices in the Workplace and Institutions of Learning vs Cultural and Religious Rights of Communities (Dress Code, and Challenges of Traditional Healers)* (hereinafter *Dress Code Report*).

40 *Dress Code Report* at 3.

41 *Dress Code Report* at 4.

42 *MEC for Education: Kwazulu Natal v. Pillay*, 2008 SA 474. The Report adopts the definition of reasonable accommodation in Paragraph 73 of the judgment: 'At its core is the notion that sometimes the community, whether the State, an employer or a school must take positive measures and possibly incur additional hardships or expense in order to allow al people to participate and enjoy all rights equally. It ensures that we do not relegate people to the margins of the society because they do not or cannot conform to certain social norms.' The Report also referred to *POPCRU v. Department of Correctional Services* (2011) 32 ILJ 2629.

43 *Kievits Kroon Country Estate Ltd v. Johanna Mmoledi*, 2012 ZALAC 22.

44 See Matthew Hassan Kukah, *Religion Power Politics in Northern Nigeria* (Spectrum Books Ibadan 1993), 233.

45 Chapter A8 Laws of the Federation 2004.

c assisting the Federal and State Governments of Nigeria and the populace by stressing and accentuating the position and roles religion should play in national development;
d serving as a forum for harnessing religion to serve national goals towards economic recovery, consolidation of national unity, and the promotion of political cohesion and stability;
e considering and making recommendations to the Federal Government on matters that may assist in fostering the spiritual development of Nigeria in a manner acceptable to all religious groups;
f making recommendations on such other matters as the Federal Government may from time to time refer to the Council.

The membership of the Council is restricted to Muslims and Christians, who are represented by 12 members each.[46] If the functions of the Council are broadly interpreted, it may well be argued that they are likely to protect religious rights if it can be established that they can receive and investigate individual and community complaints of breach of religious rights. This is plausible given the fact that the Council is mandated to make recommendations that could arguably arise from investigations of complaints. In this regard, one can imagine a synergy between the ACRA and the National Human Rights Commission to protect religious rights.

Anecdotal evidence of the work of the ACRA suggests that it is more of an interactive forum[47] that enables Nigeria's majority religions to dialogue to prevent and contain religious conflicts. Given extensive Christian and Muslim conflicts in the Northern part of Nigeria,[48] it is difficult to contend one way or another on the impact of the ACRA, because of a lack of information of the work of the Council. While the recurrence of inter- and intra-religious conflicts could suggest the ineffectiveness of the ACRA, it is also plausible to argue that such an interactive forum may have assisted in maintaining the peace. That said, the fact that there are only Christians and Muslims in the ACRA casts serious doubt as to its capacity to protect other faiths, especially adherents of Traditional African Religions. Again, the body is stated to be autonomous, even though its secretariat is statutorily located at the seat of the Federal Government of Nigeria, suggesting official influence in its work.

A framework for the protection of religious rights by National Human Rights Institutions

While the potential of NHRIs in protecting human rights in general and religious rights in particular is not in doubt, it is difficult to argue from that point that NHRIs in fact do protect religious rights by facilitating the accommodation of religious diversity, given the fact that there is need for extensive fact-finding studies of the impact of NHRIs in resolving religious conflicts and accommodating religious diversity in African States. In a wider context it can be said that it is in a handful of African countries – South Africa being the best – that we have a fairly comprehensive understanding of the interaction of law,

46 See Section 2(1) of the Act.
47 One commentator describes ACRA as an ecumenical body. See Iheanyi M. Enwerem, 'An Assessment of Government's Formal Response to Ethnic/Religious Riots, 1980–1990', in Ernest Uwazie, Isaac Olawale Albert, and Godfrey Uzoigw, eds, *Inter Ethnic and Religious Conflict Resolution in Nigeria* (Lexington Books 999), 121.
48 An idea of the widespread nature of these conflicts appears in Enwerem, supra note 23, who asserts that between the 1980s and 1990s there were 22 communal riots over religious conflicts.

religion, and human rights in the accommodation of religious diversity and the protection of religious minorities. The work of the CRL Commission should be understood in this light.

The first issue to dwell on is whether religious human rights organizations have a comparative advantage over human rights organizations in the protection of religious rights and the accommodation of religious diversity. To begin with, it is plausible to wonder why there is need for religious human rights institutions when human rights institutions exist with a mandate covers religious human rights. Allied to this fact is the proliferation of specific human rights institutions, which would further weaken NHRIs that are not performing optimally. It will be better, it can be argued, for NHRIs to be better equipped to ensure that they are better able to respond to the protection of all human rights. Even if in principle this is a feasible option, it is not a complete negation of the idea of a specific organization dedicated to protecting religious rights.

In reality, the limited resources of NHRIs will force them to prioritize their work amongst the broad spectrum of human rights as, the SAHRC, the CHRAJ, and the NHRC appear to have done. Available evidence suggests that the protection of religious rights and the accommodation of religious diversity is not a top priority for these NHRIs. The more extensive powers of human rights organizations could be of importance in protecting religious rights, given the example of the SAHRC and the CHRAJ, which have extensive investigative and prosecutorial powers. All that these NHRIs should do, it can be argued, is to prioritize the protection of religious rights. Accordingly, with an extensive resource base a human rights organization should be able to protect religious rights and facilitate the accommodation of religious diversity just as a religious human rights organization would. For example, if it is well resourced, there is no reason that the NHRC should not be able to protect religious rights in Nigeria and facilitate the accommodation of religious diversity. On the other hand, the mandate and work of the CRL Commission supports the thesis that religious human rights organizations are better suited to protect religious rights. In this regard the relative ineffectiveness of Nigeria's ACRA is essentially a design outcome, and if structured like the CRL Commission it could do more in this regard. In all, it would therefore appear that the form that an NHRI takes is not really significant, if by design and with human and material resources at its disposal the NHRI actively undertakes the promotion of religious rights.

The next issue to examine is a deeper understanding of the contribution of an NHRI in the protection of religious rights and the accommodation of religious diversity. But what can an NHRI actually do that courts are unable to do in the protection of religious rights? After all, the nature of rights and correlative duties appear best suited for judicial enforcement since precedents guide the conduct of litigants, ordinary citizens, administrators, and policy makers. However, an effective judiciary depends on crucial factors of affordability, accessibility, and quick disposition of cases. These three features cannot be said to characterize much of African judiciaries. Widespread poverty, corruption, illiteracy, and infrastructural and structural problems in many African states result in inefficient judiciaries that are distant from ordinary people. Lengthy, expensive, and drawn-out cases have a chilling effect on ordinary citizens who want to turn to the judiciary for the protection of their rights. NHRIs are attractive because they appear to be fast, simple, cheap, and informal. They also take a long-term view of their mandate by engaging in public education and enlightenment. It is therefore reasonable to be enthusiastic about the existence of numerous NHRIs in Africa, since they should be able to protect religious rights. However, even with the limited evidence at our disposal, it is clear that nothing much has been done in this regard with the exception of the CRL Commission, whose work invites reflections on the intellectual framework of a religious NHRI.

A key question to ask is whether an NHRI should be guided by the jurisprudence of national judiciaries or whether it should approach its work on an ad hoc basis, reacting as it were to the peculiarities of complaints. In this regard it is important to wonder whether an NHRI should be guided by the principle of reasonable accommodation, which is considered a crucial outcome of the combined reading of the right to freedom of thought, belief, and religion, and non-discrimination on the grounds of religion. Since the idea of positive obligations, which is at the heart of reasonable accommodation, requires equal respect for all religions more than toleration of 'other' religions, it can be forcefully argued that if a legal system has not reached this fundamental understanding of how to treat religion in public life, the judicial and non-judicial protection of religious rights will be less than forthright. When a national judiciary is not committed to the equality of religions, it is nearly impossible for an NHRI to be effective, since the work of the latter can be successfully challenged in the former.

This point comes out clearly in the work of the CRL Commission. In the review of the reports of the Commission, it is clear that the jurisprudence of the South African Constitutional Court has been central in the articulation of the intellectual foundations of the Commission's intervention in the form of recommendations. Because of lack of evidence, we cannot make the same determination for the NHRC and the CHRAJ, even though there appears enough jurisprudence to argue that to some extent the Nigerian and Ghanaian judiciaries believe in the equality of religions and the concept of reasonable accommodation. Considerable doubt remains with respect to the treatment of other religions in Nigeria because of the question of a state religion. Thus, even though Nigeria expressly states in its constitution that the state cannot declare a state religion and that she is a secular state[49] the question of a state religion refuses to go away because Nigeria is a *de facto* Christian and Islamic State. In addition to other religions, the two dominant religions in Nigeria are not treated equally in parts of Nigeria that are outside their broad spheres of influence – Christians in Northern Nigeria and Muslims in Southern Nigeria. To imagine that the NHRC would be involved in protecting religious rights and seeking reasonable accommodation without a clear articulated jurisprudence of equality would be misleading.

The use of dialogue as a means of articulating recommendations by the CRL Commission is to be welcomed, as it serves as an informal means of consensus building and public enlightenment. There are a number of procedural issues, however, that require further examination. The first issue is the generalization of the resolution of complaints into recommendations targeted at laws, policies, and plans without a direct response to individual complaints. It is plausible that such recommendations requiring administrative and legislative changes leave individual complainants without a direct response. Even if the use of recommendations appears a non-intrusive way of dealing with religious disputes, the concept of reasonable accommodation as correctly affirmed by the Commission cannot be a complete substitute for remedies directed at private and public institutions. While it is agreed that some of the issues investigated by the CRL Commission, such as the question of religious holidays, require legislative reform, there are other issues, such as annual paid leave for religious holidays and the dress code at school and workplace, which could have been dealt with by remedies – directed at the institutions in question – based on the existing jurisprudence of the Constitutional Court. One advantage of such direct response is that it would enable the CRL Commission to devise remedies that respond to peculiarities of each complaint.

49 See Section 10 of the 1999 Constitution of the Federal Republic of Nigeria.

In a continent ravaged by religious and religion-inspired conflicts, flickers of containment in the form of NHRIs are exciting. The quick, efficient, and relatively informal means of intervention by NHRIs can have far-reaching effects, especially if they are mediatory or conciliatory. If NHRIs are proactive in early detection of religious conflicts, it is obvious that they would become an indispensable mechanism for peace and harmony in many African states. It is important that NHRIs are well resourced to be able to discharge their mandate. International support for NHRIs is crucial in this regard. Regional cooperation as well as the sharing of best practices would assist.

The work of the CRL Commission is to be commended because of its intervention in protecting religious rights. The equal respect for all religions is a path that should be followed by all national judiciaries and NHRIs. Unfortunately, this will not materialize until many African countries recognize that they are *de facto* Christian and Islamic countries and address the positive obligations that arise thereby to respect rather than tolerate the 'other' religions.

11 The status of religious organizations in Poland

Equal rights and differentiation

Piotr Stanisz

Religion rights under the Polish Constitution

The Polish Constitution of 2 April 1997 is one of rather few constitutions which – next to the principle of equality of all persons before the law – *expressis verbis* includes the principle of equal rights of all religious organizations. According to Article 25 para. 1, 'Churches and other religious organizations shall have equal rights.'[1]

Similar wordings can obviously be found also in some other constitutions. In the Constitutions of the Russian Federation,[2] of the Republic of Macedonia,[3] and of the Republic of Croatia[4] it is provided that religious communities (or religious associations) shall be equal before the law. The Constitution of the Italian Republic, for its part, includes the principle of equal freedom of all religious confessions before the law.[5] In the Constitution of the Republic of Slovenia one can even find a provision referring exactly to equal rights of religious communities.[6] It ought to be emphasized, however, that despite the presence of the principle of equal rights of religious organizations (communities) in the constitutions of both Poland and Slovenia, each of these states has developed a different system of church–state relations. With reference to the three basic models (state church model, cooperation system, separation system), Slovenia should rather be considered as a state which exists 'at the separatist end of the spectrum', while Poland has adopted the cooperation model.[7] In its

1 *Dziennik Ustaw* (Polish Official Journal, hereinafter Dz. U.) 1997, no. 78, item 483, with subsequent amendments.

2 According to Article 14 para. 2 of the Constitution of the Russian Federation of 1993, 'religious associations shall be separated from the State and shall be equal before the law.' See Lev Simkin, 'Church and State in Russia', in Silvio Ferrari and W. Cole Durham, Jr., eds, *Law and Religion in Post-Communist Europe* (Peeters 2003), 264–268.

3 In Article 19 of the Constitution of the Republic of Macedonia it is stated that 'the Macedonian Orthodox Church and other religious communities and groups are [...] equal before the law.' See Stefan Kostovski, 'Church and State in Macedonia', in Ferrari and Durham supra note 2 at 203–206.

4 Article 41 of the Constitution of the Republic of Croatia of 1990 provides that 'all religious communities shall be equal before the law [...].' See Ivan Padjen, 'Church and State in Croatia', in Ferrari and Durham, supra note 2 at 62–64.

5 According to Article 8 of the Constitution of the Italian Republic of 1947, 'all religious confessions are equally free before the law.' See Silvio Ferrari, 'State and Church in Italy', in'Gerhard Robbers, ed., *State and Church in the European Union* (Nomos 2005), 211–215.

6 Article 7 of the Constitution of the Republic of Slovenia of 1991 states that 'religious communities shall enjoy equal rights.' See Lovro Šturm, 'Church and State in Slovenia', in Ferrari and Durham, supra note 2 at 329–335.

7 See Norman Doe, *Law and Religion in Europe. A Comparative Introduction* (Oxford University Press 2011), 28–39.

constitutional legislation Poland has decided to promote cooperation and agreements between the state and religious organizations (art. 25).[8]

The co-existence of the above-mentioned rules (especially of equal rights and agreements) gives rise to a number of issues.[9] Of particular importance is the question whether the principle of equal rights can actually be fully realized under these circumstances and whether it is put into practice to a full extent. In view of the clear indication that the relations between the Republic of Poland and the Catholic Church shall be determined primarily by an international treaty concluded with the Holy See (art 25 para 4 of the constitution), it is true that the form of regulating the legal situation of non-Catholic religious organizations which is provided in Article 25, paragraph 5 of the constitution (stating that 'the relations between the Republic of Poland and other churches and religious organizations shall be determined by statutes adopted pursuant to agreements concluded between their appropriate representatives and the Council of Ministers') can be perceived as an 'instrument of the realization of the principle of equal rights'.[10] However, it cannot be denied that defining the basis of the legal status of individual religious organizations in separate normative acts whose content has been agreed upon by the representatives of the interested parties assumes the adoption of distinct and hence not uniform regulations concerning individual religious organizations.[11]

Origin of Article 23 paragraph 1 of the Constitution of the Republic of Poland

In the first place, some attention should be devoted to the circumstances under which the current Constitution of the Republic of Poland was adopted and how it came to include the principle of equal rights of religious organizations. The constitution marks a kind of culmination of the process of political transformation undertaken as a result of social protest and the fiasco of the system based on Marxist-Leninist ideology and patterns applied in the Soviet Union, imposed on Poland after World War II as a consequence of the decision of the victorious superpowers. The process of political transformation and the ensuing democratization began in 1989. With reference to changes in law on religion, most important were aspirations to guarantee real religious freedom and to ensure religious organizations due freedom to act within a democratic state ruled by law. Special importance was accorded to defining the legal situation of the Catholic Church, whose members comprised about 90 percent of society. Over the previous decades it had been subjected to various kinds of repressions as one of the most significant centers of resistance to the introduced order. When the process of democratization of Polish law on religion was undertaken in 1989, the majority agreed that there were several goals to be realized at

8 See Piotr Stanisz, 'Relations between the State and Religious Organizations in Contemporary Poland from a Legal Perspective', in Wilhelm Rees, María Roca and Balázs Schanda, eds, *Neuere Entwicklungen im Religionsrecht europäischer Staaten* (Duncker & Humblot 2013), 693–694.

9 A special relation between the principle of equal rights and the principle of bilateral agreements is noticed, among others, by Marcin Olszówka, *Ustawy wyznaniowe. Art. 25 ust. 5 Konstytucji RP – próba interpretacji* (Wydawnictwa Uniwersytetu Warszawskiego 2010), 27–36.

10 Paweł Leszczyński, *Regulacja stosunków między państwem a nierzymskokatolickimi Kościołami i innymi związkami wyznaniowymi określona w art. 25 ust. 5 Konstytucji RP*: (Wydawnictwo Naukowe Państwowej Wyższej Szkoły Zawodowej 2012), 295.

11 Dariusz Walencik, *Zakres przedmiotowy umowy z art. 25 ust. 5 Konstytucji RP*, in Piotr Stanisz and Marta Ordon, eds, *Układowe formy regulacji stosunków między państwem a związkami wyznaniowymi (art. 25 ust. 4–5 Konstytucji RP)* (Wydawnictwo KUL 2013), 273.

the same time. On the one hand, it was commonly believed that the solutions used at the time of the so-called People's Poland (1945–1989) should be discarded, and the Catholic Church should be given a broad freedom of action and a legal position which would correspond to its social significance. On the other hand, however, the demands for the restoration of the state church model were rather rare. In addition, there was general agreement that new solutions should not infringe the rights of non-Catholic religious organizations.[12]

It needs to be stressed that in the independent Poland in the interwar period (1918–1939) there had already been solutions which – at least to some extent – were geared towards equal rights for religious organizations. The 1921 Constitution, although it guaranteed the Roman Catholic Church the chief position in the state, still expressed (although some commentators not without reason perceived it as contradictory[13]) the idea that all denominations had equal rights.[14]

The principle of equal rights of religious organizations, no matter how their legal situation is regulated, was already included in the Act of 17 May 1989 on the Guarantees of Freedom of Conscience and Religion.[15] It was one of the three acts concerning law on religion that were adopted on that day. Their adoption was rightly considered a breakthrough in Polish law on religion. The principle of equal rights was included in the act on the initiative of minority religious groups. Their proposals gained acceptance from the government and were not objected to by the Catholic Church. At the same time, however, the Act on the Relations between the State and the Catholic Church was adopted. It was a reference to the method of regulating the legal situation of individual religious organizations by means of separate normative acts that had already been used in Poland in the past. Moreover, on 28 July 1993, the Concordat between the Republic of Poland and the Holy See was signed. Although it had to wait nearly five years for ratification (that is until 23 February 1998[16]), its conclusion increased the anxiety of non-Catholic religious organizations about the legal supremacy of the Catholic Church. In order to reduce this anxiety, eleven acts defining the legal situation of individual non-Catholic religious organizations were adopted over the next decade.[17]

The demand for equal rights of religious organizations was clearly raised by minority religious groups also during the work on a democratic constitution, which was undertaken in the 1990s. Although most of the drafts of the constitution omitted the principle in question, it soon became one of the norms which did not raise major doubts in the course of work. The principle of equal rights of churches and other religious organizations was for

12 See Michał Pietrzak, *Demokratyczne, świeckie państwo prawne* (Liber 1999), 161–173.

13 See Janusz Osuchowski, *Prawo wyznaniowe Rzeczypospolitej Polskiej 1918–1939 (węzłowe zagadnienia)* (Książka i Wiedza 1967), 333.

14 Dz. U. 1921, no. 44, item 267, with subsequent amendments.

15 Dz. U. 2005, no. 231, item 1965, with subsequent amendments.

16 Dz. U. 1998, no. 51, item 318.

17 See Paweł Borecki, 'Zasada równouprawnienia wyznań w prawie polskim' *Studia z Prawa Wyznaniowego* 2007, vol. 10, 123–128; Henryk Misztal, 'Ustawy majowe – o gwarancjach wolności sumienia i wyznania oraz o stosunku Państwa do Kościoła Katolickiego w Polsce – z perspektywy 20 lat' in Przemysław Czarnek, Dariusz Dudek, and Piotr Stanisz (eds), *Podstawy regulacji stosunków Państwo – Kościół w Rzeczypospolitej Polskiej i Republice Włoskiej* (Wydawnictwo KUL 2010), 88–93; Józef Krukowski, 'Rewizja systemu relacji między Państwem i Kościołem w Polsce' (1993) 11 *Kościół i Prawo*, 79–97; Michał Pietrzak, 'Stosunki między Państwem i Kościołem w świetle ustaw wyznaniowych z 17 maja 1989 r.' (1991) 1 *Państwo i Prawo*, 3–15.

example included in the proposal of regulations which was jointly put forward in 1995 by representatives of various religious communities, including the Catholic Church.[18]

In the final version of Article 25 of the Constitution of 1997 the principle of equal rights of churches and other religious organizations was emphasized, as it was included in the first paragraph. Interpreting it in the context of the work conducted on the provision, one may state that its introduction – as intended by its promoters – primarily aimed at dismissing the idea of a state church model. Moreover, the following principles were expressed in Article 25: (1) of impartiality of public authorities in matters of personal conviction, whether religious or philosophical, or in relation to outlooks on life, (2) of autonomy of religious organizations and mutual independence of religious organizations and the state in their own spheres, (3) of cooperation of these subjects for the individual and the common good, (4) of regulation of the relations between the state and churches and other religious organizations by means of bilateral agreements. It was only once that the legislation clearly referred to a specific religious organization (that is, the Catholic Church), allowing for the possibility of concluding an agreement with the Holy See in paragraph 4. In the subsequent paragraph, other religious organizations were referred to, and the provision stated that their relations with the state also were to be regulated by acts adopted on the basis of agreements concluded by the Council of Ministers with their proper representatives.[19]

Subjective scope of the principle of equal rights

Article 25, paragraph 1 of the Polish Constitution refers to religious organizations (in Polish *związki wyznaniowe*). The fact that 'churches' are distinguished (as seen in the expression 'churches and other religious organizations') is only of symbolic significance, its justification being rooted in Polish traditions and contemporary religious composition of Polish society.[20]

The notion of 'religious organization' is explained in Article 2 part 1 of the Act on the Guarantees of Freedom of Conscience and Religion, as applying to 'religious communities

18 See Paweł Borecki, *Geneza modelu stosunków Państwo – Kościół w Konstytucji RP*, (Wydawnictwo Sejmowe 2008), 122–381; Paweł Sobczyk, 'Udział przedstawiciela Episkopatu Polski w pracach Komisji Konstytucyjnej Zgromadzenia Narodowego nad artykułem 25 Konstytucji Rzeczypospolitej Polskiej z dnia 2 kwietnia 1997 r.' in Antoni Dębiński, Krzysztof Orzeszyna and Mirosław Sitarz, eds, *Ecclesia et Status. Księga Jubileuszowa z okazji 40-lecia pracy naukowej Profesora Józefa Krukowskiego* (Wydawnictwo KUL 2004), 859–887.

19 See Józef Krukowski, 'Konstytucyjny model stosunków między Państwem a Kościołem w III Rzeczypospolitej' in Artur Mezglewski (ed.), *Prawo wyznaniowe w systemie prawa polskiego. Materiały I Ogólnopolskiego Sympozjum Prawa Wyznaniowego (Kazimierz Dolny, 14–16 stycznia 2003)* (Wydawnictwo KUL 2004), 79–101; Michał Pietrzak, 'Stosunki Państwo – Kościół w nowej Konstytucji' (1997) 11–12 *Państwo i Prawo*, 173–184; Piotr Stanisz, 'The Principles of the Relationship between Church and State in the Constitution of the Republic of Poland of 2nd April 1997' *Soter* 2007, vol. 22(50), 129–137.

20 See Kamila Doktór-Bindas, 'Zasada równouprawnienia kościołów i związków wyznaniowych' in Czarnek, Dudek, and Stanisz, supra note 17 at 182–183. Ryszard M. Małajny, criticizing the way in which the principle in question is expressed, maintains that the wording of Article 25 para. 1 of the Constitution 'may suggest certain hierarchization' in that it divides the subjects at issue into 'better ones (churches) and worse ones (other religious organizations)'. See Ryszard M. Małajny, 'Regulacja kwestii konfesyjnych w Konstytucji III RP (refleksje krytyczne)' in R. Tokarczyk and K. Motyka (eds), *Ze sztandarem prawa przez świat. Księga dedykowana Profesorowi Wieńczysławowi Józefowi Wagnerowi von Igelgrund z okazji 85-lecia urodzin* (Zakamycze 2002), 289.

[...] set up in order to profess and spread religious faith, having their own organization, doctrine and cultic rituals'.[21]

Polish law provides for three methods of regulating the legal status of religious organizations. The first pertains exclusively to the Catholic Church, whose relations with the state are regulated by an international agreement concluded with the Holy See and by acts (especially the Act of 17 May 1989, mentioned above). The second method consists in adopting a separate act regulating relations between the state and a certain religious organization.[22] The third and most basic form of regulating the legal situation of religious organizations is the entry in the register maintained by the relevant minister for the affairs of religious denominations (who is at present the Minister of Interior and Administration), which is done upon the request of the interested parties and after conducting registration proceedings.[23]

Without going into details about the registration proceedings and the issues concerning the conditions of the entry into the register,[24] we should however address two points. First, it should be emphasized that the number of registered religious organizations is relatively large in Poland, as it exceeds 160.[25] Second, in the course of some registration proceedings there has already appeared controversy, also known from other states, about what counts and what does not count as a religion. It is legitimately assumed that a group that does not have a religious character cannot be registered as a religious organization. Consequently, such groups as the Polish Raëlian Movement and the Church of the Flying Spaghetti Monster were refused entry in the register of religious organizations.

The doctrine of the former group was based on Claude Vorilhon's views expressed in his book entitled *Raël. The message given to me by extra-terrestrials. They took me to their planet.* The Supreme Administrative Court, investigating the complaint brought by the representatives of the Movement about the negative decision of the minister, stated that the doctrine of the Movement does not correspond to the familiar patterns of religion and rather bears the hallmarks of a program of a political party or – possibly – an association. It was noted in the judgment the aim of the Movement was to influence the policy of the state and the way power is exercised. The doctrine of the organization

21 See Tadeusz J. Zieliński, 'Pojęcie religii, wyznania, związku wyznaniowego i kościoła w Konstytucji Rzeczypospolitej Polskiej', (2007) 1 *Prawo i Religia*, 46–48.

22 This is how the legal situation of the following religious organizations was regulated: the Polish Autocephalous Orthodox Church (1991), the Evangelical Church of the Augsburg Confession (1994), the Evangelical Reformed Church (1994), the Polish Catholic Church (1995), the Seventh-day Adventist Church (1995), the Baptist Church (1995), the Evangelical Methodist Church (1995), the Old Catholic Mariavite Church (1997), the Pentecostal Church (1997), the Catholic Mariavite Church (1997), and the Union of Jewish Communities (1997). Moreover, the prewar acts are still in force, which determine the legal status of the Muslim Religious Community (1936), the Karaite Religious Community (1936), and the Eastern Old Believers' Church (1928).

23 On the forms of regulating the legal situation of religious organizations in Poland see Józef Krukowski, *Kościół i państwo. Podstawy relacji prawnych* (Redakcja Wydawnictw KUL 2000) 287–291.

24 See Monika Piszcz-Czapla, 'Rejestr kościołów i związków wyznaniowych", in Krzysztof Krasowski, Małgorzata Materniak-Pawłowska and Maksymilian Stanulewicz (eds), *Prawo państwowe a prawo wewnętrzne związków wyznaniowych. Pamiętnik VII Zjazdu Katedr i Wykładowców Prawa Wyznaniowego. Gniezno 11–12 IX 2010* (Ars boni et aequi 2010), 151–166; Michał Rynkowski, 'State and Church in Poland', in Robbers, supra note 5 at 428–429.

25 As of 9 December 2015, the register contains 161 religious organizations and 5 inter-church organizations. See: https://msw.gov.pl/pl/wyznania-i-mniejszosci/relacje-panstwa-z-kosci/13964,Relacje-panstwa-z-Kosciolami-przydatne-informacje-dokumenty-i-akty-prawne.html

does not include any references to the sacred, which should be required in the case of religious doctrines.[26]

In order to take a decision in the latter of the aforementioned cases, the registering authority requested an opinion of specialists in religious studies. The experts stated that the Church of the Flying Spaghetti Monster should be counted among joke religions, and its doctrine 'definitely shows the signs of a parody of already-existing doctrines'. Pursuant to this opinion, in 2012 the minister refused to include this group in the register of churches and other religious organizations.[27] The Voivodeship Administrative Court in Warsaw, analyzing the case, pointed out that the minister committed procedural mistakes (instead of taking the decision of refusal to include the Movement in the register he should rather have refused to initiate the registration process or discontinued the procedure, if just initiated). However, it indirectly confirmed that groups having no religious character should not be entered in the register and that the religious character of a community is determined by its adopted reference to *sacrum* and its goals concentrating on the spiritual needs of adherents.[28]

In short, then, the principle of equal rights, included in Article 25 paragraph 1 of the Constitution of the Republic of Poland, refers only to these communities which can be considered religious organizations. The constitutional provision in question does not pertain to communities not having a religious character. They obviously enjoy freedom to act within the framework provided by the constitution. However, the constitutional principle of equal rights of religious organizations does not apply to them.

Interpretation of the principle of equal rights

The general unanimity which prevailed when the principle of equal rights was included in the constitution, and earlier in the Act on the Guarantees of Freedom of Conscience and Religion, did not translate into lack of dispute about its interpretation and application. One of such disputes was heard by the Constitutional Tribunal, to which a complaint was made by the Polish Autocephalous Orthodox Church. The representatives of that church claimed that some norms concerning the regulation of its property issues are markedly different from the ones adopted with respect to the Catholic Church and several other religious organizations.

Let us explain that owing to the democratic changes, the process of partial restitution of church property nationalized at the time of the People's Republic of Poland was initiated in 1989. The relevant regulations were incorporated in all acts concerning religious organizations which were adopted as of 1989. They were also included in the act of 1991 on the Relations between the State and the Polish Autocephalous Orthodox Church. What was not regulated, however, were issues connected with the legal status of one type of property. It concerned property nationalized under the Decree of 5 September 1947 on the Nationalization of Property Left by People Resettled in the USSR, being previously owned by the units of the Greek Catholic Church. At the time when the Act of 1991 was adopted, some such property – being national property – were used by the Polish Autocephalous Orthodox

26 Judgment of the Supreme Administrative Court of 22nd January 1999, I SA 775/98 (unpublished).

27 Decision of the Minister of Administration and Digitization of 15th March 2013 (unpublished).

28 Judgment of the Voivodeship Administrative Court in Warsaw of 8 April 2014 (I SA/Wa 1517/13; LEX No. 1464959). A consequence of this judgment was the decision of the Minister of Administration and Digitization of 10 October 2014 (unpublished), pursuant to which the procedure was discontinued.

Church. It was decided that relevant regulations concerning that category of property would be adopted in the future. Moreover, in a few cases the possibility of awarding compensation was clearly excluded if it was impossible to satisfy a claim by returning property or granting replacement property. The exclusions described were considered by the Orthodox Church as not complying with the principle of equal rights, since – as it was indicated – similar exclusions were not applied to other religious organizations, and especially to the Catholic Church.[29]

The Constitutional Tribunal did not agree with the charges brought by the representatives of the Orthodox Church and stated that the disputed regulations had their justification both in the special history of the property concerned and in the entire set of relevant norms. On that occasion, which is especially important, the Tribunal articulated its own understanding of the principle of equal rights of churches and other religious organizations. According to the Tribunal, the principle means that equal treatment should be given to such religious organizations who are characterized by a common distinctive feature. Different treatment, on the other hand, is justified in the case of churches and religious organizations 'which do not have a common feature relevant from the point of view of a certain regulation'.[30] Developing these ideas in the subsequent legislation, the Tribunal furthermore noted that Article 25 para. 1 of the Constitution cannot be comprehended as creating the expectancy of any religious organization achieving actual equality with other subjects of this kind.[31] It also emphasized that what makes the differentiation of religious organizations admissible is, among other issues, the fact that the relations between them and the State are to be regulated by acts adopted on the basis of previously adopted agreements: 'the constitutional legislator thus assumes a far-reaching individualization of acts concerning religious organizations and adaptation of the content of concluded agreements, and in consequence of adopted acts, to the special situation of individual churches and other religious organizations.'[32]

The aforementioned statement of the Constitutional Tribunal was met with various responses in the literature of the subject. According to the critics of this ruling, it follows from Article 25 para. 1 of the Constitution that all religious organizations are entitled to equal rights just because they are religious organizations. It is thus unjustified to establish any criteria that would permit differentiation of these subjects.[33] Separate criticism

29 As inconsistent with the principle of equal rights of churches and other religious organizations (art. 25 para. 1 of the Constitution) they considered art. 46 para. 1 pt. 3, art. 48 para. 2 pt. 3 and art. 49 para. 1 and 2 of the Act of 4 July 1991 on the Relations between the State and the Polish Autocephalous Orthodox Church (Dz. U. 1991, no. 66, item 287, with subsequent amendments). For the solutions pertaining to the regulation of property issues of churches and other religious organizations after 1989 see especially: Dariusz Walencik, *Nieruchomości Kościoła katolickiego w Polsce w latach 1918–2012. Regulacje prawne – nacjonalizacja – rewindykacja* (Drukarnia Archidiecezjalna 2013), 233–374; Włodzimierz Bendza, *Regulacja kościelnych spraw majątkowych na przykładzie Kościoła prawosławnego w Polsce* (Wolters Kluwer 2009); Stanisz, 'Relations' supra note 8 at 699–701.

30 See the judgment of the Constitutional Tribunal of 2 April 2003 (K 13/02), in *Orzecznictwo Trybunału Konstytucyjnego* 2003, series A, no. 4, item 28.

31 See the judgment of the Constitutional Tribunal of 2 December 2009 (U 10/07), *Orzecznictwo Trybunału Konstytucyjnego* 2009, series A, no. 11, item 163; the judgement of the Constitutional Tribunal of 8 June 2011 (K 3/09), in *Orzecznictwo Trybunału Konstytucyjnego* 2011, series A, no. 5, item 39.

32 See the judgment of the Constitutional Tribunal of 14 December 2009 (K 55/07), *Orzecznictwo Trybunału Konstytucyjnego* 2009, series A, no. 11, item 167.

33 See for example Paweł Borecki and Michał Pietrzak, 'Glosa do wyroku Trybunału Konstytucyjnego z dnia 2 kwietnia 2003 r. (sygn. Akt K 13/02)' (2003) 5 *Przegląd Sejmowy*, 96–113.

concerned the idea of differentiating religious organizations depending on the relevant features they possessed.[34]

However, other authors approved of the opinion of the Constitutional Tribunal.[35] Some of them had emphasized earlier that the principle of equal rights of churches and other religious organizations, which is an embodiment of the principle of equality before the law (see Article 32 of the Constitution), could be neither absolutized nor understood in the spirit of schematic egalitarianism.[36]

The pertinence of the interpretation adopted by the Constitutional Tribunal is strongly corroborated by the established understanding of the general principle of equality, expressed in Article 32 of the Constitution.[37] It can hardly be doubted that there is a strong connection between this principle and the principle of equal rights of religious organizations. It ought to be stressed that the general principle of equality is comprehended as an obligation to give identical treatment to subjects that are to the same degree characterized by a particular relevant feature. The lack of sameness as far as a relevant feature is concerned justifies (and sometimes even forces) diversified treatment. What is more, according to the established judicature of the Constitutional Tribunal, some situations even permit different treatment of subjects possessing the same features. In such a case, there are however three conditions which hale to be fulfilled: rationality, proportion, and justification as far as values or constitutional provisions are concerned.[38]

Methods of realization of the principle of equal rights

When looking at the actions taken by the Polish legislature, it is difficult to see any comprehensive and consistent strategy for realizing Article 25 para. 1 of the current constitution. It was counter to Polish traditions and impossible in practice to adopt – what some authors consider as the best solution[39] – uniform regulation of the legal situation of all religious organizations in a single normative act.

An analysis of the decisions taken by the Polish legislature makes it possible to identify a few different methods which are interchangeably used with a view to realizing the constitutional provision under discussion. It is easy to notice at the same time that the Polish legislature basically adopted the method of 'levelling up', thus aiming to extend the rights already granted to one religious organization or some of them to the remaining religious groups with a regulated legal status. This aim is realized by means of three mechanisms.

34 Jarosław Szymanek, 'Konstytucyjna zasada równouprawnienia kościołów i innych związków wyznaniowych' *Studia Prawnicze* 2009, no. 1–2, p. 168; also: Paweł Leszczyński, *Zasada równouprawnienia Kościołów i innych związków wyznaniowych w świetle relacji między art. 25 ust. 1 i art. 25 ust. 5 Konstytucji RP*, in Andrzej Bałaban and Przemysław Mijal (eds) *Zasady naczelne Konstytucji RP z 2 kwietnia 1997 roku. Materiały 52. Ogólnopolskiego Zjazdu Katedr Prawa Konstytucyjnego w Międzyzdrojach (27–29 maja 2010 r.)* (Uniwersytet Szczeciński 2011), 399–400.

35 See Doktór-Bindas, supra note 20 at 184–186.

36 See Józef Krukowski, *Kościół i państwo*, supra note 17 at 278–280; Dariusz Dudek, *Równouprawnienie Kościołów i związków wyznaniowych na tle konstytucyjnych zasad prawa wyznaniowego*, in Artur Mezglewski, ed, *Prawo wyznaniowe*, supra note 19 at 201–205.

37 According to this provision, '1. All persons shall be equal before the law. All persons shall have the right to equal treatment by public authorities. 2. No one shall be discriminated against in political, social or economic life for any reason whatsoever.'

38 See Dariusz Dudek, *Równouprawnienie Kościoł*, supra note 36 at 203–204.

39 See for example Michał Pietrzak, *Konstytucyjne podstawy prawa wyznaniowego*, in M. Wyrzykowski, ed, *Konstytucyjne podstawy systemu prawa* (Instytut Spraw Publicznych 2001), 176.

The first one consists in the realization of the method of uniform regulation of the legal status of all religious organizations in a particular sphere. Such a situation arose for example when the Act of 26 June 1997 was adopted, pursuant to which the regulations pertaining to the right to include in a school report a grade in religion taught in religious education centers were removed from several acts concerning individual religious organizations.[40] The removal at issue was justified precisely by the need for regulating the issue in a way that would pertain to all religious organizations in the same way. Such solutions were indeed present in the Ordinance of the Minister of Education of 14 April 1992 on the Conditions and Way of Organizing Religious Education in Public Kindergartens and Schools.[41] As a consequence, the adoption of the Act of 26 June 1997 led to a situation in which the issues under discussion were subjected to regulations concerning all religious groups in the same way.[42]

The second mechanism for ensuring the realization of the principle of equal rights of all religious organizations follows from Article 18 para. 2 of the Act on the Guarantees of freedom of conscience and religion. However, we should first explain the fact that pursuant to Article 18 para. 1 most of the dispositions of this Act do not apply to religious organizations whose legal situation is regulated by separate acts. It also concerns, in principle, the regulations determining the rights of religious organizations. An exception is a situation when acts pertaining to individual religious organizations do not provide for the rights defined in the Act on the Guarantees of Freedom of Conscience and Religion. The catalogue of rights comprised in this Act can thus be considered as the minimum standard of due rights of religious organizations, irrespective of whether these rights are provided for in normative acts directly pertaining to these organizations. This solution is of particular significance for three religious communities whose legal status is defined by normative acts adopted before World War II.[43] The relevant regulations (the ordinance of the President of 1928 and acts of 1936) do not comprise many of the rights included in the legislation of 1989. Owing to the mechanism under discussion, potential gaps in this respect do not involve the deterioration of the legal situation of these religious organizations.[44]

The third mechanism was mainly involved in connection with the ratification of the Concordat. It consists in adopting subsequent normative acts in order to extend the rights granted to the Catholic Church in this international agreement to other religious organizations. Even before the Concordat became effective, a number of acts pertaining to religious organizations were altered. Due to these changes, the right to conclude civil marriages in a religious form or the right to provide religious instruction in kindergartens was extended to non-Catholic religious organizations.[45] Similar actions were also undertaken later. For example, on 13 May 2011 the act on funding the Orthodox Seminary in Warsaw from the

40 Dz. U. 1998, no. 59, item 375.

41 Dz. U. 1992, no. 36, item 155, with subsequent amendments.

42 It is worth mentioning that before signing the act the President of the Republic of Poland put forward a request to the Constitutional Tribunal for checking the constitutionality of the norms discussed above. In the judgment of 5 May 1998 (K. 35/97) the Constitutional Tribunal did not consider them as not complying with art. 25 para. 1 of the Polish Constitution (see *Orzecznictwo Trybunału Konstytucyjnego* 1998, no. 3, item 32).

43 See supra note 22.

44 See Michał Pietrzak, *Demokratyczne*, supra note 12 at 176–177.

45 See Jarosław Matwiejuk, 'Konkordat z 1993 roku a pozycja prawna kościołów i związków wyznaniowych nierzymskokatolickich', in Mezglewski (ed.), *Prawo wyznaniowe*, supra note 19 at 231–253; Wiktor Wysoczański, 'Wpływ konkordatu z 1993 r. na sytuację prawną kościołów i innych związków wyznaniowych mniejszościowych', in Józef Wroceński and Helena Pietrzak

state budget was adopted.[46] It can be considered as a response to funding several Catholic universities from the state budget.[47] However, it should be admitted that the full realization of the principle of equal rights of all religious organizations using this method would be possible only if based on the assumption of due consistency on the part of the legislator, who should consider the realization of the principle at issue as one of the basic aims and objectives of the policy on law on religion. However, no full consistency of this kind can be observed, which results in the persistence of some solutions which differentiate the legal situation of religious organizations without sufficient justification.[48]

General assessment of the degree of conformity of subconstitutional regulations to the principle of equal rights of religious organizations

At the level of ordinary acts, it is easy to notice numerous regulations which treat individual religious organizations in different ways. It is possible – as already stressed above – due to the diversification of the forms of regulating the legal situation of religious organizations and consequent application of various normative acts to these organizations.

Already at first glance it can be seen that this differentiation does not comply with the principle of equal rights of religious organizations in each case. On the other hand, it ought to be stressed that not every differentiation, however, violates the principle of equal rights. In order to illustrate the situations mentioned, let us use the examples concerning two important spheres of engagement on the part of religious organizations, that is, religious education and marriage.

According to the Constitution of the Republic of Poland, religion of any religious organization with regulated legal status can be a school subject. However, classes in a specific religion (just as classes in ethics) in a particular school are only organized when parents of at least seven students (or students themselves, depending on their age) declare that they are willing to participate in such classes. When the number of interested students is smaller, it is possible to organize religious instruction outside schools, in inter-school groups or religious education centres (but still within the system of education). According to the norms which were valid until recently, the number of students in such a group could not be smaller than three. It was possible to organize religious education in accordance with different rules (that is, irrespective of the number of reported students), but only when requested by an interested religious organization and within the means possessed by a given school. In Polish literature some authors expressed opinions that these solutions discriminated against minority religious organizations.[49] Nevertheless, the Constitutional Tribunal in the already-mentioned judgment of 5 May 1998 voiced the conviction that this regulation significantly met the needs of smaller churches and religious organizations to ensure religious education

(eds), *Konkordat polski w 10 lat po ratyfikacji. Materiały z konferencji* (Wydawnictwo Uniwersytetu Kardynała Stefana Wyszyńskiego 2008), 83–85.

46 Dz. U. 2011, no. 144, item 849.

47 Such funding is currently awarded to John Paul II Catholic University of Lublin, the Pontifical University of John Paul II in Cracow, the Pontifical Theological Faculty in Warsaw, the Pontifical Theological Faculty in Wrocław, and the Jesuit University of Philosophy and Education 'Ignatianum' in Cracow. See Michalina Duda, 'Zasady finansowania uczelni kościelnych z budżetu państwa' *Studia z Prawa Wyznaniowego*, 2012, vol. 15, 36–41.

48 They are mentioned (and overemphasized at the same time) for example by Borecki, supra note 17 at 138–154.

49 See Borecki at 143.

within the system of education. This opinion deserved approval. The regulation discussed, although it provided for diversified forms of teaching religion, was not at variance with the principle of equality of every person irrespective of their religion or with the principle of equal rights of churches and other religious organizations. These norms did not promote (or discriminate) any religious organization by name, and did not favor (or bias) any of the formally distinguished groups. They uniformly applied to all religious organizations. By diversifying the ways of organizing religious instruction they referred to the relevant feature of individual, local religious communities, that is to the number of students who were ready to receive instruction in a particular religion (or ethics). As for the differentiation of the forms of organizing religious education depending on this feature, it should not be regarded as disproportionate. For we should agree with the opinion of the Constitutional Tribunal expressed in the judgment of 5 May 1998 that the requirement to organize religious classes in religious education centres for at least three students was not excessively rigorous, especially as these did not have to be students from the same school.[50]

The solution under discussion was, however, changed in consequence of the 2010 judgment of the European Court of Human Rights in the case of *Grzelak v. Poland*. The change consisted in cancelling the limit on the number of students conditioning the possibility of organizing classes in inter-school groups or religious education centers. The Strasbourg Court examined the case of the applicant who over the entire period of his education in Polish schools received school certificates without a mark for religion/ethics because he did not attend religion classes, and ethics classes were not in the curriculum due to the insufficient number of interested students. The Court found that the absence of a mark for religion/ethics on the applicant's school certificates throughout the entire period of schooling 'amounted to a form of unwarranted stigmatization', and so there was a violation of Article 14 in conjunction with Article 9 of the Convention.[51]

What is also worth discussing at this point are the regulations on the religious form of concluding a civil marriage. As already mentioned, the right to conclude marriages in such a form was included in the Concordat with reference to Catholics, and it was extended to other religious organizations by means of subsequent acts. The problem is, however, that the possibility of acquiring this right was limited only to religious organizations whose legal situation is regulated by a separate act. As a matter of fact, this right was not granted to all fifteen subjects from this group, but only to eleven of them. The possibility of acquiring this right was completely excluded for religious organizations that are listed in the register.[52] In this case, it was the formal criterion that served as the basis for differences in treatment. It was the form of regulating the legal situation that was referred to, which certainly cannot be considered a relevant feature. For this reason, we should concur with the opinions that it is necessary to change the current law in the sphere under discussion.[53]

50 Another issue is that the limits discussed are in force on the basis of an ordinance which did not have any foundation in regulations of statutory rank. It could thus be questioned on account of Article 92 para. 1 of the Constitution. See Artur Mezglewski, *Polski model edukacji religijnej w szkołach publicznych. Aspekty prawne* (Wydawnictwo KUL 2009), 119–124.

51 See *Grzelak v. Poland*, Application no. 7710/02 (ECtHR, 15 June 2010).

52 See Artur Mezglewski and Anna Tunia, *Wyznaniowa forma zawarcia małżeństwa cywilnego* (C. H. Beck 2007), 13–17.

53 See Tadeusz J. Zieliński, 'Rozciągnięcie prawa procedowania wyznaniowej formy zawarcia małżeństwa cywilnego na wspólnoty religijne wpisane do rejestru (propozycja de lege ferenda)' (2012) 4 *Przegląd Prawa Wyznaniowego*, 169–176; Aneta Abramowicz, 'Wyznaniowa forma zawarcia małżeństwa cywilnego a zasada równouprawnienia związków wyznaniowych', *Studia z Prawa Wyznaniowego* 2014, vol. 17, 141–143.

Resolutions

The analysis of the Polish regulations in question makes it possible to draw several general conclusions. In the first place, there is some kind of tension between the principle of equal rights of religious organizations and the method of individual regulation of their legal situation, especially on the basis of previous agreements. This tension, however, does not give rise to conflicts that are impossible to resolve. When interpreting and realizing one principle, it is sufficient to take into account the meaning of the other. Moreover, the co-existence of both principles also contributes to extending the scope of rights of religious organizations, as the rights granted to one of them should be possible to obtain by the remaining religious organizations possessing identical feature. It has to be admitted that obeying the principle of equal rights in this situation requires much greater attention on the part of the legislator than in the case of defining the status of all religious organizations in a fully uniform way. However, it is not an excessive price to pay for taking into account the unique character of individual religious groups.

Second, it ought to be emphasized that according to the Polish Constitutional Tribunal, proportional differentiation of the legal situation of religious organizations that do not possess the same relevant features is in conformity with the Constitution of the Republic of Poland of 1997. Nonetheless, in Polish law one can still find solutions that diversify the rights of religious organizations in an insufficiently justified way. Their existence certainly cannot be considered as the primary feature of contemporary Polish law on religion, and problems with the full realization of similar principles can easily be noticed also in some other states. Nevertheless, the conclusion remains that introducing necessary changes which would be in complete conformity with the constitutional principle of equal rights of all religious organizations should constitute an important goal of the policy pursued by Polish authorities.

12 State neutrality and religious plurality in Europe[1]

Javier Martínez-Torrón

Defining state neutrality

Given the increasing tendency to consider religious neutrality to be one of the necessary characteristics of contemporary democratic states, defining the notion of state neutrality becomes crucial to any discussion of the relationship of religion to the state. From a pan-European perspective, the first approach is a negative one – that is, to define what state neutrality is *not*.

In this respect, it is clear that neutrality *cannot be a uniform constitutional principle*, enforced at the European level, containing a particular notion of how the relations between state and religion should be structured. The European Court of Human Rights (ECtHR) has since long held that the European Convention is aimed at guaranteeing certain fundamental freedoms – among them religious freedom – but does not impose any particular model of relations between state and religion.[2] The underlying assumption is that the state's attitude towards religion is primarily a matter of political choice, and is the result, to a large extent, of the historical tradition and the social, moral, and cultural circumstances of each country. The legal framework of the European Union – in particular, Article 17 of the Treaty on the Functioning of the European Union – is even more specific about the fact that there is no uniform European rule on the status of churches and religious communities, and that this is a matter that has to be decided at the national level.[3]

For those reasons, neutrality cannot be understood as synonymous with strict separation between state and religion. This is a strong differential factor between the analysis of issues raised by institutional religious symbols in Europe and in the United States, respectively. In the US, the courts' construction of the constitutional Establishment Clause plays a crucial

1 This chapter was begun in the context of the Project DER2011–29385, of the Spanish Ministry of Science and Innovation. An earlier version appeared as 'Institutional Religious Symbols, State Neutrality and Protection of Minorities in Europe', (2013) 171 *Law & Justice – Christian Law Review*, 21.

2 See, for further details and references, Javier Martínez-Torrón and Rafael Navarro-Valls, 'The Protection of Religious Freedom in the System of the Council of Europe', in Tore Lindholm, W. Cole Durham, Jr., and Bahia Tahzib-Lie, eds, *Facilitating Freedom of Religion and Belief: A Deskbook* (Martinus Nijhoff 2004), 216–218.

3 This is the text of Article 17 of the Treaty on the Functioning of the European Union: '1. The Union respects and does not prejudice the status under national law of churches and religious associations or communities in the Member States.— 2. The Union equally respects the status under national law of philosophical and non-confessional organisations.— 3. Recognising their identity and their specific contribution, the Union shall maintain an open, transparent and regular dialogue with these churches and organisations.'

role and prevents any use of religious symbols that can lead to an interpretation that the state is endorsing religion in general or – even less – a particular religion.[4]

The foregoing does not mean that strict separation between state and religion cannot be adopted in Europe, or that it is precluded by the ECHR. On the contrary, separation is one of the legitimate choices that European states have at their disposal. But note: the discussion about adopting or not a system of separation, as the best way to guarantee state religious neutrality, must take place at the national level – that is, at the level of each country's constitutional principles that define the framework of relations between state and religion. France and Turkey, for instance, claim to have a system of separation and proclaim a strict *laïcité* of the state. However, the countries are not the rule but are exceptions (and a detailed analysis of their respective legal systems may raise serious doubts about how real separation between state and religion is in those countries). Interestingly, most European states have adopted, explicitly or implicitly, formulas of state cooperation with religion in their constitutions and/or in their laws.[5]

Contrary to what occurs in the United States, from a pan-European perspective (i.e., from the perspective of the ECHR) neither cooperation with religion nor endorsement of religion are a problem per se. Not even the remaining systems of established churches are as such incompatible with the ECHR. One may think that those systems are the product of particular historical circumstances, and are not perhaps the best choice in contemporary times, but they are compatible with the ECHR. From a pan-European perspective, the crucial question with regard to the systems of cooperation, endorsement or establishment – as well as to systems of separation – is to guarantee that they respect

4 For a detailed and analytical explanation of the US constitutional prohibition of establishment of religion and its judicial interpretation, see, for example, Michael W. McConnell, John H. Harvey, and Thomas C. Berg, *Religion and the Constitution* (Wolters Kluwer, 3rd edn, 2011), 121ff. From a comparative perspective, see W. Cole Durham, Jr. and Brett G. Scharffs, *Law and Religion: National, International, and Comparative Perspective* (Aspen / Wolters Kluwer Law and Business, 2nd edn, 2016). For a critical analysis of the judicial approach to the non-endorsement requirement derived from the establishment clause, see, among others, from different perspectives: Douglas Laycock, 'Nonpreferential Aid to Religion: A False Claim about Original Intent', (1985–1986) 27 *William & Mary Law Review*, 875–923; Michael W. McConnell, 'Coercion: The Lost Element of Establishment', (1985–1986) 27 *William & Mary Law Review*, 933–941; Arnold H. Loewy, 'Rethinking Government Neutrality Towards Religion Under the Establishment Clause: The Untapped Potential of Justice O'Connor's Insight', (1985–1986) 64 *North Carolina Law Review*, 1049–1070; Jesse H. Choper, 'The Endorsement Test: Its Status and Desirability', (2002) 18 *Journal of Law and Public Policy*, 499–536; Thomas C. Berg, 'What's Right and Wrong with "No Endorsement"', (2006) 21 *Washington University Journal of Law & Policy*, 307–322.

5 For a succinct explanation of the relations between state and religion in the EU countries, see *State and Church in the European Union*, Gerhard Robbers, ed. (Nomos, 2nd edn, 2005). More detailed studies analyzing concrete aspects of law and religion in EU states can be found, for example, in the publications mentioned in the Internet pages of the European Consortium for Church and State Research, at http://www.churchstate.eu/Publications (accessed 28 March 2017). Interesting data and analysis can also be found in *Religion and the Secular State: National Reports*, prepared for 18th Congress of the International Congress of Comparative Law, Javier Martínez-Torrón and W. Cole Durham, Jr., eds (Complutense University of Madrid 2015). More detailed studies and law and religion in all countries of the world appear in the *Encyclopedia of Law and Religion*, Gerhard Robbers, W. Cole Durham, Jr., with Donlu Thayer, eds (Brill/Nijhoff 2016) and are gradually appearing in the *International Encyclopaedia of Laws*, Rik Torfs, ed. (Wolters-Kluwer ongoing), see http://ielaws.com/encyclopaedias/iel-religion (accessed 28 March 2017).

religious freedom and the equality principle. What the ECHR does not allow is that constitutional choices degenerate, in practice, into a repressive or discriminatory legal framework, in which, for instance, persons not belonging to the privileged religion or religions actually suffer discrimination in the exercise of their freedom of religion and belief.

This, precisely, helps us define in positive terms the European notion of state religious neutrality. Taking into account that the ECHR is not aimed at imposing a uniform model of church–state relations but at guaranteeing fundamental rights, neutrality has to be conceived as a distinctive feature of European states that constitutes a necessary requirement to adequately protect freedom of thought, conscience and religion (art. 9 ECHR) and non-discrimination on religious grounds (art. 14 ECHR). The protection of freedom of religion and belief of all individuals and groups, and not the model of church–state relations, is the point of reference to understand the common meaning of state neutrality in Europe.

In this respect, the case law of the ECtHR permits us to infer the two main coordinates that define the notion of state neutrality.

One is impartiality vis-à-vis religions or beliefs. This applies especially to religious differences or disputes. A number of judgments of the ECtHR relating to internal religious disputes (with regard, in particular, to the appointment of religious leaders or to religious splits) signal that the state cannot take sides in those matters and must act as an impartial arbiter or organizer. When facing the social tension that is occasionally created by competing religious groups, the role of national authorities is not to determine which party is right or wrong, or to eliminate pluralism as the price to guarantee social peace. The state's function is rather to organize religious pluralism in a way that ensures that all individuals are free to practice their religion, that diverging groups respect each other, and that all groups are as autonomous as possible to take care of their own internal affairs without undue external interferences. Thus, the Court has affirmed that the States exceed their power when they fail to remain neutral with regard to changes in the leadership of a religious community, when they try to force the community to come together under a unified leadership against its own wishes, or when they attempt to prevent a schism in a church for dissensions of religious nature.[6]

However, formal impartiality is not sufficient. Deeply understood, state impartiality must be based on a second coordinate: the *incompetence* of the state to judge the truth or falsity of religious doctrines, and more generally to have any judgment on strictly religious issues. In this respect, it is important to conceive *stricto sensu* the state's incompetence on religious matters. It is not that the state decides to renounce one of its legitimate competences for the sake of achieving a higher level of religious freedom. It is more than that. State neutrality implies that strictly religious issues are not part of its legitimate competences, and therefore any interference in such issues would be, *ipso facto* and *ipso iure*, an unjustified limitation on the religious freedom of individuals and groups. The state cannot say which religion is better or worse, or which religious leader

6 See, especially, *Serif v. Greece*, 14 December 1999; *Hasan and Chaush v. Bulgaria*, 26 October 2000; *Agga v. Greece*, 17 October 2002; *Supreme Holy Council of the Muslim Community v. Bulgaria*, 16 December 2004 (which refer to public authorities' intervention in leadership disputes within Muslim communities); and *Metropolitan Church of Bessarabia v. Moldova*, 13 December 2001; *Svyato-Mykhaylivska Parafiya v. Ukraine*, 14 September 2007 (which refer to public authorities' refusal to register Orthodox religious communities formed out of split from other Orthodox church).

is more or less appropriate for a religious group, because it lacks all legitimate competence on those issues.[7]

Nevertheless, it is also important to note that this notion of neutrality does not imply that public authorities must – or can – be indifferent towards the results produced by the exercise of freedom of religion or belief, or that they ignore completely the content of personal choices in this particular area of human rationality. While neutrality vetoes state judgments on strictly religious issues or doctrines, it does not preclude state action with respect to religion, which may be based on other judgments. In particular, the state may take into account the social effects of the religious activity, or the predictable effects of religious moral doctrines, including the situations in which those effects conflict with the law or with values that the legal system considers essential (consider, for instance, the case of religious groups that assert their intention to impose their doctrines through violence if necessary, or that preach violence or discrimination against some people).[8]

Two important consequences derive from the foregoing. First, state action with regard to religion shall and must be, for the most part, a legal action – that is, an action precisely defined by law, with narrow margin for public authorities' discretion that could lead in practice to value judgments on religious doctrines or customs. Second, neutrality implies recognition of the reciprocal autonomy of state and religion; therefore, state's interference with religious autonomy must be reduced to a minimum and its necessity must be clearly justified.[9] We must keep in mind that, as indicated above, neutrality is conceived not as an

7 The notion of neutrality as state incompetence on religious matters may raise some important questions with respect to European states that have established churches. Certainly, as already indicated, the ECtHR has always understood that the ECHR is compatible with such models of church–state relations. Two interrelated reasons seem to justify such compatibility. One is the fact that those systems of established churches must be understood in the light of the particular history of the country; it would probably be incomprehensible, from the perspective of current European standards, to constitute such systems now, *ex novo*. The second reason is that, in practice, there is a high degree of protection of religious freedom of individuals and groups in those countries, and the state put a serious effort in preventing that the system of established church results in the discrimination of religious or belief minorities.

8 Those factors were decisive in the ECtHR's judgments on the case *Refah Partisi and Others v. Turkey*, 31 July 2001 (Third Section) and 13 February 2003 (Grand Chamber), as well as in the decision *Kalifatstaat v. Germany* (decision on the admissibility of App. No. 13828/04), 11 December 2006. The former involved the dissolution of a large party of Islamic orientation by the Turkish Constitutional Court. The latter referred to the illegalization of an Islamic association by German authorities. For a comment on *Refah Partisi*, which is one of the most significant judgments of the ECtHR on the dissolution of political parties, see Carolyn Evans and Christopher A. Thomas, 'Church-State Relations in the European Court of Human Rights', (2006) *Brigham Young University Law Review*, 709–713; and the chapters written, respectively, by Ann Elizabeth Mayer, Christine Moe, Javid Gadirov, and Lance Lehnhof in the volume *Islam, Europe and Emerging Legal Issues*, W. Cole Durham, Jr., Rik Torfs, David M. Kirkham, and Christine Scott, eds (Ashgate 2012), 209ff.

9 The ECtHR has often emphasized this idea since the late 1990s. See, especially, the judgments cited supra, in note 5. However, in practice defining the limits of religious autonomy is far from easy, as demonstrated by some ECtHR's cases of the last years concerning the labour relations between churches and their employees. See, for example, *Obst v. Germany* and *Schüth v. Germany*, both of 23 September 2010; see also *Fernandez Martinez v. Spain,* Grand Chamber, 21 June 2014. For an interesting comment on this type of cases and on which should be the right way to deal with them from the ECHR perspective, when the German cases had not yet been decided by the European Court, see Gerhard Robbers, 'Church Autonomy in the European Court of Human Rights: Recent Developments in Germany', (2010–2011) 26 *Journal of Law and Religion*, 281–320.

aim in itself but as a means to guarantee and facilitate the exercise of freedom of religion or belief by all individuals and groups on equal grounds.

State neutrality and display of religious symbols in public places or institutions

With the background of this conceptual approach to state neutrality, we can now turn back to the question of religious symbols, well illustrated by the issue of the crucifix in public schools, which has been the subject of a heated debate in some European countries since the mid 1990s.[10] If the religious neutrality of the state is – from a pan-European perspective – intimately and inextricably linked to the protection of freedom of religion or belief, it follows that the display of religious symbols in public places or institutions is not, per se, contrary to art. 9 of the European Convention of Human Rights, as far as individuals are not subject to coercion or indoctrination.[11]

I mean it in the strictest possible sense, and therefore I must add two nuances.

First, a constitutional court may consider that the display of religious symbols in some public institutions – for example, educational centres, courtrooms, legislatures, or town halls – is contrary to the constitutional principles that define the relations between state and religion in its country. However, the European Court is not competent to adjudicate on such principles, this is the exclusive realm of national courts. As indicated above, the aim of the European Convention is – and always was – to protect freedoms and not to impose constitutional church–state models.

Second, I am not discussing here if the display of religious symbols in public places or institutions is good or bad in order to foster mutual respect and understanding between religions and beliefs in a plural setting. Such discussion, taken seriously, would lead to numerous distinctions (including different types of public places or institutions, as well as different national contexts). It would also require analysing complex questions that are far from the purpose of this chapter. The point is that, *in the absence of coercion or indoctrination*, is not for the courts – and in particular the ECtHR – to make choices with regard to the display of religious symbols in the public sphere. Within the democratic process, the decision about such displays is the domain of public policies and hence the competence of other authorities. Those decisions involve questions not susceptible of easy answers. Often they are taken at the local level. Tradition plays a role, and certainly installing a religious symbol *ex novo* is not the same as keeping it in the place where it had been for agės; in a European context of religious traditions influencing the shaping of the public sphere, both keeping and removing a symbol have a meaning, neither of which can be ignored. One-sided views are normally unfair and public authorities must take into account a plurality of interests. In any event, the function of the courts is not to substitute for the competent

10 See, for further details and references, in the context of analogous debates in other European and American countries Rafael Navarro-Valls and Javier Martínez-Torrón, *Conflictos entre conciencia y ley: las objeciones de conciencia* (Iustel, 2nd edn, 2011), 374–393. For a useful source of documentation on the issue of the crucifix in Italy, with interesting scholarly analysis from diverse perspectives, see 'La questione del crocifisso', Antonio Guiseppe Chizzoniti, ed., on the website *Osservatorio delle libertà ed istituzioni religiose* at http://www.olir.it/areetematiche/75/index.php (accessed 28 March 2017).

11 The coercive factor was present, for example, in the case *Buscarini and others v. San Marino*, 18 February 1999, in which the Court held that requiring newly elected members of Parliament to swear allegiance to the Constitution on the Gospels, on pain of forfeiting their parliamentary seats, was contrary to the provisions of Article 9 ECHR.

authorities on this type of issues. They must limit themselves to be vigilant and ensure that no rights are violated by decisions adopted by the legitimate authorities. And, of course, if they find a violation of religious freedom, they must provide the relevant evidence.

The mistake of the ECtHR's Second Section in its chamber judgment in the *Lautsi* case (*Lautsi I*)[12] was, precisely, to take for granted that the mere display of a traditional religious symbol in Italy – the crucifix – was a violation of the religious freedom of the students opposing to it and of the parents' rights under article 2 of the First Protocol to the ECHR.[13] For the Court, the crucifix was a 'powerful' symbol with remarkable potential impact on young students, and with a primarily religious meaning. Therefore, its presence in the school premises could be emotionally disturbing for some students and was restrictive of the parents' rights to decide the orientation of their children's education and incompatible with the neutrality that must preside the public school environment.[14] Naturally, the logical consequence of this rationale would be the removal of crucifixes from all public schools in Italy (and probably elsewhere). Implicit in that approach was a notion of neutrality as *exclusion of religion* from the public space, at least in the educational milieu. Such understanding of neutrality is, of course, a legitimate option but it is not the only legitimate option, and it is not for the courts – even less for the European Court – to impose their own choices on such delicate issue.

Ultimately, by making mandatory the exclusive concept of religious neutrality, *Lautsi I* axiomatically accepted a very debatable distinction between believers and non-believers, attaching the latter to the realm of reason and the former to the realm of non-rational belief. From this departure point, the logical corollary was that the particular symbols of a religion

12 *Lautsi v. Italy*, 3 November 2009. Among the immense legal literature generated by this case, see, from different perspectives, and with reference to the chamber's judgment, Pasquale Annicchino, 'Is the glass half empty or half full? *Lautsi v. Italy* before the European Court of Human Rights', (May 2010) *Stato, Chiese e Pluralismo confessionale*, 1–19 (www.statoechiese.it); Santiago Cañamares Arribas, 'La cruz de Estrasburgo. en torno a la sentencia *Lautsi v. Italia*, del Tribunal Europeo de Derechos Humanos', (2010) 22 *Revista General de Derecho Canónico y Derecho Eclesiástico*, 1–13; Nicola Colaianni, 'Il crocifisso in giro per l'Europa: da Roma a Strasburgo (e ritorno)', (2010) 24 *Revista General de Derecho Canónico y Derecho Eclesiástico del Estado*, 1–26J; Stefan Mückl, 'Crucifijos en las aulas: ¿lesión a los derechos fundamentales?', (2010) 23 *Revista General de Derecho Canónico y Derecho Eclesiástico del Estado*, 1–15 (comparing *Lautsi* with the case law of the German Federal Constitutional Law); Débora Ranieri de Cechini, 'Notable reacción europea ante otro intento laicista. El crucifijo en las escuelas italianas y la Corte de Estrasburgo', (2010) 68–69 *Prudentia Iuris*, 247–280; Joseph H. H. Weiler, 'Crucifix in the Classroom Redux', (2010) 21 (1) *European Journal of International Law*, 1–6.

13 This is the text of Article 2 of the Protocol to the ECHR: 'No person shall be denied the right to education. In the exercise of any functions which it assumes in relation to education and to teaching, the State shall respect the right of parents to ensure such education and teaching in conformity with their own religious and philosophical convictions.' As is well known, the *Lautsi* case is a result of a heated public and legal debate in Italy in the last decade about the display of the crucifix in public schools' classrooms. The applicant was the mother of two students of a public school (aged 13 and 11 at the time), who unsuccessfully had asked the school's governors to remove crucifixes from classrooms – the Italian law prescribes that there shall be a crucifix on the wall of public schools classrooms. The mother claimed that the presence of that religious symbol was against the constitutional principle of secularity (*laicità*), in which she wished to educate her children. A chamber of the ECtHR decided unanimously in favour of the applicant, considering that there had been a violation of Article 2 of the First Protocol to the Convention in connection with Article 9 ECHR. The judgment was reversed on appeal by the ECtHR's Grand Chamber.

14 See especially *Lautsi I*, § 57.

did not have a place in the sphere of public education. In this respect, it is interesting to note that a substantial part of the rationale of *Lautsi I* replicates the ECtHR's argument in *Leyla şahin* and other cases that adopt a similar approach with regard to the wearing of Islamic headscarf or other personal clothing of religious significance.[15] One of the reasons utilized to support the states' restrictive policies on personal religious garments at school was that such expressions of religiosity could lead to tension or 'pressure' on other students.

Lautsi I, like the ECtHR's decisions on Islamic headscarf cases, transmits the implicit message that imposing the absence of religious visible elements, at least in public schools, is a necessary consequence of state neutrality as guarantee of freedom of thought, conscience, and religion. The underlying assumption appears to be that religion is a factor of potential conflicts, and perhaps provocation, leading easily to confrontation and social tension. Hence the best choice would be to eliminate its visible features, and state neutrality would require

15 See *Leyla Şahin v. Turkey*, 29 June 2004 (Fourth Section), and *Leyla Şahin v. Turkey*, 10 November 2005 (Grand Chamber). For some comments on this case, among the immense legal literature it has generated, see the chapters written by T. Jeremy Gunn, Njål Høstmaelingen, Tore Lindholm, Javier Martínez-Torrón, and Ingvill Thorson Plesner in the volume *Islam, Europe and Emerging Legal Issues*, supra note 8; Natan Lerner, 'How Wide the Margin of Appreciation? The Turkish Headscarf Case, the Strasbourg Court, and Secularist Tolerance', (2005) 13 *Willamette Journal of International Law and Dispute Resolutions*, 65–85; Blandine Chelini-Pont and Emmanuel Tawil, 'Brèves remarques sur l'arrêt *Leyla Sahin*', (2006–2007) 2 *Annuaire Droit e Religions*, 607–611. Other important cases related to Islamic headscarves or analogous religious clothing include *Dogru c. Francia* and *Kervanci c. Francia*, both of 4 December 2008; *Dahlab v. Switzerland*, decision on the admissibility of App. No. 42393/98, 15 February 2001; *Köse and 93 other applicants v. Turkey*, decision on the admissibility of App. No. 26625/02, 24 January 2006; *Kurtulmus v. Turkey*, decision on the admissibility of App. No. 65500/01, 24 January 2006; and six almost identical decisions of inadmissibility of 30 June 2009: *Aktas v. France*, App. No. 43563/08, *Bayrak v. France*, App. No. 14308/08, *Gamaleddyn v. France*, App. No. 18527/08; *Ghazal v. France*, App. No. 29134/08, *Jasvir Singh v. France*, App. No. 25463/08, and *Ranjit Singh v. France*, App. No. 27561/08 (the six decisions involved applications by students punished in application of the 2004 French law that prohibits 'visible' personal religious symbols in public schools: four of them were female Muslims wearing a hijab and two of them were male Sikhs wearing a *keski*, which is a more discreet garb usually worn under the turban characteristic of Sikhs). More recently, in *SAS v. France*, App. No. 4385/11 (ECtHR Grand Chamber, 1 July 2014) the court upheld the French ban on facecoverings in public as a proportionate exercise of the margin of appreciation accorded France in preserving the cultural value of 'living together'. In *Ebrahimian v. France*, App. No. 64846/11 (ECtHR, 26 November 2015) the Court upheld the French ban on headscarves for 'the entire public sector' in its finding that a Muslim employee's loss of employment in a public hospital for refusing to remove her headscarf represents 'a wide margin of appreciation of the States Parties, and a confirmation of the acceptability of a system that elevates secularism to a constitutional principle and uses it as a basis for restricting individual expressions of religion by persons associated with the state.' See Eva Brems, 'Ebrahimian v France: headscarf ban upheld for entire public sector', *Strasbourg Observers*, 27 November 2015, https://strasbourgobservers.com/2015/11/27/ebrahimian-v-france-headscarf-ban-upheld-for-entire-public-sector/. Finally, following upon contrary opinions issued by two Advocates General in cases about firms desiring to dismiss an employee on the basis of her wearing an Islamic headscarf, the Grand Chamber of the Court of Justice of the European Union issued preliminary rulings on 14 March 2017. In the Belgium case *Achbita v. G4S Secure Solutions*, C-157/15 and the France case *Bougnaoui v. Micropole SA*, C-188/15, 'The Court found that under the right circumstances a company might be entitled to have a policy [which disallowed all religious, political or philosophical signs in the workplace]. One condition was that the policy must be in writing – in the interests of certainty and clarity. Another condition was that it must apply without distinction to all beliefs.' See Gareth David, 'Achbita v G4S: Religious Equality Squeezed between Profit and Prejudice', *European Law Blog*, 6 April 2017, https://europeanlawblog.eu/2017/04/06/achbita-v-g4s-religious-equality-squeezed-between-profit-and-prejudice/.

the protection of the individual right to build 'uncontaminated' educational environments free from religion. From such perspective, the state would become obliged to eliminate the possibility of conflict by prohibiting every visible religious symbol (when in reality conflicts and confrontation are normally produced not by religious symbols but rather by those who assert their absolute right to erase those symbols from their sight, so that they are not exposed to its presence or alleged influence). One of the predictable results of this position is that in practice non-religious ideas enjoy a superior position over religious ideas. In other words, it could lead to a design of public spaces in which an atheist can feel more comfortable than a religious believer.[16]

At the same time, it is not easy to understand how such a conception of state neutrality, with respect both to personal and to institutional symbols, can contribute to build the pluralist, inclusive, and objective educational environment that *Lautsi I* mentions.[17] Indeed, the effect of eliminating the visibility of the religious is to exclude and hide an important part of pluralism as well as to create a fictitious school setting, separated from the complexities of real life.[18] Such a school setting would not be indeed neutral, for it may transmit the subliminal message that religion, being potentially conflictive, has its place out of the school but not inside it (with the implication that atheism and agnosticism are in the opposite end of the spectrum, that is, they are considered as non-conflictive ideas, and therefore 'acceptable' at school).

Fortunately, the Grand Chamber of the ECtHR overruled the Second Section's decision one and a half years later (*Lautsi II*).[19] In *Lautsi II*, the Court rejected that the exclusive notion of neutrality proposed by the chamber was the only acceptable one, and pointed out that neutrality could also be achieved by a school environment that is inclusive and therefore open to visible expressions of both majority and minority religions or worldviews.[20]

16 See Richard Puza, 'La Cour constitutionnelle, la Bavière et le crucifix dans les écoles', (1995) 45 *Revue de droit canonique*, 373ff, commenting on the 1995 decision of the German Federal Constitutional Court on the crucifix in public schools in Bavaria.

17 See *Lautsi I*, § 47c.

18 See in this regard Malcom D. Evans, *Manual on the Wearing of Religious Symbols in Public Areas* (Council of Europe/Martinus Nijoff 2008), especially 59ff and 89ff.

19 *Lautsi v. Italy* (Grand Chamber), 18 March 2011. The *Lautsi* case has been – and keeps being – commented upon by scholars from very diverse positions. See, among Italian scholars, after the Grand Chamber's decision, and from different perspectives, Vincenzo Turchi, 'La pronuncia della Grande Chambre della Corte di Strasburgo sul caso *Lautsi c. Italia*: post nubila Phoebus', (October 2011) *Stato, Chiese e pluralismo confessionale*, where further bibliographical references, especially to Italian legal literature, can be found; and Paolo Ronchi, 'Crucifixes, Margin of Appreciation and Consensus: The Grand Chamber Ruling in *Lautsi v Italy*', (2011) 13 *Ecclesiastical Law Journal*, 287–297. See also, comparing the Strasbourg and the US approach to institutional religious symbols, John Witte Jr. and Nina-Louisa Arold Lorenz, '"Lift High the Cross"? Contrasting the New European and American Cases on Religious Symbols on Government Property', (2011) 25 *Emory International Law Review*, 5–55; and a critical view of *Lautsi II*, in the light of Canadian law and putting the European case law into a socio-cultural perspective, Lori Beaman, 'Battles over Symbols: The "Religion" of the Minority versus the "Culture" of the Majority', (2012–2013) 28 The Journal of Law and Religion, 67ff. In Spain, see Isidoro Martín Sánchez, 'El caso Lautsi ante el Tribunal Europeo de Derechos Humanos', (2012) 28 *Anuario de Derecho Eclesiástico del Estado*, 215–252; Santiago Cañamares Arribas, 'Los símbolos religiosos en el espacio público: entre la amenaza real y la mera sospecha', (April 2011) 20 El Cronista del Estado Social y Democrático de Derecho, 60–67; Silvia Meseguer Velasco, 'Símbolos religiosos en colegios públicos: ¿hacia dónde camina la jurisprudencia europea?', (2011) 5 *Anuario Jurídico Villanueva*, 202–213.

20 See especially *Lautsi II*, § 74.

According to the Grand Chamber, the decision about the presence of religious symbols in public schools falls within the state margin of appreciation. The Court was not expressing agreement (or disagreement) with the Italian government or with the Italian law on crucifixes in public schools. Its only function was to determine if there had been a violation of religious freedom. The ECtHR concluded that Italy was entitled to choose their own symbols and that, in the absence of coercion, intolerance, or indoctrination of persons thinking differently, the Court can not interfere with choices legitimately adopted in accordance with the Italian democratic legislative process.

Should religious minorities be empowered to re-shape the public sphere?

Together with the meaning of the religious neutrality of the state, the main question present in *Lautsi* was if religious minorities – or individuals – have the right to re-shape the public sphere when they feel offended by the display of the symbols that express the beliefs – or just the traditions – of the religious majority, with which they profoundly disagree.

The response of *Lautsi I* was affirmative,[21] and the Second Section categorically assumed that, in a public school, students' freedom of religion or belief implies a negative dimension consisting in their right not to be 'exposed' to the presence of a religious symbol that some may find alien or even offensive. The argument was analogous to that used in the Islamic headscarf cases (which not coincidentally are often cited in that decision); that is, that religious symbols must be avoided in the public school environment because of the hypothetical pressure they must cause on the students disagreeing with or opposing to the meaning of those symbols.

This argument does not seem very persuasive, taking into account the nature of 'static' or 'passive' symbol of the crucifix and the absence – as in the case of Islamic headscarf – of any proselytizing intention or effect.[22] There was no evidence at all that the presence of that Christian symbol was utilized in practice to affirm the 'superiority' of the majority religion in Italy, to indoctrinate students, or to foster conversions. On the other hand, the chamber's reasoning seems also in contradiction with the previous case law of the ECtHR that held – with good reason – that the religious freedom of the believers of a certain religion – be it a majority or minority religion – does not confer them the right to be exempt from criticism or to be free from the influence of contrary or even hostile ideas.[23]

Those holdings of the Second Section were corrected by the Grand Chamber in *Lautsi II*. The Court noted that the mere display of a crucifix in classrooms, as a sign of the religion of the majority of the Italian population, was not sufficient to conclude that there was a process

21 See *Lautsi I*, §§ 53–55.

22 See in this regard the essays cited in note 12 by Cañamares, 6–7, and Mückl, 8–10.

23 See *Otto-Preminger-Institut v. Austria*, 20 September 1994, § 47. See, for further references and bibliography, Javier Martínez-Torrón, 'Freedom of Expression versus Freedom of Religion in the European Court of Human Rights', in András Sajó, ed., *Censorial Sensitivities: Free Speech and Religion in a Fundamentalist World* (Eleven 2007), especially 238–239. With this same orientation, the German Federal Constitutional Court, in 2003, rejected the claim of a father demanding that the table blessing in the local elementary school attended by his son had to be discontinued because he was an atheist and those prayers violated his ideological freedom. Among other things, the German Court affirmed: 'it is not unconstitutional that all children, including those with parents of atheistic convictions, know since their childhood that there are in society people with religious beliefs that wish to practice their beliefs.' See BVerfGE, 1BvR 1522/03 vom 2.10.2003, Absatz-Nr. (1–11).

of indoctrination, and even less if taking into account that the Italian school environment was open to practices and visible expressions of other minority religions. For instance, students could freely wear Islamic headscarves, and optional religious instruction in creeds other than Catholic could be organized at school.[24] Briefly but clearly, the Grand Chamber held that the subjective feeling of some students about the crucifix was not in itself sufficient to establish a breach of the European Convention and to challenge the legitimacy of a school setting that was objectively built according to an open and inclusive concept of neutrality.[25]

It can be argued that *Lautsi II* would have been even better if it had elaborated on some points remarked in the concurring opinions of two of the judges. On the one hand, it would have been useful had the Court expressed more clearly that the value protected by the Convention is religious freedom and not secularity, notwithstanding how legitimate and traditional the latter may be in some European States.[26] As indicated earlier in this chapter, strict separation between state and religion is not included in the ECHR, but only the state neutrality conceived as a condition for the respect for religious freedom. On the other hand, the Court could have developed the idea that coercion should be the test to a violation of freedom of religion or belief, and not the subjective feeling of offense experienced by some persons in the presence of some religious symbols. Just as religious believers do not have the right to be free from criticism, atheistic believers do not have the right to be free from exposure to symbols – personal or institutional – that may offend their convictions or feelings.[27]

Such development would have been helpful to counteract the curious rationale of the Second Section in *Lautsi I*, focused on the (often hypothetical) subjective feelings of individuals. According to the chamber, religious symbols would not have a place in a public school because they could generate in the students the perception that they are brought up in a milieu marked by a particular religion – allegedly, this religion would be perceived as the state's favourite, which would be 'emotionally disturbing for pupils of other religions or those who profess no religion'.[28] Such juridical reasoning centered on emotions and subjectivity is a slippery surface, not exempt from risks and imprecisions, reminiscent of the questionable criterion of the 'reasonable observer' created by the US Supreme Court.[29]

On the one hand, *Lautsi I* took for granted that the presence of the symbol could 'objectively' cause 'emotional disturbance' on students that do not share the belief of the majority. However, the reality is that each person has, towards religious symbols, diverse

24 See especially *Lautsi II*, §§ 70–72, 74.

25 See especially *Lautsi II*, § 66.

26 Compare concurring opinion of Judge Bonello.

27 See concurring opinion of Judge Power.

28 See *Lautsi I*, §§ 54–55. A similar stance was adopted by a first instance court in Spain in 2008, when a 'secular cultural association' of the city of Valladolid required from the school board that crucifixes should be removed from all common areas of the school. The main argument utilized by the court was that the display of religious symbols in an educational center attended by minors could generate in the students the 'feeling' that the state is 'closer' to the Christian religion than to other worldviews (Juzgado de lo Contencioso-Administrativo N° 2, sentencia n° 288/2008, 14 November 2008). Note that in Spain there is no law comparable to the Italian law on crucifixes. No provision obliges public schools to place crucifixes or any other religious symbols in classrooms or other school areas. However, the school board can take that decision. In practice, there are no religious symbols in most public schools in Spain, although in some of the oldest ones – where crucifixes used to be displayed – they have been kept out of respect for the school tradition.

29 See, among others, the bibliography cited in note 23.

(and mutable) feelings and reactions. Indeed, the vast majority of people with atheistic or agnostic beliefs do not express any objection against religious symbols. Their usual reaction is indifference, sometimes accompanied by their respect for the beliefs of others and by their realization that they are often a minority in a place in which the majority belief is other (which is not a negative fact in itself, provided that public authorities ensure that minorities are not discriminated in practice). Seldom people articulate their atheism or agnosticism as intolerance of the presence of visible objects that symbolize religious ideas that they hate, despise, or simply consider false.

On the other hand, we should apply to this issue the same criteria that are applicable to the cases in which people, in use of their freedom of expression, use a language that is offensive for the religious sentiments of other people.[30] Law does not immunize individuals against mere offense. Law protects freedoms and rights, but not feelings or emotions. Law must be based on facts and on objective criteria, and feelings are, by nature, subjective and variable. Therefore, in order to determine whether the display of a religious symbol violates the religious freedom of those opposing the symbol, the test should be aimed at identifying the possible existence of coercion, or of indoctrination, which is another form of coercion, and not on the subjective feeling of offense alleged by dissenters.[31] If a court could grant to opponents to a religious symbol of majoritarian support the right to eliminate the visibility of such symbol, it would be empowering those people to impose their will, and their notion of 'educational habitat', on the majority.

Does the foregoing entail that, from the perspective of the European Convention on Human Rights, minorities, or individuals, are bound to respect the majority decisions concerning the display of religious symbols in public places? The answer must be definitely affirmative, as far as there is no coercion or indoctrination attached to such display – as would be the case, for instance, when a specific act of reverence or worship is required,[32] or when those religious symbols are used to promote intolerance or discrimination of dissenters, be they atheists, agnostics, or believers of other religions. Religion, and its symbols, are part of the culture and should be treated as such – which is not the same as affirming that the crucifix is a cultural symbol, as the Italian Council of State did.[33]

The position of Spanish and German courts

This, indeed, has been the predominant line of reasoning in the Spanish jurisprudence, which has been very open to the maintenance of religious traditions in public places or institutions, and at the same time very firm in proclaiming that no person can be obliged to take an active part in those traditions.[34]

30 See, on this topic, Martínez-Torrón in Sajó, ed., supra note 23 at 233–269.

31 As the concurring opinion of Judge Power in *Lautsi II* put it: 'The test of a violation under Article 9 is not "offence" but "coercion". That article does not create a right not to be offended by the manifestation of the religious beliefs of others even where those beliefs are given "preponderant visibility" by the State. The display of a religious symbol does not compel or coerce an individual to do or to refrain from doing anything. It does not require engagement in any activity though it may, conceivably, invite or stimulate discussion and an open exchange of views. It does not prevent an individual from following his or her own conscience nor does it make it unfeasible for such a person to manifest his or her own religious beliefs and ideas.'

32 Such was the situation in *Buscarini*, cited in note 11.

33 See Consiglio di Stato - Sez. VI. Sentenza n. 556/2006, 13 February 2006.

34 Among the Spanish legal literature on these issues, see Santiago Cañamares Arribas, 'Tratamiento de la simbología religiosa en el Derecho español: propuestas ante la reforma de la Ley orgánica de

Thus, the Constitutional Court has held that state neutrality is compatible with the presence of Christian symbols in public corporations, as far as they are linked to the history of the institution and imply neither the adherence of the state to a particular creed nor any coercion on the religious freedom of individuals. For instance, the Court has found nothing unconstitutional in the fact that a military garrison organized a solemn parade in honour of the local advocation of the Holy Virgin,[35] or in the fact that a unit of the National Police participated in a religious procession during the celebration of the Catholic Holy Week – not to guarantee the safety of the event but in its quality of a member of the relevant religious fraternity, with police officers wearing their gala uniforms.[36] However, the Court has made clear that no officer can be obliged to be present in those religious ceremonies against his personal convictions, for public events reflecting a religious tradition must be reconciled with the individuals' freedom of conscience.

For analogous reasons, the Constitutional Court held that it would have been legitimate for the University of Valencia – a public University – to keep an image of the Holy Virgin that had been traditionally present in its coat of arms, if the University governing bodies had so decided.[37] And, more recently, the Court has sustained the constitutionality of the statutes of the Bar Association of Seville, which have kept, as 'a secular tradition', the Immaculate Conception of the Holy Virgin as its honorary patron.[38] The Court noted that, being the bar association itself aconfessional, preserving this tradition does not infringe either the neutrality of public institutions or the religious freedom of non-Christians. The Court added that symbols reflect the history of institutions, and it is natural to find in the Spanish culture plenty of symbols, with religious connotations, that represent public institutions. Furthermore, the Court observed that in contemporary societies passive symbols have virtually no influence on the people's beliefs and, therefore, the religious freedom of individuals is safe, provided that no one is compelled to participate in rites or ceremonies in honour of those symbols. In the absence of such coercion – the Court concluded – the mere subjective perception of offense is not sufficient to appreciate that freedom of ideology or religion has been violated.

libertad religiosa', (2009) 19 *Revista General de Derecho Canónico y Derecho Eclesiástico del Estado*, 1–29; Alejando González-Varas Ibáñez, 'Los actos religiosos en las escuelas públicas en el derecho español y comparado', (2009) 19 *Revista General de Derecho Canónico y Derecho Eclesiástico del Estado* (2009), 1–28; Gloria Moreno Botella, 'Crucifijo y escuela en España', (2003) 2 *Revista General de Derecho Canónico y Derecho Eclesiástico del Estado*, 1–34. See also Irene María Briones, 'Los símbolos religiosos como signos de identidad y de discordia. De la libertad de conciencia y de expresión del individuo a las tradiciones religiosas de un pueblo'; Lorenzo Martín-Retortillo, 'Símbolos religiosos en actos y espacios institucionales'; and Andrés Ollero Tassara, 'Símbolos religiosos, poder, razón: una reflexión político-jurídica'; all in (2012) 28 *Anuario de Derecho Eclesiástico del Estado.*

35 See STC (*Sentencia del Tribunal Constitucional* /Judgment of the Constitutional Court) 177/1996.

36 See STC 101/2004.

37 See STC 130/1991. In this case, the supreme governing body of the University had decided the opposite, that is, to remove the image of the Virgin from the coat of arms. See Javier Martínez-Torrón, 'Freedom of Religion in the Case Law of the Spanish Constitutional Court', (2001) *Brigham Young University Law Review*, 720–724; Santiago Cañamares Arribas, 'Religious Symbols in Spain: A Legal Perspective', (2009) 11 *Ecclesiastical Law Journal*, 189–191.

38 See STC 34/2011. See Tomás Prieto Álvarez, 'Colegios profesionales, aconfesionalidad y patronazgo religioso. Comentario a la STC de 28 de marzo de 2011', (2011) 79 *Revista Andaluza de Administración Pública*, 137–156.

A comparable position was adopted by the Superior Court of Justice of Valencia in 2011,[39] when it refused to decree the removal of huge cross placed on a mountain since the eighteenth century and rebuilt several times by popular initiative. The Court declared that 'in our country, as in many others of similar cultural and religious traditions ..., there is a visible presence of religious symbols in public places ...; their maintenance is just a manifestation of respect for those traditions and not an imposition of particular religious beliefs, and therefore they cannot be understood as expressing intolerance of non-believers.'[40]

Another interesting case – widely spread by the media – concerning the presence of the crucifix in a public space, and more precisely in the city hall of Saragossa, was decided in 2010 by a court of first instance.[41] A group of left-wing councilmen demanded the mayor to order the removal of an old crucifix from the plenary hall, where the city council meetings were usually held. The mayor – of the Socialist Party – refused to remove the crucifix, making reference to its historical and artistic value as well as to the significance of respect for traditions – that particular crucifix was linked to the life of the Saragossa's city council since the seventeenth century. The issue was put to a vote and the majority of the council decided in favour of keeping the crucifix. The court of first instance confirmed the legitimacy of the council's decision. Interestingly, the court analyzed the issue from the perspective of judicial self-restraint. For the court, the right question was not how or if the council could justify the display of a historic crucifix in the plenary hall but, on the contrary, to elucidate if there was any reason why a court must prohibit the council from having that crucifix in its plenary hall. The court did not find any reason for the prohibition, considering that the principle of secularity does not entail erasing the visibility of religion from public life, and noting that the display of the crucifix was not aimed at imposing a particular religion over other religions or beliefs – it simply reflected the history of a city council more than nine centuries old.

In the educational environment, another case that attracted considerable media attention was resolved by a decision of the Superior Court of Castile and León in 2009.[42] Its origin was a complaint about the crucifixes that hung on the classrooms of a public school in Valladolid. A cultural 'secular' association, following the unsuccessful request of some students' parents to the school board, demanded that the crucifixes were removed from all classes and common spaces of the school. The court of first instance decided in favour of the plaintiffs and ordered the immediate removal of all the crucifixes, on the ground that the display of religious symbols in an educational centre could generate in young students the 'feeling' that the state was 'closer' to the Christian religions than to other worldviews.[43] On appeal, the Superior Court overruled partially the first instance decision. On the one hand, the Court rejected – as contrary to Article 16 of the Constitution and to the case law of the Constitutional Court – any 'maximalist' or 'extreme' interpretation of the constitutional principle of secularity (*laicidad*) that prompted to erase all traces of religion from public life. On the other hand, the Court held that state neutrality obliged to take away from school those religious symbols whose presence could be 'emotionally disturbing' for students and contrary to the parents' rights to have their children educated in accordance with their

39 STSJ Valencia 648/2011 (*Sala de lo Contencioso-Administrativo, Sección 5^aa^*), 6 September 2011.

40 STSJ Valencia 648/2011, FJ 9.

41 *Juzgado de lo Contencioso-Administrativo* Nr. 3 of Saragossa, Judgment Nr. 156/10, 30 April 2010.

42 STSJ Castilla y León 3250/2009 (*Sala de lo Contencioso-Administrativo, Sección 3^a^*), 14 December 2009.

43 See *Juzgado de lo Contencioso-Administrativo* Nr. 2 of Valladolid, Judgment Nr. 288/2008, 14 November 2008, FJ 4.

convictions. As a consequence, in a sort of Solomonic judgment, the Court decreed that crucifixes should be removed only from the school common areas and from those classrooms attended by students whose parents had explicitly complained about their presence; they could remain in the rest of rooms if the school board so determined. It is interesting to note that the Superior Court's judgment was openly grounded on the ECtHR's decision *Lautsi I*. Had *Lautsi II* already been rendered – overruling the chamber's decision – we may conjecture that the Court might have decided differently.

In Germany, the Federal Constitutional Court has adopted a stance closer to an exclusive notion of state neutrality, although giving some margin of appreciation to the states (*Länder*) to accommodate the differing views with respect to the display of religious symbols in public schools.

One of the main conflicts was raised, two decades ago, when some students' parents challenged the Bavarian laws according to which a crucifix had to be placed on the wall of every classroom of public schools. The parents, of anthroposophical convictions, argued that they did not want their children exposed to the daily influence of a religious symbol consisting in the representation of a 'human agonizing body'. The *Bundesverfassungsgericht* declared that aspect of Bavarian law unconstitutional, in a judgment that has received numerous criticisms by German scholars.[44] Among other things, it has been noted that the alleged moral conflict of the students could have been prevented, or accommodated, in other ways, more appropriate to generate an atmosphere of reciprocal tolerance between diverging worldviews. For instance, the crucifix could have been removed from that particular classroom, or moved to a place in the classroom where it would not be noticeable by the objector students. Indeed, such had been the practice of the Court in similar conflicts until then.[45] A few months after the judgment, the Bavarian government modified the law on public schools in order to keep the display of crucifixes in classrooms. When there is an objection by some student – or his parents – the school authorities shall seek an agreed solution to the conflict; and, if this proves to be not possible, they will endeavour to find a balance between the diverging religious and ideological convictions of the students, without losing sight of the majority position.[46]

44 BVerfG, 1 BvR 1087/91 vom 16.05.1995. For an analysis of this judgment and its consequences, see Alexander Hollerbach et al., *Das Kreuz im Widerspruch: der Kruzifix-Beschluss des Bundesverfassungsgerichts in der Kontroverse*, Hans Maier, ed. (Herder 1996). See also Axel Freiherr von Campenhausen, 'Zur Kruzifix-Entscheidung des Bundesverfassungsgerichts', (1996) 121 *Archiv des öffentlichen Rechts*, 448–464; Josef Isensee, 'Bildersturm durch Grundrechtsinterpretation. Der Kruzifix-Beschluß des BverfG', (1996) *Zeitschrift für Rechtspolitik*, 10ff; Detlef Merten, 'Der Kruzifix-Beschluß des Bundesverfassungsgerichts aus grundrechtsdogmatischer Sicht', in Joachim Burmeister, ed., *Verfassungsstaatlichkeit, Festschrift für Klaus Stern zum 65. Geburtstag* (C.H. Beck 1997), 987ff.; Dietrich Pirson, 'Kruzifix in Unterrichtsräumen', (1995) *Bayerische Verwaltungsblätter*, 755–758. In Spain, see Tomás Prieto Álvarez, *Libertad religiosa y espacios públicos. Laicidad, pluralismo, símbolos* (Thomson-Civitas 2010), 81–88, 126–129.

45 See Gerhard Robbers, 'Religious Freedom in Germany', in Javier Martínez-Torrón, ed., *La libertad religiosa y de conciencia ante la justicia constitucional* (Comares 1998), 203–204.

46 Article 7.3 of the *Bayerisches Gesetz über das Erziehungs- und Unterrichtswesen* (BayEUG): 'Angesichts der geschichtlichen und kulturellen Prägung Bayerns wird in jedem Klassenraum ein Kreuz angebracht. Damit kommt der Wille zum Ausdruck, die obersten Bildungsziele der Verfassung auf der Grundlage christlicher und abendländischer Werte unter Wahrung der Glaubensfreiheit zu verwirklichen. Wird der Anbringung des Kreuzes aus ernsthaften und einsehbaren Gründen des Glaubens oder der Weltanschauung durch die Erziehungsberechtigten widersprochen, versucht die Schulleiterin bzw. der Schulleiter eine gütliche Einigung. Gelingt eine

A more hesitant stance towards neutrality was adopted by the Federal Constitutional Court in the *Ludin* case, in 2003, with respect to the wearing of personal religious symbols in public schools, in particular the Islamic headscarf, or *hijab*, by a female teacher.[47] The conflict was raised by a Muslim woman, born in Afghanistan and legal resident in Germany since 1987, who had passed the public examination necessary to take the position of primary school teacher. The education authorities of Baden-Württemberg – one of the German *Länder* or states – excluded her from the possibility to have such position at public schools, because of her firm decision to wear a *hijab* while teaching, despite the fact that she was equally determined to avoid all kinds of indoctrination or proselytism. The state authorities alleged that the Islamic headscarf was a political and religious symbol, incompatible with the neutrality that should permeate the German system of public schools. The plaintiff rejected a notion of state neutrality consisting in the eradication of visible symbols of religious or philosophical ideas, and claimed that true neutrality cannot lead to conceal from students the religious plurality actually existing in German contemporary society. Moreover, she declared that never in her teaching experience had she experienced any situation of tension with her students or with their parents for reason of her *hijab*.

A divided Court decided in favour of the plaintiff,[48] with a reasoning that has raised some doubts among many German scholars. The Court admitted that there were constitutional rights and values – state neutrality, as well as the parents' and the students' rights – that could justify a limitation on the plaintiff's religious freedom, including her disqualification from teaching at public schools, provided that there was a sufficiently specified legal basis. According to the majority of the Court, such specific legal basis was lacking in this case, and therefore a sole 'abstract danger' for those other legal interests was not sufficient to justify a restriction on a constitutional right. The Constitutional Court emphasized three points. First, there are legal interests that undoubtedly can support imposing on teachers of public schools a prohibition from wearing a *hijab*. Second, those interests must be grounded on a specific legislative provision. And third, the states (*Länder*), by virtue of their competences

Einigung nicht, hat sie bzw. er nach Unterrichtung des Schulamts für den Einzelfall eine Regelung zu treffen, welche die Glaubensfreiheit des Widersprechenden achtet und die religiösen und weltanschaulichen Überzeugungen aller in der Klasse Betroffenen zu einem gerechten Ausgleich bringt; dabei ist auch der Wille der Mehrheit, soweit möglich, zu berücksichtigen.'

47 BVerfG, 2 BvR 1436/02 vom 3.6.2003, Absatz-Nr. (1–140). In Spain, this judgment has been analysed by María Ángeles Martín Vida and Sven Müller-Grune, '¿Puede una maestra portar durante las clases en una escuela pública un pañuelo en la cabeza por motivos religiosos?', (2004) 70 *REDCo*, 313–336; Irene María Briones, 'El uso del velo islámico en Europa: un conflicto de libertad religiosa y de conciencia' (2009) 10 *Anuario de Derechos Humanos – Nueva Época*, 35–42; Ángel López-Sidro, 'Breve comentario sobre la sentencia del Tribunal Constitucional Federal de Alemania, de 24 de septiembre de 2003 (2 BvR 1436/02), sobre el velo islámico de una profesora en centro escolar público', (2003) *Revista General de Derecho Canónico y Derecho Eclesiástico del Estado*, 1–3; Jaime Rossell, 'La cuestión del velo islámico y la vestimenta religiosa en la República Federal de Alemania', in Agustín Motilla, ed., *El pañuelo islámico en Europa* (Marcial Pons 2009), 187–193. Among German legal literature, see Gerhard Robbers, 'Muslimische Lehrerinnen, das Kopftuch und das deutsche Bundesverfassungsgericht', (2003) 50 *Österreichisches Archiv für Recht & Religion*, 405–417; Stefan Mückl, 'Der Islam im Staatskirchenrecht des Bundesrepublik Deutschland', in Hartmut Kress, ed., *Religionsfreiheit als Leitbild. Staatskirchenrecht in Deutschland und Europa im Prozess der Reform* (LIT Verlag Münster 2004), 119–139; Johann Bader, 'Cuius regio, eius religio – Wessen Land, dessen Religion', (2004) 43 *Neue Juristische Wochenschrift*, 3092–3094; and, before the Constitutional Court's judgment, Stefan Mückl, 'Religionsfreiheit und Sonderstatusverhältnisse – Kopftuchverbot für Lehrerinnen?' (2001) 40 *Der Staat*, 96–127.

48 The decision was taken by five votes to three.

on education, can enact laws that prohibit teachers from wearing personal religious symbols at school. For the Court, the states are free to legislate on such a sensitive issue in an increasingly plural society, for plurality is positive as far as it facilitates tolerance and open-mindedness, but may have some problematic aspects and constitute a potential source of conflicts.

A number of German states understood the *Ludin* judgment as an invitation to legislate on the issue as they considered appropriate, beginning by Baden-Württemberg, which modified its law on education six months after the judgment[49] in order to forbid every external expression by teachers that could harm the state neutrality vis-à-vis the students or their parents. In particular, the law prohibits all behaviour that may lead to conclude that a teacher is violating human dignity, the equality of rights, fundamental rights, or democratic order. Until now, eight out of sixteen *Länder* have enacted laws on this matter, with diverse nuances.[50] Experience, however, demonstrates that this legislation will not necessarily end judicial conflicts on the issue of Islamic headscarf, in which sometimes the plaintiffs demand an equal treatment with regard to Catholic nuns that are permitted to wear their habits while teaching.[51]

Neutrality as inclusion, neutrality as exclusion

In the light of the preceding discussion and of the current debates about the place of religion in public life that are developing in Europe, and generally in the West, one may wonder if the display of a particular religious symbol in a public space – a symbol of the majority religion in the country – is the best way to promote pluralism and mutual respect between different religious and belief communities. A direct and unconditional affirmative response would certainly be questionable, and a number of distinctions and nuances should be taken into account. For instance, it would be important to differentiate between the various types of public spaces, to determine who took the initiative to set the symbol in a public place, or to consider if the symbol can be easily removed upon request and if other religious symbols are allowed in the same area. A small crucifix on the wall of a hospital, which can be easily detached or substituted by a symbol of other religion, is definitely not the same as a big cross presiding a courtroom.

In any event, as has been repeatedly mentioned in this chapter, it is not for the courts to decide on public policies regarding religious symbols, and even less for the European Court of Human Rights. Courts are not policy makers. Their role is to apply the law of the land, to adjudicate on rights. In the case of the ECtHR, its role is to resolve if the display of a religious symbol in a particular context entails an element of coercion or indoctrination that constitutes a violation of the freedom of thought, conscience, or religion guaranteed by

49 More precisely, Article 38 of its Law on Schools (*Schulgesetz*). See Alejandro Torres Gutierrez, 'Neutralidad del Estado y empleo de los símbolos religiosos en centros públicos en Alemania: la sentencia del Tribunal Constitucional Alemán de 24 de septiembre de 2003', (2005) 5 *Laicidad y libertades*, 295–297.

50 For an interesting source of information and documentation on the evolution of the laws enacted by the German states (*Länder*) after the Federal Constitutional Court's judgment, see the Internet pages of the *Institut für europäisches Verfassungsrecht* of the University of Trier: http://www.uni-trier.de/index.php?id=24373 (accessed 28 March 2017). See also, in Spain, Rossell, supra note 47 at 193ff.

51 See, for further details and references, Navarro-Valls and Martínez-Torrón, supra note 10 at 354–355.

Article 9 ECHR. With particular reference to the *Lautsi* case, a law that imposes the presence of the crucifix in all public schools of the country is probably not a good idea. It would likely be more appropriate to take such decision at the local level. But, again, the role of the courts is not to validate the appropriateness of such political solution but only to ascertain if the static presence of a small crucifix on the wall of a classroom amounts to coercion or indoctrination. And the Grand Chamber of the ECtHR rightly concluded that it did not.

It has been often said, and it is true, that the realm of education is particularly sensitive with regard to the presence of religious symbols – institutional and personal – and other external expressions of religion, for it involves the transmission of values to young generations, the right of parents to decide the religious and moral orientation of their children's education, and the state's obligation to abstain from indoctrination against the parents' wishes, out of respect for the freedom of choice in matters of religion or belief (*forum internum*). In essence, two basic approaches are possible in this matter. One is based on an exclusive notion of state neutrality, which leads to prohibit religious symbols in public schools with the aim of eliminating the visibility of religion; an extreme conception of this kind is followed by France, whose law excludes even noticeable personal garments that reveal the student's religion.[52] The other is based on an inclusive notion of neutrality, and allows for a variety of symbols, institutional and personal, that can coexist and are part of the ordinary 'landscape' of the public school.[53]

Although both approaches are legitimate from the perspective of the ECHR, and in general from the perspective of international standards on religious freedom, certainly the preferred approach is the one based on an inclusive concept of neutrality, among other things because it is more realistic than creating an artificial school atmosphere characterized by the absence of religion. It seems unreasonable to require, in a country enjoying religious peace, that no religious symbols are visible either in classrooms or in the students' or teachers' clothes, instead of making possible that students can see in their own school an evidence of the religious pluralism existing in society. Allowing spontaneous expressions of religious pluralism seems to be more consistent with a neutral attitude of the state, and probably also more educative for students than imposing the fictitious absence of religion.

52 *Loi n.° 2004–228, du 15 mars 2004, encadrant, en application du principe de laïcité, le port de signes ou de tenues manifestant une appartenance religieuse dans les écoles, collèges et lycées publics.* This law and its conception of state neutrality have been ratified by the *Charte de la laïcité à l'École*, produced by the French Ministry of Education (circulaire n° 2013–144 du 6-9-2013); text available at http://www.education.gouv.fr/pid25535/bulletin_officiel.html?cid_bo=73659 (accessed 28 March 2017). For a critical comment on the 2004 French law, see Alain Garay, 'Secularism, Schools and Religious Affiliation: For a Demanding Account of Law no. 2004–228 of March 15, 2004', in W. Cole Durham, Jr., Tore Lindholm, and David M. Kirkham, *Islam and Political-Cultural Europe* (Ashgate 2012), 117–145. In the broader context of relations between state and religion in France, see Blandine Chelini-Pont and T. Jeremy Gunn, *Dieu en France et aux Etat-Unis. Quand les mythes font la loi* (Berg 2005). In Spain, see Santiago Cañamares Arribas, *Libertad religiosa, simbología y laicid del Estado* (Aranzadi 2005), 70ff; Alejandro González-Varas Ibáñez, *Confessioni religiose, diritto e scuola pubblica in Italia. Insegnamento, culto e simbologia religiosa nelle scuole pubblich* (CLUEB 2005), 229ff; María José Ciáurriz, 'Laicidad y ley sobre los símbolos religiosos en Francia', in Motilla, *El pañuelo islámico en Europa*, supra note 47 at 91ff.

53 This is the line that seems to be suggested by the *EU Guidelines on the promotion and protection of freedom of religion or belief*, approved by the Council of the European Union on 24 June 2013 (see especially §§ 34, 37, 46), text available at http://consilium.europa.eu/uedocs/cms_data/docs/pressdata/EN/foraff/137585.pdf (accessed 27 March 2017).

Unless there is a *specific* risk for the public order or the social peace, or unless the presence of religious symbols actually puts pressure on people disagreeing with them, a strict prohibition of external signs of religion – institutional or personal, Christian or of other religions – is not necessary either to preserve state neutrality or to protect the freedom of choice of members of the school community in belief matters.

Indeed, such prohibition could transmit a wrong subliminal message to the young generations. If the school is supposed to be the realm of reason, culture, and values, that is, the domain of civilization, excluding religion from school could be easily understood as implying that religion does not belong in school (while other non-religious beliefs do). It can hardly be seen as a manifestation of neutrality.

Part IV

Conclusion

13 Religious pluralism

Peace or poison?

W. Cole Durham, Jr. and Donlu D. Thayer

The ideal and the problem

We have undertaken in this volume to explore aspects of the sociological reality that seems to have become the irreversible destiny of mankind: that we live in an increasingly pluralized world. Even once religiously homogeneous societies are becoming increasingly diverse. While we remain convinced that religious freedom is modernity's most profound if sometimes forgotten answer to the resulting social pressures, we acknowledge the tide of pluralization that threatens to overwhelm that freedom's stabilizing force.

This volume has been aimed at exploring differing ways of grappling with the resulting tensions, and then asking: Will the tensions ultimately yield poisonous polarization that erodes all hope of meaningful community? Or can the tradition and the institutions protecting freedom of religion or belief be developed and applied in ways that (still) foster productive interactions, stability, and peace?

An often quoted passage from one of the leading religious freedom decisions of the European Court of Human Rights articulates the challenge:

> [While] it is possible that tension is created in situations where a religious or any other community becomes divided, … this is one of the unavoidable consequences of pluralism. The role of the authorities in such circumstances is not to remove the cause of tension by eliminating pluralism, but to ensure that the competing groups tolerate each other….[1]

The difficulty, of course, lies in understanding the social forces in play, and determining concretely how to achieve the social peace and toleration that the Court recommends. How do 'authorities' *ensure* toleration among competing groups? And even if it could be achieved, is 'toleration' enough to ensure peace? Are there ways to influence a kind of mutual understanding that transcends mere toleration and goes to the core of what 'peace' actually is?

A vital starting point for analysis is that there is in fact wide-ranging respect for religious freedom ideals. As the European Court of Human Rights recognized in a landmark 2008 opinion:

> While religious freedom is primarily a matter of individual conscience, it also implies, inter alia, freedom to 'manifest [one's] religion' alone and in private or in community

1 *Serif v. Greece*, App. No. 38178/97 (ECtHR, 14 December 1999), para. 53.

> with others, in public and within the circle of those whose faith one shares ... The autonomous existence of religious communities is indispensable for pluralism in a democratic society and is, thus, an issue at the very heart of the protection which Article 9 [on religious freedom] affords.[2]

The ideal of religious freedom has long constituted the most significant response to the challenge of religious pluralism. A key insight of modernity is that respect for religious difference can be a source of stability as well as a source of tension. Only a generation ago, the right to freedom of religion or belief seemed securely ensconced as a fundamental and even a 'first' freedom. This was clearly true in Western bloc countries, and protections spread further as a result of the collapse of Soviet-style communism and the ripple effects of that transformational change in many other parts of the world. As of late 2018, 171 countries have ratified and six more have signed the International Covenant on Civil and Political Rights, with its Article 18 on freedom of religion or belief.[3] This basic principle of international human rights is reinforced by numerous regional instruments,[4] and most national constitutions have provisions designed to protect this freedom.[5]

Despite the widespread formal commitment to this ideal, however, the practical realities are far less encouraging. Data gathered annually by the Pew Research Center on Religion and Public Life over the past decade indicates that at least 42 percent of the 198 countries and territories included in the studies had high or very high restrictions on religion (combining both government restrictions on religion and social hostilities towards religion), and since these countries include many of the most populous countries on earth, nearly 80 percent of the world's population lives under such conditions.[6] Significantly, Pew studies have shown a steady increase in both government restrictions on religion and social hostilities involving religion in the years 2007 through 2012, reversing slightly in 2013 and 2014, and increasing again in 2015 and 2016, as reported in 2017 and 2018.[7]

The Pew data show not only that more than three-quarters of the people in the world live in countries where they experience high or very high government restrictions on religion but that correlations between such restrictions and majority religious populations, mostly

2 *Religionsgemeinschaft der Zeugen Jehovahs v. Austria*, App. No. 27540/05 (ECtHR, 25 September 2008).

3 See the UN Human Rights Office of the High Commissioner's 'Status of Ratification Interactive Dashboard' at http://indicators.ohchr.org/.

4 The European Convention on Human Rights (of the Council of Europe), the American Convention on Human Rights (of the Organization of American States), the African Union, for example, and more indirectly such entities as the Association of Southeast Asian Nations (ASEAN). Further reinforcement of these norms is provided by the political commitments made by participating states in the Organization for Cooperation in Europe.

5 See overview of constitutional protections in an appendix, 'Comparative Constitutional Provisions on Religion and Religious Freedom around the World, § 37:20 of William Bassett, W. Cole Durham, Jr., and Robert T. Smith, *Religious Organizations and the Law* (Thomson Reuters 2018, updated annually). See also Javier Martinez-Torrón and W. Cole Durham, Jr. 'General Report', in *Religion and the Secular State: National Reports* (Faculty of Law of Complutense University of Madrid 2015).

6 The most recent data analyzed comes from 2016, reported in Pew Research Center on Religion & Public Life, 'Global Uptick in Government Restrictions on Religion in 2016 (Nationalist parties and organizations played an increasing role in harassment of religious minorities, especially in Europe)', 21 June 2018, at http://www.pewforum.org/2018/06/21/global-uptick-in-government-restrictions-on-religion-in-2016/ (accessed 10 July 2018).

7 See Pew Research Center, 'Global Uptick in Government Restrictions on Religion in 2016'.

Muslim, are high. At the same time, the greatest increase reported for the 2015 data (13%) was in social hostilities against Muslims occurring in Europe (from 58% of countries to 71% of countries) and in Sub-Saharan Africa (from 25% to 38% of countries). In contrast, perhaps not surprisingly, social hostilities in that year against Muslims decreased in the Middle East and Northern Africa by 10%, from 75% to 65%.[8] The 2015 data covers trends for a year bracketed by deadly terrorist attacks in Paris, where in January avowed Islamist extremists killed 12 people at the offices of the satirical magazine *Charlie Hebdo*, a policewoman, and four people at a kosher supermarket; and in November a series of coordinated terrorist attacks killed 130 people and injured nearly 400 more. The European refugee crisis also began in 2015 and with it fears of ISIS militants hiding in the streams of mostly Muslim migrants fleeing from Muslim-majority countries and flooding Europe in search of asylum or economic aid.

Another major issue resulting in heightened consciousness of problems of religious pluralism involves blasphemy laws. In Indonesia, for example, despite concerted efforts by major NGOs and testimony by 49 national and international experts, the Supreme Court in 2010 upheld the country's blasphemy law. The law was widely seen by legal experts in Indonesia and around the world to be unconstitutional, but the Court asserted it was designed 'to protect all religions from desecration and to ensure religious harmony between faiths' and should therefore be preserved.[9] More recently (May 2017) in Indonesia, 'Ahok', the popular Christian governor of Jakarta was sentenced to two years in prison for blasphemy after allegedly insulting the Qu'ran in a comment during a campaign speech.[10]

In Pakistan blasphemy – making any 'imputation, insinuation or innuendo' against the Prophet Muhammad – carries a mandatory death sentence. Most notoriously, a Christian mother of five, Asia Noreen Bibi, had by late 2018 spent eight years in prison under sentence of death for blasphemy as a result of what she insisted were the baseless accusations of co-workers. In January 2011, the governor of Punjab, Salman Taseer, was killed by his own bodyguard after visiting Bibi in prison and expressing sympathy for her cause. A few months later, Shahbaz Bhatti, the only Christian minister in the Pakistan government, was assassinated for opposing the blasphemy law and expressing sympathy for Bibi. It is important to note that while no death sentence has been carried out under the Pakistani blasphemy law, hysteria surrounding blasphemy charges 'has led to the targeting of minorities, fake allegations, and at least 69 vigilante murders since 1990.'[11]

During the campaign that saw him elected Prime Minister of Pakistan in 2018, Imran Khan voiced strong support for the blasphemy law, though he had been known in the past to be critical of it. The son of Shabaz Bhatti accused Khan of political opportunism,

8 Kayatoun Kishi, 'Muslims, Jews Faced Social Hostilities in Seven-in-Ten European Countries in 2015', 12 April 2017, http://www.pewresearch.org/fact-tank/2017/04/12/muslims-jews-faced-social-hostilities-in-seven-in-ten-european-countries-in-2015/.

9 See Arghea Desafti Hapsari, 'Experts Insist Blasphemy Law Undermines Freedom', *The Jakarta Post*, 25 March 2010, at http://www.thejakartapost.com/news/2010/03/25/experts-insist-blasphemy-law-undermines-freedom.html (accessed 10 July 2018).

10 On this, see, for example, Joe Cochrane, '"Rot at the Core": Blasphemy Verdict in Indonesia Dismays Legal Experts', *The New York Times*, 11 May 2017, at https://www.nytimes.com/2017/05/11/world/asia/indonesia-blasphemy-governor-jakarta-ahok.html (accessed 10 July 2018). See also Tim Lindsay, 'Retreat from Democracy', *Australian Foreign Affairs* #3, 9 July 2018.

11 Memphis Barker, 'Imran Khan Criticised for Defence of Pakistan Blasphemy Laws', *The Guardian*, 9 July 2018, https://www.theguardian.com/world/2018/jul/09/imran-kahn-accused-over-defence-of-pakistan-blasphemy-laws.

cowardice, and supporting murderers and mob violence: 'This law is persecuting people, it is not respecting our prophet.'[12] A part of Khan's political platform was the stated goal of fostering peace with neighboring India, where the another majority, this one Hindu, faces increasing international criticism for persecution of religious minorities.[13]

These and countless other problems, recurring in myriad forms across the daily headlines of news media around the world,[14] underscore the pervasiveness of the challenges of pluralism. In such situations, actions to curtail a flourishing religious pluralism by a majority that feels challenged, undermined, or otherwise threatened, have been justified in the name of various public interests – some legitimate but many not. Contrary to those who see religious pluralism as an ultimate societal 'poison,' however, we contend that it is in fact an important foundation for peace. As Tore Lindholm argues, social stability 'is not jeopardized by but *requires* plurality at the foundations of the right to freedom of religion or belief'.[15]

Achieving stabilizing pluralism

Demographic data make it clear that mere plurality – in the sense of people of diverse ethnicity, heritage, and belief systems sharing cultural and legal space, the 'co-presence of many'[16] – is the sociological reality of our times. But this says little the various forms that this plurality may take. This is not the place to undertake a comprehensive review of theories of pluralism.[17] Pluralism that can provide a stable basis for modern society requires more than mere plurality. At a minimum, it is helpful to make a distinction between 'plural' and 'plurality', on the one hand, which refer to the fact of sociological diversity, and 'pluralist' and 'pluralism' on the other hand, which connote 'a cognitive or evaluative "stance to plurality"'.[18] But there are, of course, a broad range of stances one can take towards pluralism, and much depends on the modality of pluralism that is adopted.

Clearly, any meaningful type of pluralism presupposes a community in which communication is possible. Good faith communication is the key to solving many of the challenges of pluralism. It is for this reason that the importance of dialogue is so often stressed as a vital factor in achieving social stability. For example, Pope Francis is reported to have said:

> When leaders in various fields ask me for advice [about peaceful coexistence], my response is always the same: dialogue, dialogue, dialogue. The only way for individuals, families and societies to grow, the only way for the life of peoples to progress, is via the

12 Barker.

13 See 'Imran Khan Bats for Cooperation with India to Ensure Regional Peace', *The Times of India*, 9 July 2018, at http://timesofindia.indiatimes.com/articleshow/64922356.cms, and Kannan Sundaram, 'As intolerance grows, India needs a brand of secularism that keeps a distance from religion, caste', *Scroll.in* Opinion, 9 July 2018, at https://scroll.in/article/884179/as-intolerance-grows-india-needs-a-brand-of-secularism-that-keeps-a-distance-from-religion-caste.

14 See International Law and Religion Headlines at https://www.iclrs.org/internationalheadlines.

15 Tore Lindholm, 'Philosophical and Religious Justifications of Freedom of Religion or Belief', in Tore Lindholm, W. Cole Durham Jr., Bahia G. Tahzib-Lie, Elizabeth A. Sewell, and Lena Larsen, *Facilitating Freedom of Religion or Belief: A Deskbook* (Brill Nijhoff 2004), 21.

16 Lindholm at 20 (fn 6).

17 For comprehensive recent studies, see Jacob T. Levy, *Rationalism, Pluralism, and Freedom* (Oxford University Press 2015); Victor M. Muñiz-Fratricelli, *The Structure of Pluralism: On the Authority of Organizations* (Oxford University Press 2014);

18 We follow a distinction here used by Ian S. Markham, *Plurality and Christian Ethics* (Seven Ridges Press, rev ed, 1999) and deployed by Tore Lindholm, supra note 15 at 20 (fn 6).

> culture of encounter, a culture in which all have something good to give and all can receive something good in return. Others always have something to give me, if we know how to approach them in a spirit of openness and without prejudice. This open spirit, without prejudice, I would describe as 'social humility', which is what favours dialogue. Only in this way can understanding grow between cultures and religions, mutual esteem without needless preconceptions, in a climate that is respectful of the rights of everyone. Today, either we take the risk of dialogue, we risk the culture of encounter, or we all fall; this is the path that will bear fruit.[19]

Of course, dialogue must have certain key elements if it is to constitute the kind of authentic dialogue that is necessary for achieving stabilizing pluralism. Kristen Looney, Director of the Religious Freedom Forum Institute in Washington, DC, has outlined skills helpful in creating a culture of civility and respect, including key elements useful for 'promoting dialogue among people of all religions and none'.[20] Referring to the Greek notion of *dialogos* as 'thinking together and seeking understanding', Looney suggests that authentic dialogue is not discussion, debate, deliberation, mediation, conflict resolution, or problem solving. Skillful dialogue involves an open attitude, listening, speaking, responding, and reflecting. It is not an exercise in conquest. And it does not require that one surrender or repudiate one's deepest beliefs.[21]

Beyond authentic dialogue, there is a need for what can be called 'engaged dialogue'. Such a stance is described in some detail by Diana Eck, founder and director of The Pluralism Project at Harvard University, who defines pluralism as the 'energetic engagement with diversity and, beyond mere tolerance, the active seeking of understanding across lines of difference'. Diversity and tolerance alone do not require encounter, relationship, mutual understanding, all of which a robust pluralism requires. And '[m]ere diversity without real encounter and relationship will yield increasing tensions in our societies.' Though tolerance 'is a necessary public virtue', observes Eck, 'it does not require Christians and Muslims, Hindus, Jews, and ardent secularists to know anything about one another. ... In the world in which we live today, our ignorance of one another will be increasingly costly.'[22] Eck's recommendation is to engage a 'new paradigm', an 'encounter of commitments' that 'means holding our deepest differences, even our religious differences, not in isolation, but in relationship to one another'.[23]

How is such a stance – how is such pluralism – effectuated? What are the costs and compromises of achieving stabilizing pluralism? Other authors in this book, beginning with Sandberg and Thompson, delineate and explore possibilities and paths. As we consider the

19 Cited in Norberto Padilla, 'Religious Pluralism: The Argentine Experience', Chapter 8 of this volume. Full text available at http://www.vatican.va/holy_father/francesco/speeches/2013/july/documents/papa-francesco_20130727_gmg-classe-dirigente-rio_en.html (accessed 10 July 2018).

20 See Kristen Looney, 'Bridging Cultural and Personal Divides: Creating a Culture of Civility and Respect', presentation at the Religious Freedom Annual Review, Brigham Young University, 21 June 2018.

21 For a more extensive discussion of key features needed for meaningful dialogue across deep divides, see Leonard Swidler, 'Freedom of Religion and Dialogue', in Lindholm, Durham and Tahzib-Lie, *Deskbook*, supra note 15 at 761–776. Particularly helpful is his 'Dialogue Decalogue', reproduced at pages 772–775 of his chapter in the *Deskbook*.

22 Diana L. Eck, 'What Is Pluralism?' *The Pluralism Project, Harvard University*, 2006, http://pluralism.org/what-is-pluralism/.

23 Eck.

objectives, hopes, and challenges, it is worth continually asking ourselves and suggesting to others the difficult questions: Does pluralism require that, for the sake of peaceful coexistence in our increasingly diverse societies, we must be actively complicit in 'error'? Does it require accepting the notion of religious (even moral) relativism? Does it mean that there is no 'real' truth, but only subjective perceptions – my perceived reality and your perceived reality? Asher Maoz states the issue in stark terms: 'If you know that truth lies with you, why should you tolerate contrary teachings? Why should you sanction the freedom to practice a religion that you know is false?'[24]

These questions may be even more difficult if one strives to engage Eck's engagement paradigm. If, as Eck asserts, pluralism requires 'dialogue ... give and take, criticism and self-criticism ... both speaking and listening [in a process that] reveals both common understandings and real differences', what compromises does engagement entail? If pluralism 'involves the commitment to being at the table – with one's commitments'[25] (without expecting change in the commitments of others), can we do it? Should we do it? In practical terms, what does such a process look like? Can a group take a seat at the pluralistic table without compromising its principles? Can it keep its fundamental commitments intact while pursuing reconciliation, or will distinctive differences be lost in the process? Does the religious pluralism that the 'Western world now takes for granted' necessarily compromise the 'moral fragmentation' resulting from the Protestant Reformation of the sixteenth and seventeenth centuries, when civil government could no longer 'assume that society rested on any sort of religious consensus'.[26] Richard John Neuhaus has asserted:

> Genuine democratic pluralism depends upon dualism. It depends on an acknowledgement that nobody has the correct fit between the ultimacies of God's self-revelation and the penultimacies of the ordering of our political life .... It is difficult for certain communities to affirm genuine democratic pluralism when they believe that other groups are misleading people to damnation.[27]

This leads to a first dilemma, which Tore Lindholm articulates as follows: 'How can I reasonably respect proponents of doctrines and practices that contradict my own serious commitments without, somehow, renouncing those commitments?'[28] Many, says Lindholm, will see this as merely 'an alleged (and "outdated") dilemma'.

> Their position in this regard would be sound if the challenge of accommodating mutual respect across fundamental normative divides were already widely understood to be properly resolved. However, it is not. Surely, in many contemporary societies the problem of mutual respect across normative divides is no longer held to be a major issue. But in many contexts this remains a live issue that needs to be candidly addressed.

24 See Asher Maoz, 'Religious Freedom and Pluralism: A Judaic Perspective', Chapter 4 of this volume.
25 Eck, supra note 22.
26 Frederick Mark Gedicks, 'The Religious, the Secular, and the Antithetical', (1991) 20 *Capital University Law Review* 118, citing Richard John Neuhaus, *The Naked Public Square* 172 (2d ed. 1986).
27 Richard John Neuhaus in Markham, supra note 18 at 182, 185.
28 Lindholm, supra note 15 at 23.

> Accordingly, we have reason not to repress or paper over the troublesome foundational question lurking beneath the pluralist surface of modern public life.[29]

Even supposing this first dilemma to be suitably settled, Lindholm identifies a second and even more troubling dilemma stemming from the presence of conflicting premise systems in plural societies:

> A plurality of sets of incompatible premises, each of which may constitute internally well-grounded support for freedom of religion or belief, appears as a whole to be incoherent and hence not a reasonable public grounding.
>
> The two dilemmas of justifying freedom of religion or belief across normative divides may in given circumstances trigger threats to social peace and stability. For example, the first dilemma can lead to conflict between rival 'fundamentalist' communities within a larger political order. ... The second dilemma calls attention to stability hazards of plural societies that have failed to spell out and entrench a shared public understanding of the basis for moral solidarity across religious and life-stance divides.[30]

We agree with Lindholm that these dilemmas need to be taken seriously, both because of their historical validity 'either as explicit premises or as unstated assumptions behind much of human discourse concerning freedom of religion or belief' and 'because they help identify hurdles that must be overcome, and a direction in which we need to move, to accommodate recalcitrant challenges to plural public justifications and to attain stable backing for religious and life-stance pluralism'.[31] However, as Lindholm himself has recognized, less is needed to achieve (and justify) stable pluralism than is often thought.

Contrary to what is often assumed, stability does not depend on religious homogeneity (or some weaker religious common denominator of shared values) and can be reconciled with deep religious differences. What is needed, according to Lindholm's analysis, is 'public espousals of differing yet overlapping justifications of the right' to freedom of religions or belief.[32] What counts, in his view, is

> not whether religious people appreciate other beliefs and practices or whether they admit of alternative paths to salvation ... [but] whether each, on sound internal grounds, supports the public doctrine of the equal inherent dignity and inalienable freedom of all human beings, irrespective of their religion, life stance, or any other differences, and that each reasonably understand[s] or else trust[s] that other[s] similarly support general freedom of religion or belief.[33]

That is, what is necessary for social stability and peace is not shared religious doctrines in general, but a much more limited agreement to respect the publicly accepted notions of dignity and inalienable freedom, and the ability to find overlapping justifications of the right to freedom of religion or belief. This more limited agreement should not be unduly difficult,

29 Lindholm at 23.
30 Lindholm at 23–24.
31 Lindholm at 24. Note that Lindholm uses the term 'life-stance' to 'capture nonreligious positions referred to by the term "belief" in the human rights-locution "freedom of religion or belief" ...' id. at 21 fn 8.
32 Lindholm at 21.
33 Lindholm at 46.

because it is the mirror image of the respect that the individual claims for him- or herself. Pluralism that reflects this minimal constraint is likely to promote stability, because protection of this inner core of freedom and dignity earns the gratitude and loyalty of the individual (or group) thus protected. The linkage of respect and toleration with social stability was a central insight of John Locke's political theory,[34] has been vindicated by over two centuries of experience, and continues to be validated by empirical research today.[35]

Of course, one might worry that conditions have deteriorated sufficiently that these time-tested principles can no longer be looked to for realistic solutions. Lindholm and Eck were writing in 2004 and 2006 respectively, and Pope Francis was speaking in 2013. These statements came after 9/11 but before the violent extremists of the Islamic State of Iraq and al-Sham began beheading journalists on camera in 2014, and before the horrors of the conflicts in Syria that claimed 400,000 lives between 2011 and 2018. What do 'social humility' and a 'culture of encounter' look like as the second decade of the twenty-first century draws to a close? How does dialogue take place in a post-ISIS world?

In these circumstances, it may be difficult even to contemplate engaging in authentic dialogue in the rancorous political atmospheres now present in many countries of the world – East, West, Global North, Global South, and everywhere in between. But what alternative is there? Neither dissent into social chaos and violence nor subjugation to non-pluralistic autocracy are welcome alternatives. As we have tried to suggest in this book, the best hope lies in cultivating deeper understanding of the issues, and it proceeds with a commitment to applying principles known to be conducive to social stability and human flourishing and to counter eroding their foundations.

Protecting the foundations of stable pluralism

The foregoing analysis helps to explain why freedom of religion or belief is such a vital aspect of stable pluralism. There are, to be sure, longstanding challenges in a significant number of the world's countries where the ideals of freedom of religion or belief have not been uniformly held or protected, and where in fact, as described earlier, intolerance in the form of government restrictions on religion and social hostilities towards religion continue to increase. There are also critical emerging challenges to fostering a climate protective of these ideals in places where they have for centuries been fundamental. In a number of such societies hostilities and restrictions are also rising, as a variety of converging trends combine, not necessarily to diminish the ideals themselves but to lower their priority, to erode the scope of religious exceptions and, in general, to weaken the commitment to protecting religious freedom itself.

One of the most corrosive threats to stable pluralism is fear. A major ground for tensions in pluralistic settings is that each sub-community has fears that it will be exposed to persecution by others, or will lose levels of privilege and recognition it has held in the past. An excellent example of this is what Russell Sandberg has described as the 'moral panics' arising in our 'post 9/11 world', in which concerns about Islam, including a fear of sharia, have become commonplace.[36]

34 John Locke, *A Letter Concerning Toleration* (first published in 1689; cited edition: Library of Liberal Arts 1990).

35 See Brian J. Grim and Roger Finke, *The Price of Freedom Denied: Religious Persecution and Conflict in the Twenty-First Century* (Cambridge University Press 2011), ch. 7 and Appendix.

36 Russell Sandberg, 'Conclusion: In Pursuit of Pluralism', in Rossella Bottoni, Rinaldo Cristofori, and Silvio Ferrari, eds, *Religious Rules, State Law, and Normative Pluralism – A Comparative Overview* (Springer 2016), 395.

> These apprehensions existed before 2001 and had previously given rise to moral panics across the globe. However, in the twenty-first century these panics have become more frequent with concerns about fundamentalism overflowing into debates about the wearing of religious dress and symbols in the public sphere, the appropriateness of the publication of words and images that satirise religious imagery and the operation of courts and tribunals who apply religious rules.[37]

That these panics often manifest a fear of sharia 'is simply a convenient short-hand' for deeper anxieties, says Sandberg, arising from widespread uncertainties induced by the accelerated social change of the late twentieth century. Dilution of distinctive political differences; the falling away of age-old traditions and forms of employment, of geographic barriers, and of consensus concerning gender roles and sexual orientation; 'mass communication, information overload and instant access to people at all social levels'; achieved identity becoming more important than ascribed identities. 'These profound changes … have had a significant effect upon religion.'[38]

Refining conceptions of pluralism

One of the ironies in responding to the challenges of pluralism is that, sometimes, dealing with the consequences of pluralism requires even greater pluralism, or at least a deeper understanding of pluralism. In this regard, Russell Sandberg and Sharon Thompson open this volume with a discussion of this paradox of pluralism: that too often 'the pluralist focus is not pluralist enough'.[39] Their contention is that in order to have an adequate approach to the problems of pluralism, we need to be able to take into account the rich variety of ways that individual agency interacts with different sub-communities within society, as well as with the state, if we are to arrive at an adequate account of the full complexity of pluralism. It is too easy in the process of criticizing a particular pluralist view to short-change the importance of other pluralist perspectives.

Sandberg and Thompson give the insightful example of Ayelet Shachar's critique of the 'right to exit' argument (i.e., the notion that a group's norms should be respected so long as its members have a free right of exit). Shachar maintains that this imposes 'the burden of solving conflict upon the individual' whilst 'relieving the state of any responsibility for the situation.' Sandberg and Thompson note how Shachar is critical of a binary approach that sees the individual either as a member of a group or a citizen of the state, but then point out how this analysis fails to give a sufficiently refined notion of how interaction with groups shapes individual identity. In the paradigm of Sandberg and Thompson, 'reference to differing perspectives and a move away from binary solutions provides a step forward.'

In similar ways, secular defense of certain rights can too easily fail to give full value to religious rights and religious identity in balancing conflicting interests. In this regard, the decision in June 2018 of the United States Supreme Court in *Masterpiece Cakeshop, Ltd. v. Colorado Civil Rights Commission* (584 U. S. ___ (2018)) provides an important reminder. Whatever one's views on whether the baker, Jack Phillips, should have been able to refuse on conscientious grounds to make a wedding cake for a gay couple, it was important to

37 Sandberg, 'Conclusion: In Pursuit of Pluralism' at 395–396.
38 Sandberg at 396.
39 Sandberg and Thompson at 4.

remember the importance of affording equal and neutral respect to the religious convictions of the baker, even while seeking to vindicate the rights of the gay couple. Failure to give fair weight to the rights of the religious freedom claimant risks unraveling the core principle necessary to sustain pluralism for all in a world of deep difference.

A judgment of the Supreme Court of Canada issued two weeks after *Masterpiece Cakeshop* in the US provides perhaps an even more important reminder of how the conflicting interests might be balanced in the courts, in a decision that, in the words of the Canadian Conference of Catholic Bishops, is 'a harbinger for serious disputes to come'.[40] In *Law Society of British Columbia v. Trinity Western University* (2018 SCC 32) the Court held, 7–2, that provincial law societies could refuse to admit lawyers trained in the law school of a university where students were required to sign a 'Community Covenant' pledging to uphold the university's Christian character while studying at the school. Among the requirements of covenant is avoiding 'sexual intimacy that violates the sacredness of marriage between a man and a woman'.[41] 'Hailed a triumph by gender-identity activists, [the] decision is described by critics as a "severe blow" to religious freedom in Canada and throughout the West.'[42]

Much has been and will be written about this landmark case.[43] It will suffice us here to quote constitutional specialist Iain Benson, one of the authors of this volume:

> Whether they realize it or not, the Supreme Court of Canada is demonstrating textbook secularism, which is increasing marginalization and privatization of religion in Canada ... a project designed to make religion and religious irrelevant to culture.[44]

In the words of Barry W. Bussey, one of the lawyers involved in litigating the case, 'Simply put, these decisions are going to have a lasting effect on how we understand and apply the Charter right of religious freedom in Canada.'[45]

Finding principled grounds for compromise

Part of what makes stable pluralism possible is that people adhering to different belief systems can often find grounds for agreeing on a range of issues despite deep difference on a variety of key issues. There are any number of ways this can happen. Sometimes this may be because while certain core beliefs are inconsistent, there is no disagreement in other areas, where overlapping consensus exists. Sometimes core beliefs about caring for others will override lesser beliefs about taking moral stands against conduct that is disapproved. That is, while public attention focuses on those cases in which someone for conscientious reasons objects to being even loosely connected with conduct of others which he or she finds

40 Celeste McGovern, 'Canadian Top Court Renders "Severe Blow" to Religious Freedom in Trinity Western Case', *National Catholic Register*, 28 July 2018, at http://www.ncregister.com/daily-news/canadian-top-court-renders-severe-blow-to-religious-freedom-in-trinity-west.

41 Trinity Western University, Community Covenant Agreement, at https://www.twu.ca/sites/default/files/twu-community-covenant-agreement.pdf.

42 McGovern, supra note 40.

43 See, for example, 'Trinity Western', International Law and Religion Headlines at https://www.iclrs.org/common/headline.php?contentId=1673&search=Trinity+Western.

44 McGovern.

45 Barry W. Bussey, 'Trinity Western University, Charter Values and Charter Right', *ipolitics*, 22 June 2018, at https://ipolitics.ca/article/trinity-western-university-charter-values-and-charter-rights/.

morally objectionable, there are many other cases where showing care or respect for others may override the complicity concerns.

Another example, perhaps derivative from one of the prior grounds for agreement, is found at the core of modern human rights and international standards for assessing religious freedom claims. Under typical human rights and constitutional standards, where there is a substantial burden on or interference with a religious freedom claim, that claim will prevail even against compelling or pressing state interests, if there is a less burdensome way of pursuing the state interests in question. For example, in its decision in *Hobby Lobby v. Burwell* (573 U.S. ___ (2014)) the United States Supreme Court sustained the conscientious objection of a for-profit business corporation and its owners to a federal regulation requiring provision of health insurance coverage for its female employees. The Court ultimately determined that it was possible for the coverage in question to be provided without requiring the corporation and its owners to violate conscience. Where there is good will, it is often possible to find such accommodations. Given the significance of the freedom of religion claims at stake, some willingness to make accommodations on both sides seems justifiable in the spirit of making stable pluralism possible.

Another example is the compromise on religious liberty and sexual orientation claims that was worked out in Utah, the home state of this chapter's authors. This was a compromise made possible by deep commitment of religious leaders and political leaders to find a workable compromise that respected the rights of both religious believers and the LGBT community.[46]

On the one hand, this compromise provided as much protection for LGBT groups as had been provided in most of the more liberal states that had previously approved same-sex marriage. The Utah legislation protects LGBT individuals from employment and housing discrimination, and provides reasonable workplace accommodations, including for transgender individuals, who have often been left unprotected elsewhere. Moreover, it provides a system that allows government officials who object to same-sex marriage to keep their jobs, while assuring that marriage will be available to all, even in rural areas, and will be provided in ways that do not single out LGBT individuals in ways that might be demeaning. At the same time, the Utah legislation provides more extensive protections for religious groups, assuring that the religious communities can remain true to their beliefs and that the religious character of religiously affiliated institutions and religious buildings owned by denominations will be respected. The exemptions are crafted with sufficient breadth to cover religiously affiliated institutions, such as religiously affiliated schools and charitable institutions. It adds affiliates, religious associations, societies (including a special mention of the Boy Scouts) to existing carve-outs for small employers, religious corporations, and their subsidiaries.

The 'Utah compromise' also included exemptions that had been adopted in all or virtually all other states that approved same-sex legislation. Thus, it exempts clergy from officiating at same-sex marriage ceremonies if this is contrary to their religious beliefs, and it similarly exempts religious organizations from providing such services. It protects those who object to same-sex marriages from private law suits and public penalties. Somewhat less typical but important is an explicit provision exempting religious marriage counseling courses or retreats from the obligation to serve same sex couples. It allows adoption agencies to maintain their

46 Utah State Legislature, SB 296 Antidiscrimination and Religious Freedom Amendments, signed 12 March 2015, and SB 297 Protections for Religious Expression and Beliefs about Marriage, Family, or Sexuality, signed 20 March 2015.

existing placement policies, even if that means they do not provide adoption services for LGBT couples.

While typically referred to as a 'compromise,' which indeed it was in many respects, it is significant than key figures on both sides regard it as a determination that was made without sacrificing core principles.[47]

Different US states will no doubt reach different accommodations. In the aftermath of such Supreme Court opinions as *Obergefell v. Hodges* (576 U.S. ___ (2015)) (the decision authorizing same-sex marriage nationwide in the United States) and *Masterpiece Cakeshop* (finding a violation of a baker's free exercise rights in the Colorado Civil Rights Commission's animus toward his religious objection to providing a cake for a same-sex wedding ceremony), countless ripple-effect issues will be encountered. Parallel tensions are certain to be encountered in Europe and other parts of the world as they wrestle with the implications of changing mores (at least in the belief systems of some) around the world. The question going forward is whether we will be able to find accommodations that can make all citizens feel safe in their dignity and differing life stances. The important point is that we need to understand the important role that churches and religious leaders can play in working out compromises that respect the rights and principles both of religious believers and the rights of individuals in other sectors of society.

Weathering impediments to religious freedom

Among the emerging challenges to a climate hospitable to religious freedom are such phenomena as secularization, the rise of the 'nones' (the 'nonreligious', those professing no affiliation with organized religion), moral/religious relativism, the 'privatization' of religion; apathy regarding religious freedom, erosion of the presumptive value of religion; the development of equality, privacy, and other 'new' rights that seem to automatically trump religious freedom rights; the steady expansion of state authority; the rise of identity politics, and the legitimate but often overemphasized concern with security. Each of these social trends needs to be analyzed carefully to make certain that they don't result in inappropriate erosion or undervaluing of rights to freedom of religion or belief.

Secularization, the process through which societies move from close identification with religious values and institutions toward nonreligious values and secular institutions, weakens the bonds society feels for religion, thereby undermining the perceived importance of religious freedom. In most Western countries, increasing secularization erodes the presumptive value of religion, pushing it from the public square. At the same time, it is frequently asserted that religious freedoms are best protected in a 'secular' society free from the imposition of the values of a state religion.

47 For information about this process from a scholar and a legislator who helped craft the legislation, see the work of Professor Robin Fretwell Wilson, Roger and Stephany Joslin Professor of Law and Director, Epstein Health Law and Policy Program; Director, Family Law and Policy Program, University of Illinois College of Law at, for example, 'Summary of the Utah Compromise' (March 24, 2015) at SSRN: https://ssrn.com/abstract=2584543, and 'Marriage of Necessity: Same-Sex Marriage and Religious Liberty Protections', 64 *Case Western Reserve Law Review* 1161 (2014). See also the chapter by Utah State Senate Majority Whip J. Stuart Adams, 'Taking Colliding Trains off a Collision Path: Lessons from the Utah Compromise for Civil Society', in Robin Fretwell Wilson, ed., *The Contested Place of Religion in Family Law* (Cambridge University Press 2018).

While secularity of state institutions is often a critical factor in helping to assure the equal freedom for all that is vital for stable pluralism, it is important to distinguish between secularity in this sense and secularism that manifests varying degrees of hostility for religion. The contrast between secularity and secularism was worked out in detail in a general report prepared for the International Academy of Comparative Law in 2010.[48] Whereas secularity constitutes a religion–state regime characterized by flexibility and openness to a variety of world views, secularism is itself an ideology that promotes secularism as an end in itself. For believers, secularism is often experienced as a competing world view, unlike secularity, which is an accommodating framework welcoming a broad range of belief systems, both religious and secular. Brett Scharffs has further elaborated this contrast in a number of articles. As he describes it,

> Secularity is an approach to religion-state relations that avoids identification of the state with any particular religion or ideology (including secularism itself) and that endeavors to provide a neutral framework capable of accommodating a broad range of religions and beliefs. Secularism, in contrast, is an ideological position that is committed to promoting a secular order.[49]

Needless to say, secularity is much more likely to serve as the basis for a stabilizing type of pluralism, whereas secularism can accentuate tensions between religious and secular outlooks.

The collapse of Soviet communism led to a pronounced shift toward greater secularity in former Soviet bloc countries in the 1990s, but at present we are seeing retreat from these positions in a number of countries. The retreat from secularity can involve a shift toward more aggressive secularism on the one hand, or resurgence of a dominant religion on the other. The relapse in Russia has been in the direction of heightened influence of the Russian Orthodox Church. Among other things this has been evident in the overreach of anti-extremism legislation, which among other things has led to the dissolution of the Jehovah's Witnesses and expropriation of their property.

Such shifts are not limited to former Soviet space, however. Turkey has shifted from a harsh version of secularism to a system that exhibits greater dominance of Sunni Islam. Unfortunately, this means we are witnessing a retreat from only recently developed secularity and its protections of religious freedoms, including the rights of religious minorities, in both Russia and Turkey, two of the three Council of Europe Member States with the greatest number of human rights judgments against them.[50]

48 See Javier Martinez-Torrón and W. Cole Durham, Jr., *Religion and the Secular State: National Reports* (Complutense University of Madrid Faculty of Law 2015), 1–64.

49 Brett G. Scharffs, 'Secularity or Secularism: Two Competing Visions for the Relationship between Religion and the State in the New Turkish Constitution', in *International Congress on Constitutional Law: Book of Papers*, 362 (2011), http://digitalcommons.law.byu.edu/faculty_scholarship/122. See also 'Four Views of the Citadel: The Consequential Distinction between Secularity and Secularism', (2011) 6 *Religion & Human Rights* (4) 109–126.

50 For the period 1959–2016, of all judgments involving Article 9 of the European Convention on Human Rights (freedom of religion or belief), Greece has the most negative judgments (13, many of them involving property disputes), followed by Turkey (11), and Russia (9). For total of all human rights judgments, Turkey has by far the most (3,270), followed by Italy (2,351), and Russia (1,948). See table, European Court of Human Rights, Violation by Article and by States (1959–2016), at http://www.echr.coe.int/Documents/Stats_violation_1959_2016_ENG.pdf.

In Turkey, the constitution provides for freedom of conscience, religious belief, conviction, expression, and worship; and prohibits discrimination based on religious grounds. However, following the attempted coup in 2016, a government crackdown on suspected supporters of the self-exiled Muslim cleric Fethullah Gulen resulted in the dismissal or suspension from state institutions more than 100,000 government officials and the arrest of more than 50,000 individuals on alleged terror-related grounds. Rights of non-Muslim minorities and of a heterodox Muslim group, the Alevis, were curtailed.

> The Ministry of National Education implemented an extensive revision of the school curriculum, which secular individuals and other citizens said increased the Sunni Muslim content in the textbooks and undermined the country's secular education system. Non-Sunni Muslims did not receive the same protections as recognized non-Muslim minorities, although both experienced difficulty operating or opening houses of worship, challenging land and other property claims, or obtaining exemptions from mandatory religion classes. The government continued to train Sunni Muslim clerics, while restricting other religious groups from training their clergy, and continued to fund the construction of Sunni mosques while restricting land use of other religious groups. Ecumenical Patriarch Bartholomew of the Greek Orthodox Church continued to call on the government to allow the Halki Seminary to reopen as an independent institution to train Greek Orthodox clerics in the country.[51]

Another fundamental problem for the protection of strong religious freedom protections is the instrumentalization of religion by political authorities. Turkish scholar Bugra Kalkan has explored the reasons for such a process.

> The first and the obvious reason is that governments want the dominant religion as their ally in order to stabilize the political system. For sure, being a member of a religious community facilitates the collective action, in this case, the political action. The control of the dominant religion by the state – or the control of the state by religious leaders – will increase loyalty of the citizens towards the political system. Therefore, when the state becomes an ally of a religion or a denomination, the freedom of the other religions or the denominations will be restricted in order to strengthen the political power. This happens in Muslim-majority countries almost all the time but it often happens in non-Muslim-majority countries as well. / … [W]hen the monopolization tendency in religious markets meets the need of political legitimacy, being loyal to the dominant and 'legitimate' religion will be an utterly important political issue. And the outsiders will be a great danger to both the religious and the political society. This is what happens in Middle East to varying degrees. On the other hand, in Western Europe, because religion is not the prime source of the political authority, the monopolization tendency in religious markets does not require the destruction of religious pluralism. Because the risks of religious freedom are not that high. But as the religious terrorism rises in Western Europe, the political demands to limit religious freedom are increasing.[52]

51 United States Department of State, *International Religious Freedom Report for 2017 – Turkey*, at https://www.state.gov/j/drl/rls/irf/religiousfreedom/index.htm?year=2017&dlid=280968#wrapper.

52 Bugra Kalkan, 'Why Governments Regulate Religion?', *Istanbul Network for Liberty*, 3 May 2017, http://istanbulnetwork.org/why-governments-regulate-religion/.

Another factor shifting the contours of pluralism relates to important cultural shifts away from organized religion. In the West, suggests Oxford-educated American pastor James Emery White, there is at the heart of secularism a *functional* atheism. 'Rather than rejecting the idea of God, our culture simply ignores him.'[53] White has explored both the 'swift and dramatic' rise of the 'nones' – especially among the 'Millennials' (people born between 1981 and 1996) and the significance of 'Generation Z' (born between 1993 and 2012), whom White also calls the 'first post-Christian generation'.[54] This latter group, who make up more than 25 percent of the current population of the United States, seem 'poised to challenge every church to rethink its role in light of a rapidly changing culture'.[55] Recent reports show that in contrast to results of nationwide surveys from the 1970s and 1980s, when fewer than one-in-ten adults in the US reported no religious affiliation, almost a quarter now describe themselves as atheists, agnostics, or 'nothing in particular'.[56] Studies conducted by the Pew Research Center for Religion & Public Life report that 'Millennials' are less religious than older Americans. 'The fastest growing religious identifier among this generation is "spiritual but not religious."'[57]

In discussing this group, White notes some significant characteristics:

> First, they have a strong desire to make a difference with their lives and are attracted to what will enable them to make that difference. A faith that is privately engaging, but socially irrelevant, will not attract them. Second, traditional morality will be a tricky conversation, as they are not only sexually fluid themselves, but consider relational acceptance and lifestyle affirmation to be synonymous. Individual freedom is simply a core value. Third, a final faith question will revolve around their amazingly deep sense of awe and wonder about the universe. More than any other generation, Generation Z has an openness to spirituality via cosmology.[58]

The rise of the nonreligious in the United Kingdom has been even more dramatic. According to the 2015 British Election Study, the nones in the UK, who represented a mere 3 percent of the population in 1963, now represent 44.7 percent of all adults and 66 percent, a full two-thirds, of adults aged 25 and under.[59]

The increasing numbers of 'nonreligious' people in many Western societies is 'reshaping civil societies and geopolitics'.[60] In fact, Lois Lee, director of the Understanding Unbelief

53 James Emery White, *Meet Generation Z: Understanding and Reaching the New Post-Christian World* (Baker Books 2017), 20.

54 See James Emery White, *The Rise of the Nones: Understanding and Reaching the Religiously Unaffiliated* (Baker Books 2014).

55 White, *Meet Generation Z*, supra note 53.

56 Gregory A. Smith and Alan Cooperman, 'The factors driving the growth of religious "nones" in the U.S.', *Pew Research Center Fact Tank*, 14 September 2016, http://www.pewresearch.org/fact-tank/2016/09/14/the-factors-driving-the-growth-of-religious-nones-in-the-u-s/. See also Michael Lipka, 'Why America's "nones" left religion', *Pew Research Center Fact Tank*, 24 August 2016, http://www.pewresearch.org/fact-tank/2016/08/24/why-americas-nones-left-religion-behind/.

57 Jonathan Merritt, 'Forget Millennials. How Will Churches Reach Generation Z?', *Religion News Service Column: On Faith & Culture*, 1 May 2017, http://religionnews.com/2017/05/01/forget-millennials-how-will-churches-reach-generation-z/.

58 Merritt, 'Forget Millennials', (interview with James Emery White).

59 White, *Meet Generation Z*, supra note 53 at 26–27.

60 Lois Lee, 'The Nonreligious in the World Today', *The Association of Religion Data Archives*, 31 January 2017, http://globalplus.thearda.com/globalplus-the-nonreligious-in-the-world-today/.

program at the University of Kent, has noted, 'Depending on how they are counted, the nonreligious today may be considered the world's third largest "religion," trailing only Christianity and Islam.'[61] The bad news is that the rise of a generation of young adults who characterize their religious affiliation as 'none' exacerbates the secularist trend, and contributes to a growing apathy with respect to religious freedom. Indeed, what happens is worse than apathy: the general populace no longer understands what is at stake, and assumes all is well so long as police don't prevent people from attending worship services. The result is that religious freedom ceases to be a political priority, and religion is no longer seen as a critical value deserving special protection.

Lee suggests that, worldwide, 'the makeup and balance of religious and nonreligious populations … matters in ways both small and large', ranging from 'the transformation of rites accompanying events such as the birth of a child to the challenges posed by the rapid integration of religious immigrants from ethnic minorities in increasingly nonreligious European nations. The fate of governments themselves can stand in the balance of relations between the religious and nonreligious.'[62]

Lee cites as one example the election of Donald Trump to the US presidency 'with support from an estimated 81 percent of white Christian voters who identified as "born again" or evangelical … a constituency that perceived itself as being marginalized and ignored in an increasingly secular, even anti-religious public square'.[63]

Modern secular societies are increasingly hospitable to various versions of religious or moral relativism. This is taken not as a sign of deep difference deserving special protection, but as evidence that distinctive conscientious beliefs do not represent important differences warranting social protection. Consequently, religious freedom rights are increasingly seen as deserving less weight than a series of other interests, such as privacy rights and equality rights. The point here is not that these other rights aren't also important, but that there is an increasing tendency to assume they automatically trump religious rights. Equality is increasingly given unthinking priority over liberty.

Religious subjectivism, a form of or at least a posture of tolerance towards moral relativism, is an aspect of the privatization of religion. Privatization can be more subtle in its effects than a clear move toward secularism or an admission of no formal religious affiliation, but its various effects are profound, as they tend to shunt religion out of the public realm.

Privatization may plausibly refer to a number of phenomena in addition to religious subjectivism, including separation of religion from public concerns, the emergence of religion without churches, and the replacement of a strong sense of religious community with the notion of a 'religious marketplace'.[64] The result is a loss of commitment to and within religious communities, with a concomitant erosion of traditional values of personal improvement and service to others. 'Another big change that comes with the growth of nonreligion', observes Lois Lee, 'is the decline of institutions as a forum for engaging with existential ideas or rituals.'[65] When religion has reached this point, why should religious 'worship' be more worthy of legal protection than, say, regular participation in nature hikes or birdwatching, physical fitness groups, or in motivational sales meetings for a multilevel marketing company?

61 Lee.
62 Lee.
63 Lee.
64 See Stephen Hart, 'Privatization in American Religion and Society', (1987) 47 *Sociological Analysis* (4), 320–321.
65 Lee.

These converging trends have implications across the spectrum of religious practice, from the wearing and display of religious symbols, to religious argumentation,[66] and in general, for any public manifestation of religion. Even in political systems with robust protection for freedom of expression, religious argumentation becomes a second-class citizen in the marketplace of ideas. The presumptive value of religion is eroded. Media coverage focusing on violent religious extremism, sex-abuse scandals, hypocrisy and misbehavior of religious leaders and believers, and other manifestations of the negative behavior of professed religious believers undermine public confidence in religion.

All of this happens against the background of ever-expanding state authority. Whether this takes the form of totalitarian states, rising authoritarianism, populism, or more innocuous social welfare states, expansion of the state has permanently transformed the context in which religious freedom rights exist. 'Pressing social needs' or 'compelling state interests' are more evident on every front. Bureaucrats tend to assume (and argue as a matter of job protection) that the program he or she administers has compelling justification. After all, how else do budgets get renewed? State paternalism is assumed to be the norm. The presumption of state authority reverses the presumption in favor of religious freedom. The problem is of course even more severe in the context of authoritarian regimes.

Fear of immigration points to the final two items in our list of impediments to the preservation of religious freedom: the rise of identity politics, and concerns over security.

A tension is increasingly clear in new sources of pressure on religion emanating from the politics of gender and sexual orientation. New forms of nationalism, or resistance to globalization and neo-colonialism can lead to restrictions on religious groups with international profiles. Fear of immigration may also have repercussions for the religious rights of immigrant groups. Such fear is only one part of widespread, often legitimate concerns with the need for security. Such concerns often lead to exaggerated constraints on religious freedom rights. These concerns have played roles in bans on headcoverings, beards, kirpans, and in calls for border walls and curtailment of immigration or even visits by certain classes of foreign nationals.

The foregoing impediments are obviously not the only social forces leading to the erosion of religious freedom, but taken together, they constitute a seemingly overwhelming set of pressures increasingly tending to outweigh religious freedom concerns in social consciousness. The point is not that these various trends are likely to be overcome or reversed. Rather, they help emphasize the fragility of religious freedom rights. The various forces serve to heighten tensions among various factions of pluralist societies, without simultaneously strengthening the core freedom protections that are vital to stabilizing pluralism. Religious communities have a longer tradition of developing toleration than secular ideologies, and while the record is far from perfect, it would be hazardous to assume secular world views – even secular equalitarianism – will in fact do better at tolerating rival views.[67]

66 See 'Religion and Political Theory', *Stanford Encyclopedia of Philosophy* (substantive revision 15 January 2016), https://plato.stanford.edu/entries/religion-politics/#Raw. 'Assume that, in religiously pluralistic conditions, religious citizens have good moral reason—perhaps even a moral obligation—to pursue secular reasons for their favored coercive laws. Assume as well that secular citizens have good reason to pursue religious reasons for their favored coercive policies (if only because, with respect to some coercive laws, some of their fellow citizens find only religious reasons to support them). What should citizens do, religious or secular, when they cannot identify these reasons?'

67 Steven D. Smith, 'Die and Let Live? The Asymmetry of Accommodation', in Timothy Samuel Shah, Thomas E. Farr, and Jack Friedman, *Religious Freedom and Gay Rights: Emerging Conflicts in North America and Europe* (Oxford University Press 2016), 191–199.

Conclusion

The types of pressures sketched above generate what Professor András Sajó has called the 'tragedy of liberty'.[68] The difficulty is that liberty tends to remain an abstract value that cannot survive without supportive and dedicated public conviction.[69] But in fact other passions or pressures, such as those just identified, will tend to overwhelm the desire for freedom. The story of Dostoevsky's Grand Inquisitor recurs in myriad modern forms: the masses appear to prefer bread (understood to represent all material wants and needs) to freedom. The emotional burden of freedom can be too great.

It is important to bear in mind that the 'tragedy of liberty' Sajó is identifying is a tragedy not of *religious* liberty but of liberty more generally. Liberty is permanently at risk due to the blandishments of the modern welfare state. However, religion is one of the few things that people care deeply enough about to generate the 'supportive and dedicated public convictions' capable of countering the tragedy of liberty. This is one of the reasons, in the words of the famous aphorism of Ernst-Wolfgang Böckenförde, that 'A free, liberal, and democratic state can only be built and sustainable on a foundation that it itself is unable to create.'[70] Religion is one of the few facets of life that people value more than life itself, and that people will prioritize over other state incentives or demands. The deep concern for religious liberty, by creating 'supportive and dedicated public convictions' in favor of liberty for a variety of deeply different world views, ends up being a guarantor for liberty more generally in modern pluralistic societies. If that liberty collapses, a bulwark for all other liberties will be gone.

This is not to say that everyone attaches such value to religion, but to recognize that many do, and that others can understand and respect the depth of these promptings of conscience. Religious leaders and religious institutions play a vital role in helping others (both within their own faith traditions and in the public at large) to understand that the concern for religious freedom goes to the core of human dignity. If that is violated, not only does fundamental injustice occur, but serious social instability is the likely result as well.

Most troubling about recent developments is that increasingly, the rise of an equality paradigm in social consciousness eclipses the rival freedom paradigm. This is not to question the value of equality. The difficulty, however, is that religious rights are too often given little or no weight in constitutional balancing. The case that others are making is important, and in some cases religious rights must give way to other rights and values. But those cases will be rare, and much more rare than those succumbing to the lure of other interests assume.

One of the reasons religious freedom rights are so important is that they protect not only the particular interest of religious claimants and religious claims, but also the broader interest within pluralistic societies of assuring that the dignity of difference will not be threatened, so that everyone can feel secure in that which they hold to be most important and most sacred. If religious liberty is subject to erosion by every wind of social passion, its fundamental role of making society safe for deep differences will be destroyed. If wedding cake bakers, photographers, and others may be coerced to provide services against conscience, even when other service providers are readily available, we send signals that religious freedom rights have been reduced to second-class status not only in the public sector, but in the

68 András Sajó, 'Liberty and its Competitors', in Renata Uitz, ed., *Freedom and its Enemies: The Tragedy of Liberty* (Eleven International Publishing 2015).

69 Sajó.

70 Ernst-Wolfgang Böckenförde, 'Die Entstehung des Staates als Vorgang der Säkularisation (1967)', in Ernst-Wolfgang Böckenförde, *Recht, Staat, Freiheit: Studien zur Rechtsphilosophie, Staatstheorie und Verfassungsgeschichte* (Suhrkamp 1992), 112.

commercial sector as well. We need to be able to protect not just the currently dominant world view, but the right to have rival and incompatible world views. We need to understand and be better at making clear that it is not only the special interest of religious communities that is at stake if religious freedom rights come unraveled, but the broader fabric of liberty itself.

In the days ahead, it will be particularly important for religious communities to work together to articulate the importance of religious freedom norms in persuasive ways, and to work out compromises that can adequately address the increasingly complex conflicts that we face.

In conclusion we find profound significance in the words of Professor Lindholm:

> Taking for granted that human beings now and for the foreseeable future do disagree in matters of religion or life stance, my overriding concern is to grasp how we may, in the religiously discordant social world that is ours, reasonably secure both principled solidarity based on mutual respect across religious and life-stance divides and unflinching doctrinal integrity of, and commitment to, our differing normative traditions. Reasoning in a virtuous circle, my answer draws on the modern tradition of internationally recognized human rights. This tradition is, I submit, rooted in an emerging worldwide public commitment to heed as inviolable the inherent dignity of every human being. Dignity is a value that may resonate within and across difference. ... Also vital is the development of legal techniques that can forestall the recurring temptation for political actors to exploit religious identification in the pursuit of power.[71]

As lawyers and believers, we join with like-minded friends worldwide, notable among them the contributors to this volume, in working to secure the blessings of stable pluralism, which is in turn grounded in freedom of religion or belief and its deeper grounding in human dignity.

71 Lindholm, supra note 15 at 22.

Index

For Product Safety Concerns and Information please contact our EU representative GPSR@taylorandfrancis.com Taylor & Francis Verlag GmbH, Kaufingerstraße 24, 80331 München, Germany

Batch number: 10726294

Printed by Printforce, the Netherlands